Though I have never worked in the Empire State Building, I believe its owners committed a great mistake when they replaced the old belt-hook windows with ones that tilt in. Tilt-ins do just that, they tilt inward at their base so that they can be cleaned without anyone having to go out.

But that is the high point (no pun intended) of a window cleaner's day: to hook myself to the side of a building, stand out on the ledge and feel the wind's tug; to look out and survey the city, to see it as the skyscraper does; to sense the quiet calm a silent high-rise offers once I've shut the window that connects me to everyday occurrences.

I am outside, apart from everyone, alone with the ledge. The Empire State Building has lost part of its heritage. I am sure that both the building and its window cleaners miss those hooks. Before I cleaned windows, such details didn't matter to me. But that was before I became a part of the sky-line. Have I imbued such buildings with too much personality? Or have I become more like them? I think the answer lies somewhere in between.

LIFE ON THE LEDGE

Reflections of a New York City Window Cleaner

a memoir by
IVOR HANSON

Two Dollar Radio
since 2005

Author's Note: All incidents in *Life on the Ledge* took place. I have, however, compressed them so that they occur over the course of one year. For the sake of privacy, I have changed some names and slightly obscured some identifying details.

Some of the events recounted in this book were first mentioned in "Allure of the Ledge," a piece I wrote for the The New York Times that can be found in the anthology *New York Stories: The Best of the City Section of The New York Times*, published by New York University Press.

———————————————

Published by Two Dollar Radio, 2006.
Copyright 2006, Ivor Hanson.

For more information, visit twodollarradio.com.

ISBN: 978-0-9763895-3-8
Library of Congress Control Number: 2006906352
All rights reserved.
First printing.

Cover Photograph: Fred R. Conrad/The New York Times.
Author Photograph: William Philpott/Five-o Images.

Two Dollar Radio
since 2005
Because we make more noise than a $2 radio.
twodollarradio.com
twodollar@twodollarradio.com
Two Dollar Radio is distributed to the trade by Biblio Distribution.

For Christina,
who made this book and so much more
-- Anikka comes to mind --
possible.

ONE

Before I rang the apartment's buzzer, I took a step back from the doorway on Lower Broadway and looked up at the windows of the old, narrow brick building. When given the chance, I like to see where I'll be working; I like to know from where I might fall. Despite the midday sun in my eyes and the mid-May heat wave it had sprung on New York City, I did manage to spot belthooks in the ancient wooden window frames. I wiped some sweat from my neck. This job couldn't be that bad if the hooks were usable, if they were safe. But if the hooks were no good, I could only hope the ledges were wide enough so that I could stand out on them without being hooked in. Ten inches or so would be fine, I could live with that.

I glanced at my watch. One o'clock was the time and one o'clock was the appointment. I always try to be right on schedule if I can manage it. Apart from making for a smoother day, if nothing else, it's one less thing a customer can hold against me. I pressed the doorbell and waited, wondering if I would be buzzed in or be asked to catch a set of falling keys dropped down by the client. After a few seconds, the door's buzzer sounded and I pushed it open, entering once more what I call "Windowland:" my world at work. At the foot of the wide and steep staircase, its worn steps undeniably slanting leftwards, I looked up and glimpsed the customer standing at the top of a landing beside her door on the third floor.

"Hey there!" I called out, my voice ricocheting in the fluorescent-lit, grey-walled entryway. "It's the window cleaner!"

"Hullo," she said in an English accent. "I can certainly see that. Come on up."

In her echo chamber of a stairwell, my footfalls resounded step by step, as did my squeegees and mops and tools as they bounced about in my bucket. Even the metal clasps on my window cleaner's belt — what would, with any luck, let me hook onto this pre-war building — squeaked loudly, reminding me of the Tin Woodsman from *The Wizard of Oz*. I just wished that image wouldn't occur to her.

Even when I know my jobs don't require my heavy window cleaner's belt, I wear it anyway. This is mostly due to the chance that a "belt" job may well come in during the day, or that a new window cleaning customer may not know what sort of windows they have, like this one. She had only been able to tell my boss that she had "very old, very large, and very tall" windows. So, I need to be prepared. But I also know that my window belt sets me apart. It shows — to other window cleaners at least — that I don't just do easy windows: tilt-ins, switchers, and storefronts. I go out on the ledge. Sure, I admit it, I take status where I can find it.

I reached the top of the stairs.

"Hi," I said, putting down my bucket and pole and extending my hand to her. "I'm Ivor."

"Hi," she said. Her hand was quite smooth, making me suddenly quite conscious of how callused my own were. "My name's Sylvia. I'm so glad you're punctual. I do hate waiting around, and these windows are a mess. My God, it's hot!"

"Fortunately, the morning job up on Fifth went well," I said. "The windows there behaved themselves and then the subway was right there at the station, and now here I am. And, yeah, it is hot."

I liked her face. It was long and narrow with Victorian pale skin offset by bright-blue eyes, thick eyelashes, arched eyebrows, and a small mouth. Her dirty-blonde hair had been noticeably but fashionably streaked in lighter shades and cut in a shoulder-length bob. Her face and hair went well with her short black skirt, her white cotton blouse that buttoned down the front, and her black pumps. I also liked her voice. Though clipped, with an air that hinted at impatience, it wasn't strident or high-pitched. Instead, her tone possessed assurance, along with a trace of drama. She seemed like an affable ice princess in her mid-to-late twenties.

I followed her through the ajar steel door and found myself in a large, long, high-ceilinged loft; a loft the way it should be, open and devoid of clutter, clean and stark. The room emphasized what makes living in such an apartment a near-decadent experience: emptiness. Wasting space in Manhattan is a wonderful crime to get away with. Only a few pieces of furniture defined the living area. A modernist black leather sofa had been placed near but not against a wall of exposed brick — as if to stress the place had room to spare. In front of the couch stood a discrete steel and glass coffee table. Opposite it, two matching armless black leather chairs staked out the border of this part of the loft. Close by, a tall, whirring steel fan atop a shiny pole watched over them all. In the middle of the room, the sun cast a long shadow across an unobstructed floor: a portrait of a window frame in black, white, and grey. Despite the dirt on the panes, I liked how the image appeared to be brushed upon the canvas of wooden floor planks.

"Well, let's see how these windows will treat you," Sylvia said, pointing at the panes I had observed from the street. "I think they will be the most difficult."

"Looks that way," I said.

She was right. In a pallid stab at ventilation, a brick held up one of the windows, meaning that at least one set of old, unpredictable ballasts — the weights that enable a window to be raised — would soon taunt me. I guessed that the upper and lower panes of these two oversized windows each measured about six feet by four feet. Additionally, both window frames sported a feature I hadn't noticed from the street below: a long, narrow "transom" window above each upper pane. I would need to affix my squeegee to my pole in order to clean them both inside the apartment and out on the ledge. Now I really hoped the belt hooks worked. The prospect of balancing myself out there hookless and working with a pole did not appeal to me at all. But I didn't have to deal with that just yet. Instead, I had to prepare for and price the job. I found an easy-to-find empty space to put my things and unslung my bag from my shoulder.

"Wow, what a great place," I said, kneeling as I fashioned my things into a small pile by the door. I meant it, but it was also something to say, an icebreaker, if not a conversation starter.

"Oh, thanks," Sylvia said. She had continued to stride across the room and now stood near the opposite wall, in the kitchen area. "It's my boy-friend's. Would you like a glass of water?"

"Sure, that would be great," I said without looking up. I didn't want to look at her too much. She might notice me doing so.

"So, tell me," Sylvia said. "Is it always this bloody hot in May? We've had to go ahead and arrange for some air conditioners to be installed later this week, it's been so awful. Here you are."

I stood up and walked over to the sink and the offered water. Putting my bucket down, I took the glass and smiled. I just love that term "bloody."

"Thanks," I said. "No. Let me assure you that it isn't usually so bad this time of year. May is usually quite nice. But this heat wave is a drag. I saw in the paper this morning that it's supposed to hit ninety-five today, but we'll get through it. Do you mind if I take a look at the rest of the windows so I can give you a price?"

"Oh, sure," Sylvia said, "But I really wouldn't worry about that."

We walked over to the living room windows that looked out on Broad-way and other low-lying loft buildings across the street. Midtown and its high-rises — where I was due next in a couple of hours — seemed very far away.

"Now, ordinarily we charge ten dollars per belt window," I said. "But since these are oversized, and you've got transoms, I'll have to charge you fifteen each."

"That's fine," she said. Sylvia's voice had lost its clipped quality, lending her words some warmth.

Walking through the rest of the loft, I saw that the apartment's minimal-ist theme continued. Like the coffee table, the rectangular dining table, too, was made of steel and glass — so that the crystal vase of yellow tulips set at its middle seemed to float above the floor. The bedroom towards the back was also sparse, containing but a bed, two dressers, a small fan, and a wall-length closet; even so, I would have to move the mattress to get at the window. A den area in the very back was similarly spaced, with a black leather couch like the one in front, an industrial-style steel coffee table that rolled on casters, and a large black television set on the floor. A fan identical to the one in the living room whirred here as well. But, like its twin, the blades seemed to merely push the stale air around the loft, rather than provide relief.

"This really is a nice place," I said, ignoring my last observation. They'd have air conditioners soon enough.

"Yes," she said. "I guess it looks all right, but I don't find it particularly comfy. Except the bed."

I didn't know whether to ignore her playful remark or make light of it. Surprising myself, I opted for the latter: "Oh, well, that's a relief," I said.

Sylvia smiled. Her eyes now seemed bluer. Then she turned on her heels and continued with her tour. The remaining seven windows were all relatively new tilt-ins — windows with frames that pivoted downwards like the gate of a pick-up truck. I could clean them entirely indoors, with a minimum of risk. These I would charge the standard eight dollars each. So $56 for them and $30 for the front two made a total of $86. As she'd predicted, Sylvia didn't mind the price. Apparently it would just be a meaningless number written on a check.

"So, how long have you lived in New York?" I asked as we walked back to the kitchen and my bucket.

"I just got here a few weeks ago," she said. "I mean, I've been to New York, I've visited, but I've never lived here. And I've never been here when it's been this muggy."

I laughed and began to fill the bucket at the sink.

"Well, I must warn you then," I said, "that this sort of heat and humidity will be an every day thing come August, or even July."

"Oh, great," Sylvia said. "Can't wait."

Now that I was standing next to her, nearer to her, I breathed in a familiar scent: Chanel N°5. Though this was what my mom wore, I wasn't about to hold that against Sylvia. She still smelled good after all. Besides, an old girlfriend had worn the perfume as well. I breathed in a bit of the fragrance and decided to learn a bit more.

"Where are you from in England?"

"London."

"Oh really?" I said. "I remember being there a few summers ago during a hot spell and how the newspapers warned everyone to stay indoors. 'Heat Wave Strikes! Mad Dogs Spotted!' That sort of thing. But it was barely eighty degrees."

"Oh, come now," Sylvia said. "That's hot enough for us!"

"Okay," I said, pleased again at how easily I could joke with her. Looking down at my now nearly full bucket, I turned off the tap. "Well, time to work."

Walking over to the front windows, I did my best not to slosh water from my bucket as my shadow and I ruined the still-life portrait of the window frame on the floor. I'd filled the bucket higher than usual since old wooden frames and single pane windows let quite a lot of dirt and dust seep in from outside. Even so, I anticipated having to change my water midway through these "insides" and would certainly have to rinse out my chamois cloth a number of times. But that was okay; these built-in breaks would give me convenient chances to gulp down some water. They might even let me talk some more to Sylvia.

Putting my bucket down to the side of the windows to reduce the chance of my knocking it over, I looked up at the oversized panes: "Worst for first," the flip side of "Best for last." The tilt-ins out back would be my reward. I jumped up onto the sill to more closely inspect the windows. They were in pretty bad shape, as much of the caulking that secured these panes to the frames had worn out or fallen away. This meant that since I couldn't put much pressure on the panes without risking their falling out to the street, I couldn't wash the windows as thoroughly as I would have liked. A stark, but easy choice, then: almost clean windows still in their frames or pristine shards of glass down on the sidewalk — or in somebody's head. I'd have to be careful and take more time. I jumped back down to the floor, took a mop from my bucket and, without squeezing off the excess water, attached it to my brass pole, extending my reach by fifteen feet. Maybe I should have charged her twenty per window.

My workday mantra of "mop, squeegee, chamois" was about to kick in: mopping down a window, squeegeeing it clean, and then chamoising its edges dry. I gingerly wetted down one of the transoms with my mop and, though my pole reduced my feel for the glass, I could see the dirt on the pane resisting my efforts. These windows hadn't been cleaned in quite a while, years at least. I continued lightly pushed the mop up and down and left and right, hoping the plentiful water dripping off it could sufficiently clean the window. This seemed to be working. Next, I placed my twenty-two inch squeegee, my "22," atop my pole and then wiped away the water, relieved by how much dirt had been removed. After a second round of mopping, squeegeeing, and chamoising, the transoms were done. They looked pretty good considering how dirty they had been.

"So, why were you in London?" Sylvia asked.

Startled, I turned my head away from the window and saw her sitting at the dining table looking up from a fashion magazine of some kind. Had she been watching me the whole time?

"I was there with my band," I said, removing my squeegee and then dunking my mop into the bucket. "We'd gone there to play and to try to get signed to a label." I rested one knee on the ground as I, by routine, automatically squeezed off the excess water from the mop with my hand. I then dunked it once more. The large panes, too, needed more water and care than usual.

"And did you land a deal?" she asked, putting the magazine aside and resting her head on her hands.

"Eventually we did, yes," I said.

I looked at the large windows before me. If they were anything like the transoms, I was pretty confident most of the dirt and grime would come off with two rounds of my mantra, perhaps three. But not all the dirt. With such windows I have to simply accept that perfection is not possible. Hopefully, of course, the customer will, too.

I am at times struck by how much I've linked what I've thought of myself, my self-worth, to how well I've cleaned a window. But then, this is how I spend my day. I've also wondered how good a drummer I'd be if I could spend the eight to ten hours that I do with my squeegee with my drumsticks instead. Moving closer to the window, my thoughts were distracted by how hot it indeed was. Even with the thick layer of dirt on the pane's other side, the window seemed to magnify the sunlight streaming into the room. Sweat began to trickle down my face and onto my neck; my tee shirt was quickly becoming damp. Where was a breeze when I needed one?

"You scored a deal?" Sylvia said. "Brilliant! Please, tell me more! I just love hearing about this kind of stuff."

"Sure," I said, pleased that she was interested and that she'd used the word "brilliant." It's such an English adjective, sounding much more impressive than, say, the word "great" — its American equivalent, at least in terms of describing bands. "But just a sec. I've just got to get started over here.

I stood and carefully removed the brick from beneath the window frame; I didn't want the window to crash down on my hand. I needn't have worried. The frame stayed still, warped into place. But with a light push, the window closed completely, snugly. I then climbed onto the sill, mop in hand, and began wetting down the upper oversized pane. To enable the mop to reach the window's top edge, I grasped the bottom of the mop's handle. As I reached and scrubbed — standing on my tiptoes, slightly arching my back, and stretching my right arm as far as I could — mop water ran down my hand, wrist, forearm, and bicep, lightly washing me with dirt.

Despite their delicate state, compared to the transoms these windows seemed easier to clean since I didn't have to use my pole. But as I gently mopped down the glass expanse of these two windows' upper and lower frames, their widths each nearly matching my arm span, their heights each nearly matching my own six feet, much of the dirt withstood my mop. I really should have charged her twenty per window. Maybe I'd try to later.

"We got signed to this little label and then they ended up putting us through the wringer," I said, facing the window as I spoke.

"That label doesn't sound very nice," Sylvia said.

"Well, no, they weren't," I said.

With the window now quite wet, I could just begin to see a blurry, distorted reflection of Sylvia at the table. I liked how she meshed, albeit quite messily, with my own image in the glass. My blonde hair and blue eyes looked faint and obscured for sure, as did my narrow face and slender body. My black tee shirt and black jeans seemed in shadow, nearly invisible. I wondered whether my chat with Sylvia was interrupting my window cleaning or if it was the other way around. Still, I liked that I had something I could talk to her about, my "other" life.

"But we got a record out and we did get some good press. At one point NME and Melody Maker both gave us a Single of the Week, so that was cool."

"Two Singles of the Week at the same time?" Sylvia said. "That's impressive."

"Thank you," I said as I drew my squeegee from its holster. "I got to admit, we were pretty happy." NME and Melody Maker were England's two leading music weeklies.

I held the "22" in my right hand somewhat loosely. Cleaning a window well all comes down to the wrist. Were I to press the brass and rubber tool too hard against the pane, it would simply skitter across the glass leaving streaks, and I would have to mop and squeegee the window again. So, I let the squeegee and window dictate the angle my wrist should assume. Ordinarily, the rubber blade should pass quickly and effortlessly along. But these windows were so dirty that I could still feel some resistance from the glass. Time for another mopping.

"Here's a question I'm sure you hate answering," Sylvia's voice called out. "What kind of rock do you like?"

I could hear a slight smirk in the way she said "rock," but I didn't mind. Sylvia sounded mischievous, as if she were interviewing me for a fake radio show.

"I like rock that has great hooks, great melodies, and isn't afraid to sound well-recorded," I answered. "Does that make me a rock snob?"

"If it does then we can be snobs together," Sylvia said. "Okay, now I have to ask you something I'm sure you resent even more: What kind of music do you play?"

"No, no," I lied, "I don't mind. I just try and come up with a different description every time. I guess you could've filed us under 'alternative rock' then. Someone wrote that we were 'melodic with a smattering of distortion,' which I thought wasn't too far off."

My musical progression had begun by drumming in punk bands in Washington, D.C. We played ultra-fast songs that audiences slam danced to and recorded for an esteemed local label, Dischord Records. The punk icon, Henry Rollins, had fronted one of my bands; another punk hero, Ian Mackaye, had fronted another of my groups; Ian's brother, Alec, had sung for a third. But over the years, in these various groups and on several records, the songs that my long-time bandmate, Michael, wrote became, well, more musical. When he started singing and fronting our fourth group together, the tunes were undeniably catchy. Some in the punk scene had derided us as popsters, sell-outs. But we hadn't craftily calculated this change in our music; we had simply evolved. And we certainly hadn't seen fortune or fame as a result. We hadn't made it to the cover of Rolling Stone, or even come close to being mentioned in it. Instead, after leaving the Dischord fold, we'd been screwed over by two record companies, the English independent label and a major American label that I'd decided not to mention to Sylvia. And I was still window cleaning. At present, we weren't even signed to a label, though I wasn't about to tell Sylvia this; I didn't even like reminding myself of that.

"But now," I said, "we sound more...."

"Laid back?" Sylvia asked. Her tone balanced deftly between helpful and slightly mocking.

"Let's just say slower and experimental. We're in the studio now trying to figure that out." Actually, I was trying to figure out a lot about the band — like if I was really in one. But I wasn't about to tell her that either.

I smiled as I dabbed my chamois cloth along the edges of the window frame. Seeing Sylvia now quite clearly in the glass, I could feel a crush coming on, sparkling excitement laced with a sprinkling of giddiness. That, or at least strong physical attraction. As I began squeegeeing the second window's interior, I decided to thwart it, or at least try to.

"What's your boyfriend do?" I asked.

"He works down on Wall Street for a brokerage firm."

"And how long has he been in the States?"

"Well," Sylvia said, "his whole life. He's American."

"Oh."

What was someone like her doing with an American Wall Streeter boyfriend? Since I hadn't noticed any photos of him in the loft, I immediately envisioned a loud, beefy ex-jock frat boy who'd followed his father into high finance. Words of Michael's flashed in my mind: "Ditch the loser!" It was a running joke he and I had, what we said under our breath whenever we saw a beautiful girl who was with a guy that we didn't think measured up to her — who wasn't either of us, in other words.

And yet, Sylvia's boyfriend did have taste. Apart from his girlfriend, I also liked the furniture he had, and his loft. I chided myself for being surprised that we would like the same things. But what did I know? It wasn't like I knew him, had met him, or even had an idea of what he actually looked like. Still, I did resent that he could afford my tastes and I couldn't.

"Does he like his work?" I asked.

"He likes it quite a lot," she said. "It's demanding, but he gets paid well. He's got this apartment, he's got his things. His office has a nice view. But his hours are crazy. It can be rather frustrating. Oh, I should stop this whining. But I guess I just like to complain."

"And, what do you do?" I asked, pleased that the glass beneath my squeegee had at last begun to be smooth, that Broadway had become a bit more visible, and that I had changed the subject to Sylvia.

"Well, that's just it. I haven't really decided. I like writing, writing about music actually. But I also like graphic design, and clothes, and sleeping late, for that matter. I just figured I'd take the summer to figure out what I wanted to do."

"That sounds like a nice plan," I said, trying not to sound envious of Sylvia's time off and ignoring the image I had of her sprawled in the bed barely covered by sheets, disregarding an alarm clock.

Silence returned as I worked on the windows, squeegeeing and mopping large sections of glass. Removing the streaks and missed patches from long-dirty windows has always heartened me. I liked that my efforts now revealed how portions of the ancient glass rippled, imperfections from a long ago manufacturing process. I looked forward to seeing what these panes would look like once they were totally done. I also looked outside to see if the window hooks sported hairpins or paper clips — what window cleaners leave behind to remind themselves (and warn other window cleaners) that the hooks are dangerously loose. Fortunately, these hooks were not so tagged, but I'd check their sturdiness anyway before I went out there. I then wiped up a nearly black puddle of water from the windowsill and took a break. I needed a drink. I also had to change the bucket's water. It was nearly black, too.

Standing at the sink, I took advantage of the moment and quietly tapped the kitchen counter: Ti ti ti tisis! Ti ti ti tisis! Ti ti tis boom-bap! Ti ti tsis boom-bap! Ti ti tisis boom-bap!

The drum beat for Michael's newest song had come to me earlier in the day, while overlooking Central Park at the morning job. Now I was trying to hold on to it so I could play it for him tonight in the studio. Nicely enough, we'd lucked out with a string of early evening sessions; we would be going in at 6 pm instead of, say 10 or 11 pm. But what was going on here? Recalling the rhythm was proving harder than usual. Maybe, I realized, it was because it wasn't a totally original — and therefore more memorable — beat. It hit me that I was sort of ripping off the drum part Stewart Copeland had laid down for "Roxanne," one of *The Police*'s signature songs. Well, hopefully Michael wouldn't notice; he hated *The Police*. But if he did nail me, I'd just tell him I was shooting for something reggae-ish.

"So, where are you from?" Sylvia asked from her chair.

I stopped my drumming, picked up the glass of water I had filled, my second, and turned to lean against the sink. She was leaning back, too, supporting the back of her head with both her hands. The pose emphasized her face, her blouse, and her torso. Ditch the loser indeed.

"Well, since my father was in the Navy, we moved around a lot. So I kinda grew up all over the place," I said and then took a quick sip. "My family lived in Japan, Hawaii, California, and Brazil, and my twin brother and I were born in Taiwan. But, I'd say that courtesy of the Pentagon, Washington, D.C. was my hometown. I haven't lived there for a long time though."

"That all sounds quite lovely and exotic."

Sadly, Sylvia had gone back to leaning over the table and resting her head in her hands. Aesthetics aside, I now appreciated the glass table for not hiding her legs.

"Yes," I said, taking my eyes off her by retrieving some ice cubes from the freezer for my next glass of water. "I guess you could say that. Then again, we did live on a Navy base in Norfolk, Virginia, at one point. But at least the house was nice."

"So, that makes you a Navy Brat?" Sylvia seemed pleased she knew the term.

I laughed.

"Yes, you could say that, or a Navy Junior." I said. "My dad was in the Navy for quite a while, thirty-two years."

"That is a long time," she said. "He must have done rather well."

"Well, yes, he did all right," I said, trying to temper my pride with modesty. "He retired as a Vice Admiral."

"An Admiral? That's very high indeed."

"Yeah," I said, "you see, when my dad was ten years old and his class was studying world geography, the teacher went around the room asking her students what the largest body of water they'd ever seen was. This being working-class Tucson, Arizona, in the late 1930s, most of the students' families didn't have a lot of money to spend on travel. But a number of kids had seen the Gulf of Mexico, a few had seen the Pacific Ocean, and one or two had even seen the Atlantic Ocean. And then it was my dad's turn, and his answer was the YMCA pool. So, the family joke has been that on that day, my father swore he wouldn't just see, but would sail all of the world's oceans and seas!"

Sylvia laughed as I hoped she would. I always liked telling that story.

"Actually," I said, "when my dad delivered the Saturday Evening Post as a kid, a retired Naval officer who was one of his customers got him interested in the Navy."

And then Sylvia asked what I thought she would, what others had also asked: "And what does the Admiral think of you cleaning windows?"

As I gulped down some water before responding, the Navy recruiter whose office windows I had once cleaned came to mind.

He had essentially asked me the same question. This enlisted man was dumbstruck that an Admiral's son would wash windows. It just didn't make sense. He didn't go so far as to ask what was wrong with me, but he was curious why I had the occupation I did. I explained that squeegeeing served as my day job, allowing me to be in my band, and that I actually liked a lot of what the work entailed. He was not swayed by this explanation, however; he thought that I should aim high. I didn't point out that was the Air Force's recruiting slogan. Instead, I told him that I was "aiming high" with my band. A part of me liked the incongruities of my job, my band, and my father's rank; I didn't have to mention them after all. I just didn't like when they were held against me — or when I held them against myself.

I had considered telling the recruiter that at 16, I had a Navy uniform of my own as a member of the Sea Cadets. I had joined this nautical take on a scout troop because I thought I wanted to follow my father's lead and go to Annapolis, the Academy. The fact that the Sea Cadets mainly sent its members off to the Navy as enlistees — we studied the sailor's bible, the Bluejackets Manual — didn't matter to me. Being a member of the Dalhgren Division, wearing my uniform, would give me a taste of the Navy in some way, in my own way, and not only make my father proud, but also allow me to connect with him.

After a few months of my uniform being found not quite "ship shape," after not really caring about what "Bluejackets" needed to know, after marching around for no reason other than it took up a bit more of the Saturday afternoon that I was already wasting at the Washington Navy Yard, I stopped going. The Sea Cadets weren't for me. The Naval Academy wouldn't be for me either. I didn't like the regimentation, I didn't like taking orders from the ersatz commander, nor did I like giving them. I didn't like inspections.

My dad didn't seem that taken by my experience, perhaps because of its enlistee emphasis. But I don't really know. We never talked about it.

Eventually, a letter from the Dahlgren Division arrived, informing me that I had been dropped from the rolls. I joined my first punk band less than a year later.

"The Admiral doesn't mind my cleaning windows," I said, answering Sylvia's question, "as long as I don't fall."

"Oh, come now," she said with a laugh. "He must be a bit..." Sylvia paused before deciding on her next word, "baffled."

I appreciated her choice. I'd heard "distressed" and even "disappointed" on other occasions, with other customers.

"I would say," I said, "that he struggles at times to understand why I do this and why my twin brother works as a paralegal to support his acting, for that matter. As for me, look, obviously this is dangerous work. But at least my dad gets why I play music, even if he's not a fan of the style. He played sax in a jazz band four nights a week when he was a kid, and he sings and plays guitar now. Still, I do wonder sometimes if he thinks I should just quit this crazy, dangerous job of mine and move on, and grow up."

Sometimes I wondered this myself, though I wasn't going to admit this to Sylvia. It might spoil the moment.

"Well, good luck with all that," Sylvia said, returning to photo spreads of outfits and catwalks.

While lugging my full bucket back to the windows, I stopped by my pile. I had to don my window cleaner's belt and pick up my crowbar. Now I felt all the more weighed down as I approached the sill. Time to do the exteriors. Usually when I encounter a warped frame, one I know I can't raise without a fight, I pull on the window's ballast chains so that their dropped weight can help me out. But since I didn't trust these chains — they looked so old they might break, making the window all but impossible to raise — I struggled to lift the frame with the crowbar's aid. I nudged it up a quarter of the way, a few inches at a time.

Though the window wasn't as high as I would have liked it to be, I did now have just enough space to pull myself through to the ledge, albeit with a bit of squirming and shimmying. And at least the window's ballasts worked well enough that the frame wouldn't slam down on me on my way out. I did not, however, look forward to the impending tussle to raise the window once more on my way back in, or opening the other window. Before settling myself onto the sill, I wetted down all four of my mops, two long, two short, and placed them out on the ledge, which I wished was not so narrow.

Once I had "limbo-ed" myself out to a sitting position on the ledge, I reached up with my right arm and attached the first of my belt's two metal clasps — one for my right side and the other for my left — to the belt hook built into the window frame's right side. The clasp's strong spring snapped its catch tightly against the hook, a round steel knob with a squared-off tip. I checked it by pulling up hard on the attached clasp in a harsh, sudden motion, as if to catch it off guard. I now felt safe; despite looking like they were in bad shape, they hadn't given a bit. I grasped the attached belt clasp and pulled myself up so that I stood on the ledge. Now I could see why the hook was so strong — the bolt that held it in place went through the window's exterior frame, through the building's brick wall, and through the window frame inside the apartment. It had been firmly in place for decades, since whenever the building had been put up.

Once I had attached the second clasp, I turned my head and did as I always do before cleaning a tricky window: I took a moment to take in the view. Why not? This look might well be my last. I smiled. How perfect: another window cleaner was out on his own ledge overlooking Broadway, a few buildings to the south. This one was using his chamois far too much. His customer was only going to enjoy a view with a lot of smudges.

Before I had ever picked up a squeegee, whenever I saw window cleaners working on-high, I had simply thought they were crazy; for that matter, before I started window cleaning, I never really noticed how many dirty windows there are in New York City. Early into my window cleaning, I realized that I was indeed in denial about the job's dangers because it took seeing someone else risking their life with a squeegee to appreciate that I, too, was risking my own. But I eventually got over that. I have, however, never gotten over all of the city's dirty windows.

The guy just down the street I now simply regarded as competition, as a job that Pat and I should be doing instead. Pat's my boss, Patrick Shields. He's a struggling-aspiring screenplay writer who went to college with my twin brother and started Shields Window Cleaning close to fifteen years earlier. I'd been working for him for seven years, just like an indentured servant I would occasionally joke.

I looked three long stories down. Delivery trucks and cars and cabs passed beneath me, or worse, sat and honked. Brief but regular moments of relative quiet occurred between these onslaughts, courtesy of well-timed stoplights. Considering all the exhaust these vehicles gave off, Sylvia (and, yes, her boyfriend) would be lucky if she had clean windows for a few weeks. The early afternoon traffic had also engulfed Broadway's sidewalks. People on their way to and from Soho and elsewhere darted below me, most dressed in black. Considering the hour, these folks were most likely reluctantly returning to their jobs after lunch, a bustling but not particularly inspiring sight. They resembled lemmings traveling tightly in a pack, and I felt like one, too, when I was down there amidst them.

I pulled my pole out onto the ledge from where I had leaned it on the sill and then, with my right foot, gently tried to close the window. Instead, it slammed down. So much for delicacy. At least the glass hadn't cracked. It had happened to me before with other windows. I attached a mop to my pole and wiped away some sweat from my face with the crook of my arm. While I ordinarily like to hold on to a hook with one hand while I clean with my other, the height of the windows and the care with which I needed to handle the pole prevented me from doing that. It would have to be a hands-free job. So, I leaned back and gave myself over to my belt, the building's hooks, and the ledge. They would have to hold me.

Not surprisingly, out here, too, the dirt on the glass proved stubborn, as mop water drizzled from the pole upon my head and shoulders. I'd been able to avoid this self-made waterfall inside, but on the ledge my belt curtailed my movements. Eventually, after a few washings, the dirt gave way. Replacing the mop with the squeegee, the rubber blade then moved along the transom's pane and the water, too, relented, leaving a shiny rectangle. To get ready to clean the main windows, I carefully leaned the pole back against the window frame's left side, trying my best to wedge its plastic tip back up against the decrepit wood.

Cleaning the window's exterior didn't really match my experience of cleaning its interior since, of course, I was not merely standing on an apartment floor, but strapped to the side of a building. And though I did have to keep many things in mind — not dropping the pole, not losing my footing, not dislodging a window pane, not leaving a streak — the joy of risk won out. I felt free and exposed, above the city and apart from the building. I mopped, squeegeed, and chamoised; mopped, squeegeed, and chamoised; mopped, squeegeed, and chamoised. Another stream of water ran down my arm. Slowly, the dirt on the pane departed, revealing a comparatively transparent sheet of glass. Despite the heat and despite the bits of wood that fell away from the frame as I cleaned, all was well.

But then I looked to my left, over at the next window, and saw that one of its ballast chains was broken, who knows for how long. Damn! I would have to cross over to that window from the outside. At least there weren't any hairpins or paper clips. Inspecting the window I'd just cleaned for streaks, I espied Sylvia watching me work from the table. I resisted the urge to wave.

I don't always mind crossing over. Beyond adding another thrill to the ledge, doing so also saves time, since I don't have to go back inside through one window only to come out again through another. Still, I prefer not having to do it, as the maneuver can be not just risky, but truly dangerous.

To get to the second window, I began by grasping both left and right hooks with my respective hands and then leaning my body to the right and removing my belt's metal clasp from the right-side hook. I then took baby steps to my left along the edge of the ledge, avoiding my mops along the way, and pushed my body up against the window frame's left side, the side I remained attached to. The moment of pure danger had arrived: I now had to detach my remaining clasp from the left-side hook, leaving me standing unhooked on the ledge. Though I was "only" fifty or so feet up, I was nonetheless high enough to die, or at least high enough to be paralyzed in a fall.

I had to remove this second clasp, my left-side clasp, so that I could then immediately attach the right-side clasp in its place. This would allow me to reach around the view-obstructing brickwork that separated the two windows with my left-side clasp in my left hand and attach myself to the next window's closest hook, sight unseen and untested. More excitement.

Lifting the clasp with my left hand and pulling back the catch's spring with my thumb, my feet tingled and my temples throbbed as the clasp came clear of the belt hook, and Windowland instantly and solely became that naked belt hook just inches from the clasp in my right hand. I had to reach it. As the clasp in my hand shot forward, various disasters flashed before me: one of my shoes slipping out from under me; the clasp knocking the pole from its place and my falling to the street along with it; a freakish wind blowing me off the ledge; the clasp missing the — the clasp clanged down hard upon the hook.

The last time I'd faced such a pronounced "grab the hook or else!" moment had been a while back. But since the ledge I'd been on was high above 13th Street, the street that I live on, the incident still seemed fresh since I walked below that close-call nearly every day. To have fallen to my death just two blocks from my apartment? Well, New York City can indeed be a small town.

With my right hand tightly gripping the clasp that was now attached to a belt hook once more, I reached my left arm around the brick column and sought the belt hook of the next window. I found it quickly, instinctively, since experience gave me a good idea of where it would be: waist-high and at arm's length. I clamped my clasp down on it and pulled up hard. I felt the belt hook remain in place.

Now hooked securely to both window frames, I swung my left leg from the first ledge to the second, pulling my body along as well, so that I straddled the brickwork between both windows. I faced not glass, but masonry, an always incongruous moment. Letting my hands go of both belt hooks, I knelt down and leaned back towards the first window's ledge, grabbed the mops from it, and moved them to the second ledge. I then did the same with the pole. Finally, I put myself on that ledge, carefully moving my belt's clasps from hook to hook, and got to work on the windows. When these panes were also done, I returned the mops and pole to the previous ledge and then crossed back myself to get to the first ledge and inside.

Damn it! If I could only get the window open, that is. I'd forgotten to bring my crowbar outside with me. Since the lower window's exterior was in such shoddy condition from exposure, much worse than on the inside, I couldn't risk pushing up the wooden frame too forcefully for fear that it would simply separate from the window pane. Perhaps it was just as well that I didn't have the crowbar. The weather-beaten wood could simply crumble against the metal tip. I needed help. I knelt down, peered inside, and softly knocked on the window frame. My soaked shirt clung to my back.

"Hey! Sylvia!" I shouted. "Can you come over here? Please?"

She abandoned her magazine and walked across the loft towards me, stood before the window and smiled.

"Are you stuck out there?" she asked through the glass, her arms akimbo, inspecting the scene.

"Uh, yes, I'm afraid I am."

Sylvia leaned forward, placing her hands on the sill and suddenly our faces were just inches apart, separated only by the shimmering window. It didn't matter that the ripples in the glass stretched her countenance this way and that. She was so close.

"How hilarious," Sylvia said with a laugh. "But the windows look great!"

"Thanks!" I said. Could she see I was blushing?

It was a bit embarrassing, a window cleaner stuck out on a ledge. This happened to me every so often. Once, when I had been ledge-bound on an overcast winter afternoon, the height-fearing customer had been so afraid to approach me that I had to convince the woman to cross the room to help raise the window. Her trip took nearly ten very cold minutes. Despite my slightly purple fingers, I nonetheless enjoyed that, instead of her talking me down from the ledge, I was coaxing her towards one. But at least she was home. When no one is, I simply have to work the window open and risk hurting my fingers, if not the window frames, to do so.

"Would you mind using the crowbar?" I asked Sylvia, pointing down at the windowsill.

"My pleasure," she said. "Do you think it's me?" Sylvia asked, picking up the steel bar and clutching it to her chest.

Sylvia then jammed the steel bar underneath the window frame and I stuck my fingers underneath as well. On a count of three, she pushed downwards, while I pulled upwards. Despite our obvious enthusiasm — she smiled broadly and grunted loudly; I dug my hands into the frame and whispered to the window, "Come on! Come on! Come on!" — the window barely moved. I could feel wooden splinters threatening to go under my fingernails. With Sylvia there, I hoped I wouldn't have to let the splinters advance any further. She'd have to do more of the work this time.

"Let's try it again," I said.

"I don't think we have much of a choice!"

With another go, the window did yield a bit and rise enough so that I could safely work my fingers underneath the wooden frame. Suddenly, I envisioned a squeegee-influenced production of a certain Shakespearean tragedy featuring a window-cleaning Romeo not on Juliet's balcony, but her ledge. I put the scene out of my head. This was getting silly.

"Okay," I said. "Once more."

On the third try, we raised the window to nearly the height it had been when I had gone out on the ledge. I handed Sylvia the pole, but spared her the mops. After releasing one belt clasp and then the other, I shimmied and "limbo-ed" back into the living room.

"Bravo! Brilliant! Well done!" Sylvia said as I set myself slowly back onto the floor.

"Thank you, thank you," I said. "But there will be no encore."

"Oh, that's a shame," Sylvia said as she handed the crowbar back to me. "I quite like this thing. It's so strong."

"Yes," I said, regretting that the moments of the smartly dressed Sylvia wielding the rather downscale crowbar had come to an end. "It does come in handy."

I took the tool over to my pile and left it and my window cleaner's belt there. Though I didn't need Sylvia's help for the remaining tilt-in windows, she tagged along anyway. She asked me about New York. I asked her about London. She asked me about my job. I asked her about...anything that came to mind. I almost always liked talking to customers. It helped pass the time and could also be regarded as customer relations, since clients were more likely to call back if they got along with me and Pat. But this was different. It felt more like a blind date, although one that involved squeegees and water breaks — and a crowbar.

As I dumped my bucket's last load of water down the sink, Sylvia leaned against the kitchen counter to my left, a few feet away.

"You really are a mess, Ivor," she said. "Just look at you."

I didn't have to peek at a mirror to know that Sylvia had spoken the truth. The afternoon's grime covered me, leaving layers of grey and black upon my arms and hands, and, I suspected, my face. Sweat now drenched my shirt, and I could taste salt and grit along my lips. The weather and the windows had taken their toll. I smiled.

"Oh, it comes with the job," I said as I inspected the squeegee I was rinsing. Cold water ran over the brass handle and my hand. "But I'm fine. It's just a bit of dirt."

A pause followed, and then Sylvia took a step towards me.

"You can wash up here, if you like," she said, her voice slow and soft. "Do you want to take a shower?"

Her fingers brushed lightly down the sleeve of my shirt. As they grazed my upper arm, the warmth of her skin contrasted with the sharpness of her fingernails. Her hand casually dropped away once her fingers reached my elbow.

I turned in her direction. Sylvia had tilted her head slightly, so that though some hair fell across her face, the angle nonetheless accentuated her raised eyebrow and her more than friendly smile. I wouldn't be bathing alone.

If I were Tomas, the doctor turned window-cleaning Valentino from Milan Kundera's *The Unbearable Lightness of Being*, I would have been quite pleased with myself: another seduction on the way. Instead, I took after Wallace, the good-hearted, window-cleaning claymation character from Nick Park's short film series, *Wallace & Gromit*. In one episode, Wallace becomes quite tongue-tied and awkward when smitten with Wendolena, the new customer whose windows he is washing.

I'd been propositioned before. A customer on the West Side, probably in her late forties, had answered her door at midday in a silk bathrobe and flirted with me the whole time I was working. She told me how she'd been a dancer so many years earlier, told me how crazy and "out there" she'd been, told me how much fun she'd had. When I'd finished, she ran a hand through her tightly curled hair and asked quite suggestively: "So, are windows all you do?" I told her they were. When I'd finished another job, the handsome young customer asked me out on a date. I told him I was flattered but that I was also straight.

With Sylvia, however, I was tempted. That was obvious. We'd certainly hit it off, and we were, apparently, attracted to each other. Moreover, her boyfriend wouldn't be home for hours. It would be so effortless, a clichéd soft-porn fantasy coming true. Unbelievable. The shower waited just steps away, the "comfy" bed, a few steps further. All I had to say was "Yes."

"Oh, no, that's okay," I said, looking back down at the squeegee that I now held quite tightly. "But thank you. I'm actually running late for my next job."

I really was: I was due at 38th and First in ten minutes, and there was no way I was going to get there on time, even if I splurged and took a cab. It was a one-hundred dollar job. And a time-consuming one, at that. If I didn't get there soon, the work staff at the Corinthian or the customer himself might not let me in, since they would deem me too late to start the job. But more than that, sticking around at Sylvia's would mean getting to the studio much later than I already would be. And that would not have been cool — it was a rare early session — even though I would have had a "brilliant" story to tell.

Despite my rationalization, I felt like such a.... I couldn't decide. A dork?

I certainly hadn't followed through, hadn't seized my chance. Unimaginative? I certainly considered my response to her line a bit feeble. Running late. Couldn't I have been at least a little clever?

But any scenario I pictured just included complications. What if it turned out badly, the sex that is. For that matter, what if it turned out really well? What if I fell in love with her? What if we were caught? Even though I wasn't seeing anyone, I didn't want to cross that line, at least not like this.

"Oh, all right," she said, turning and walking away to the dining table. She seemed much farther than just across the room.

Sylvia or the studio. The studio or Sylvia. The choice I'd just made rattled through me as I skipped washing the rest of my tools and simply tossed them into my bucket. Similarly, by the door while gathering up my stuff, I didn't strap my window belt back on, but threw it in my bucket as well.

Sylvia or the studio.

As I stood in the doorway, Sylvia handed me the check, her face now severe and taut. So much for trying to get twenty dollars per window.

"Here you are," she said coolly. "Thank you again." The ice princess had returned.

"Thank you," I said, taking the piece of paper from her without checking the amount. I could feel myself also becoming detached; walls were building themselves back up, windows were being shut. "Take care."

I heard a half-hearted "Cheers" as she closed the door, and I was banished.

Despite my attempt to leave quietly, as I descended the stairs my footsteps, my window cleaner's belt, and my bucket of tools echoed once more; even the building's door slammed loudly behind me. Usually when I've finished a job that isn't absurdly high up, I try to admire my handiwork from the sidewalk. But I didn't this time. Not that I thought Sylvia would be looking down at me from her windows, I just didn't want to look up. I didn't want to look back. Instead, I looked ahead as I made my way up the shady side of a crowded Broadway en route to the subway, the Spring Street stop on the 6 line.

Sylvia or the studio. That I had turned her down made me virtuous at some level, I guess. I had done the right thing. She did have a boyfriend. Plus, I did not want to be late yet again to the studio. Windowland had been delaying me a lot during these early sessions. Still, I'd crossed a line of some kind back there: if I had stayed and "showered" with Sylvia, I was quite sure

I would have enjoyed the tryst much more than a recording session. That sounds patently obvious, but really, it shouldn't be for me. For the studio not to come before sex, or at least be tied for first place, well....

Looking out at the Manhattan skyline, I didn't dwell too much on being just inches from a fifty-five story plunge. Nor did I fixate on the gusts of wind that could make my fall more likely; the blasts of air felt almost welcome against the heat. Instead, right before I drew my squeegee and entrusted myself to the slender ledge I now stood on, I took in my latest potential "last look." This one ranked as a classic. Four blocks north on 42nd Street, the Chrysler Building glistened in the late afternoon sun, not quite dusk's magic hour that filmmakers love, but close enough.

In terms of falling, I didn't particularly relish being so high up, but I did appreciate how cleaning the ten windows of this high-in-the-sky apartment gave me ten potential last looks that were far more satisfying than what I'd seen from Sylvia's third floor. My perch at five-hundred and fifty-five feet put me at nearly the same height as the Chrysler's chromium-nickel gargoyles that guard the building's upper reaches.

I squinted at the Art Deco rocket ship, but its gleaming white ceramic bricks and shiny stainless steel ornamentation proved too bright for my eyes. So much for truly savoring that view. I focused on the Chrysler's neighboring buildings. Not surprisingly, they seemed to simply recede, admitting their lesser stature.

Having had to give up on the Chrysler Building, I sought another dramatic view by looking to my left, crosstown, at the Empire State Building, just four blocks south. The sun accentuated its steel spandrels so that a harsh band of light raced down this skyscraping pencil's trim. I squinted and smiled at my lack of luck; my little daily doses of melodrama were being squelched. Still, I've never worn sunglasses out on a ledge. Apart from them possibly slipping off my face, shades leave me feeling too removed from my surroundings and make spotting streaks on the windows I've cleaned that much harder. And though I occasionally cover my head to shield myself from the elements, I never wear baseball caps: they make me look like Mike Love of the Beach Boys.

Seeing the Empire State Building reminded me, once more, of a famous Life magazine photo from the 1940s. The shot features a woman who fell to her death from the building, then the world's tallest. She landed on an automobile. The sedan's roof is crumpled, a mangled mess. But the woman, strangely, is not. She looks so peaceful, even graceful, lying on her back, a forever sleeping beauty at 33rd and Fifth. That's how I'd like to look should a window ever best me. I looked away and got back to work.

Ignoring the sun and the wind, I felt my heart not beat, but pound. I bent my knees slightly, took a deep breath, and with my left hand, grasped the metal window frame made hot to the touch by the day's still-high temperature. I then tested my left shoe's grip on the apartment's interior windowsill by slightly tensing and moving my foot. It held.

The customer had been pretty cool about my being late. But then he had asked if I would take my sneakers off to reduce the chances of my scuffing anything in his place. I wondered if this was some passive-aggressive way of punishing my tardiness. Actually, when I hear such requests I do fight back asking the client if they are out of their fucking mind. What are they thinking? But I had politely rejected his request, explaining that socks just do not provide enough traction on the sills and ledges. If he had insisted that I remove my shoes, I would have threatened to walk away from the job. I wasn't about to die so that he could simply avoid what should be accepted as normal wear-and-tear to an apartment in New York City: if you're going to get your windows cleaned, the window cleaner will wear sneakers or even work boots to do them.

I then tested my right shoe's hold on the building's exterior ledge. This I did a bit more tentatively, as the ledge was narrower than my sneaker and angled downward. I didn't want to put too much weight on that foot. Satisfied that my "half-in, half-out" stance was safe enough, I nonetheless streched forward a little more than I would have liked to, since I sought to line my squeegee up against the far side of the glass pane I had just wetted down with my mop. I wanted to clean as much of the window's far side as I could in one swipe. I wanted to get this job, this window, over with.

Lowering the squeegee and myself to the next wet section of the glass, I again pulled the blade first downwards and then back towards me, stopping once more at the window's half-way point. Another dry and clean swath appeared — with no streaks to the buildings glassy skin. I repeated this motion a third time in a squat-like crouch to reach the bottom section of the window pane, making sure as I pulled my squeegee back towards me that I didn't totter over (and down), to become a little ball of screaming window cleaner on his way to meet his maker, or, at least, the pavement.

Once I'd pulled the squeegee back towards me, I took the chamois cloth from my window cleaner's belt, rolled it around the tip of my squeegee — known as a "chamois on a stick" — and dabbed the window's far corners and edges, removing the stray drips that remained beyond my arm's reach. There. I'd finished half of the window. Now, just the nearer part of the pane remained dirty.

I'd never liked doing windows at the Corinthian. Curved edges and clusters of semi-circular rooms defined this striking high-rise, making its light chocolate-brown bricks seem to ripple outward and seemingly ever upward. Even now, years into this job, I dreaded the building. Whoever designed this apartment house certainly had a distinctive look in mind, but they obviously didn't concern themselves with what window cleaners would have to deal with as a result of their handiwork: very dangerous windows. What was the point of such narrow ledges? And, why should they angle downwards? Did the architect want to assure that I experience my final moment on Earth decades earlier than I would have preferred? Didn't he think about those who would have to cling to the building's side as a result of his folly? What an idiot.

I'd thought my Corinthian qualms would wane as I got to know the building. They hadn't. But I shouldn't have been too surprised — its ledges' widths and angles hadn't changed either. My way of dealing with this, then, had been to turn these tricky windows — my way of both describing and denying especially hazardous panes — into a challenge. I would conquer them. Still, whenever I've finished a job there, I've always felt that I hadn't actually beaten the windows. Rather, the windows had simply let me get away with cleaning them. I was now half a window from believing that the ten windows in this living room had let me squeak by once more. They would be giving me a pass.

Standing on the building's ledge and windowsill, I knelt and picked up the mop beside my left foot, my inside foot, and wetted down the remaining dirt on the window pane's exterior. Drops of water fell from the end of the mop and blew away, scattered by the wind. This high up — as high as the Washington Monument — I would never, of course, see the drips land. When I work on lower floors, much lower floors, I do like to watch the water drops complete their journey and transform from perfect spheres to ugly splotches on the sidewalk. At times, I have imagined myself falling with them. Then, I quickly recall the aplomb of the Empire State Building woman and this — she — somehow reassures me.

"Ti ti ti tisis! Ti ti ti tisis! Ti ti tis boom!"

Stop! No! Stop! Not now! I did my best to banish the new song's drum beat. Now was not the time for it to kick in, to take over. Still, perhaps this was a sign that it was at least a little good? To get the beat out of my head, I simply looked down. And joked to myself.

Were I to fall, what should I take out? Crumpling a car had been done already. Besides, the Corinthian was set so far back from the street that hitting any vehicle was out of the question. So, how about a hedge? Or a large pedestrian? Or a yapping dog?

My Corinthian Fear should not be confused with my daily and essential on-the-job Fear. That feeling, that pit in my stomach, that wariness I've experienced since my first day of window cleaning, I had come to regard as a companion, a life saver. We have a simple bond, really, a clear understanding between us: Fear has kept me aware; being aware has kept me alive. And we'd been true to each other thus far. I've remained scared and on the ledge, not fearless and, well, dead. Surprisingly, the first time I experienced a close-call, wry resentment flashed through me: so this is how it ends, dropping off a damn window ledge. But then pure appreciation quickly followed, and I relished touching the window frame's belt hook.

After a close call, I'm simply glad not to be splat on the sidewalk beneath me. Like status, with this job I've learned to take delight where I can find it and when I have the chance. Call them low-key epiphanies.

Man, did I wish the Corinthian had hooks.

I wiped the window's midsection, and then had to mop and squeegee the pane a second time, as my angle hadn't been quite right. This happened sometimes. Why hadn't I simply refused to work in the Corinthian? An easy trinity answers that question: I didn't want to let the windows "win;" I didn't want to let down my customers who live there; I needed the money. I squatted once more and squeegeed and chamoised the last third of the pane. There, I'd finished the window, completed the job.

Rising from my crouch, I stood again, half-in and half-out, and looked at the now clean window a final time for streaks and missed spots. Though washed panes are not mirrors by any means, I did catch a muted reflection of myself in the glass. Then I looked beyond me, continuing my search for splotches, for mistakes. I don't like seeing myself out on Corinthian ledges. Doing so means I can't deny what I am doing.

I looked up from the clean piece of glass. New York seemed so peaceful fifty-five stories up, so manageable. Being that high, above the sidewalk and the people strolling or jostling, above the trees, grass, and bushes, above the taxis and buses and cars, above plenty of other buildings for that matter — above the world — hassles and worries fall away for the moment. They're all down there, irrelevant. But height alone does not prompt me to feel this way. My work does its share as well. Cheating death by standing out on a narrow ledge burns away the superfluous, leaving only the essential: I am alive.

I turned away from Midtown and came down from the ledge. The time had come to put things back in place on the sill. A few books and a lamp reclaimed their spots, as did a telescope and a pair of binoculars. The farther up people lived, it seemed the more often they had their spyglasses out and at the ready.

As I repeatedly wiped down one section of the window sill, doing my best to remove some slight markings my shoes had indeed left, I looked about the room and silently decried this customer's taste. He was no boyfriend of Sylvia's! His couch was simply a blob of black leather. The bookshelves were a deep, dark red, while the coffee table was made of grey steel flecked with black paint. I might as well have been in somebody's low-budget office, except I'm sure this guy had spent a lot of money on this junk. While I do enjoy seeing how other people live, working in tacky surroundings does lessen the pleasure I take in my job.

I looked back down at the smudges and after conceding that the marks would not disappear, I discretely placed a few magazines on top of the spots, and then turned and addressed the customer. His reflection in the glass had let me see him walk into the room and stand at its doorway. He was a largish man in his forties, with a balding head, a clipped beard, and wire-rim glasses. I motioned to the telescope to distract him from inspecting the windowsill.

"See anything good lately?" I asked in an off-hand way.

The man laughed, and his face turned slightly red.

"Oh, that thing. No, not really. Not in this neighborhood."

Now it was my turn to chuckle.

"Come on," I said, making a point to sound light-hearted. "You must see all kinds of things from this high up."

The customer paused.

"Well, yeah," he said. "I take a look around every so often. But, really, people have blinds and even when they are up, most everything is so far away."

"That's true," I said, nodding my head in agreement. Many times when I've checked out people with telescopes, their acts, be they vacuuming or having sex, have seemed remote and out of context; albeit up-close, there's no connection.

"May I?" I asked, pointing to the binoculars.

"Oh, sure."

I picked up the lenses clad in heavy black metal, looked down and brought into focus a five-story brick building a few blocks south on 35th Street. Few of its windows had shades. Some men and women in their teens and twenties came and went through the building's front doors, or chatted on the sidewalk near the entrance.

"That place down there could be interesting," I said. "I mean, I've just noticed a bunch of young people hanging out in front of it."

"Yeah," the customer replied, "You'd think so. But, no, not really."

I smiled to myself. I had lived in the building some years earlier. Indeed, I'd been living there when I first started cleaning windows — with blinds that were rarely drawn. Now, however, curtains prevented me from seeing into an ex-girlfriend's place. But I didn't mention this, preferring to enjoy my secret. Besides, telling him would have only put him on the spot and embarrassed him — and possibly cost me a tip. So I kept my mouth shut, put the binoculars back down, finished making the windowsill presentable instead of harrowing, and then went to the kitchen to rinse out my tools.

My first day of window cleaning now seemed so long ago, and not simply because it *had* been long ago: my embracing so many aspects of the job that had at first thrown me had also added distance. Over time, I had come to know how to handle a squeegee, how to handle myself on a ledge, and how to handle customers. I know how much to charge for any given window: $8 and up, depending on type, size, and difficulty, with a minimum charge of $42 for a job. Moreover, I had also come to appreciate the risk and voyeurism that accompany the work. The heights and sights were unknown elements that now I saw as near-essential perks.

On my first day, I found it strange to be walking about in a stranger's apartment, having the run of it. This wasn't like when I'd delivered newspapers down in D.C. as a kid and stood in the hallway, or perhaps sat on the couch, and waited to be paid. Those once-a-month stops would prompt only occasional glimpses, random clues.

At one house, I recall that while an elderly customer searched her purse for a pen, I saw that since my last visit, an American flag folded neatly into a triangle had taken the place of her husband in his reading chair. When the woman saw me glancing at the Stars and Stripes, she quietly began to cry. I left a few minutes later with a smudged check written out to The Washington Post.

During my first day of window cleaning nothing so sad had taken place, but revealing moments occurred regularly along the way. At the first job, a tony duplex on Central Park West, my boss, Pat, had encouraged me to take a look around, as the customer was not home, just the maid. I felt like an intruder going from room to room. But I did have a reason to be in each one: I had to count how many windows there were to price the job.

Later, Pat pointed out a stack of boxes containing Amway household products that lined the customer's kitchen wall; they had not been there on his last visit a few months earlier. Since the cartons were still full, and since the maid had not been using any Amway cleaners that morning, Pat guessed that this customer had fallen on hard times in some way and was now considering selling Amway as a new livelihood. As Pat wrung out his chamois in the sink, he wished the customer luck since this expensive pad of theirs would be hard to hold onto. A few months later, Pat and I spotted the apartment listed for sale in the back of The New York Times Magazine. We recognized its staircase in the photo. Had Pat been correct? We never found out. The customer never called us again, but a doorman in the building did tell us that this tenant had indeed moved.

The next job that day found me and Pat at a much more downscale dwelling, a modest one-bedroom rental in a plain modern building on the East Side. The schoolteacher who lived there talked with Pat as I acquainted myself with my squeegee, learning my novel mantra of "mop, squeegee, chamois." By the job's and their conversation's end, Pat had learned that years earlier the woman had dated the acerbic comedian and actor Dennis Leary. Deep in reverie, the woman said that Hollywood should really cast Dennis as a romantic lead. The public hadn't seen that side of him, he could really be.... Her voice trailed off and I had an unkind thought. Had they broken up because she hadn't been cool enough for him? I then realized, that, though my question didn't matter, I did enjoy what prompted it: hearing her story. Knowing this bit of her life helped to make up for my now exhausting mantra, my raw hands, and my dirty clothes. I had naively worn a white collared shirt that day in deference to being in upscale surroundings. It was now ruined, and we still had one more apartment to do. I began wearing my all-black ensemble the next day. It wasn't a stretch. I'd been wearing essentially black jeans and black tee shirts ever since my junior year at Vassar, the look of the artsy crowd I floated in.

Pat and I had concluded that first day of mine at another duplex, an ornate penthouse on Park Avenue. There, I quite willingly went from room to room to count the windows, taking my time to admire the grand piano in the living room, the marble staircase that spiraled upwards to the second floor, the billowy canopy bed in the guest room, the brass-plated bathroom fixtures, the view of the Armory across the way. The maid in her gray and white uniform made sure we took note of the new raw silk curtains in the dining room. In a thick Russian accent, she had both informed and warned us that we were to get no water or dirt on them, or to harm them in any way. That would upset the lady of the house very much.

It turned out that Pat and I upset the lady of house the moment she stepped into her home simply by our presence. She had wanted us to be done and gone by the time she got back. But we had been running late and so had not yet departed. She chewed us out while Pat prepared to go out on a dining room window's ledge.

As Pat pulled himself up and out of the window, the lady of the house suddenly interrupted her rant with a sharp yell: "Be careful!" This outburst of humanity surprised and pleased me. She wasn't so horrible after all. Then the lady of the house finished her sentence: "...of the drapes!" Oh. We hadn't brought out the worst in her, just the truth.

I looked up from my bucket as I finished placing my now-rinsed tools back into it, and called out to the bearded Corinthian customer that I was done. Time to get paid, time to finally be on my way to the studio. He entered the kitchen as I wiped down the counter.

"So, how much do I owe you again?" he asked, pulling out his wallet.

I smiled, as that meant cash.

"Oh, same as last time," I said. "We charge ten dollars a window here and I cleaned ten windows, so that's a total of one-hundred dollars."

"Are you sure?" the man asked. "That sounds kinda high. I thought it was nine dollars a window."

"Ah, well, actually," I said, stalling as I gauged how blunt I would be. "We've been charging ten per window here for a while. I mean, your windows are outright dangerous."

I was not about to haggle over Corinthian windows. In fact, I felt insulted that he had questioned the price. Indeed, if I could have, I would have charged more for these panes.

I waited in silence. Was he going to acquiesce or be a jerk?

"Oh, right," he said after a few seconds. "Of course. Here you go."

He counted out five twenties.

I thanked him as I took the money and put it in my wallet. Damn! No tip. Cash can work against you when customers have expected to pay less, and so see more money leaving their billfold than they anticipated. Plus, it wasn't, say, $102, a number he could have responded to by giving me $110 and telling me to keep the change. Also, he may have mistakenly thought that I would pocket the entire amount for myself, "off the books." Or perhaps he'd come across my sneaker marks? No, I'm sure he would have pointed them out. But it wasn't for me to find out the answers to such questions. And, of course, he didn't have to tip me. Still, I did wonder what this guy would charge if he were about to go out on the ledge and clean some Corinthian windows.

I picked up the in-house phone and called the Service Elevator, telling its operator that I was on the fifty-fifth floor and waiting for him. I then picked up my bucket and the rest of my gear, and bid goodbye to the customer.

"Enjoy the view," I said.

"Thanks," he said as he closed the door behind me. "I'll enjoy it even more now."

I pictured the guy walking over to his telescope and binoculars. I just hoped he didn't move those magazines.

The Corinthian boasted one of the fastest, most modern Service Elevators I'd ever ridden in the city. It didn't simply go up and down, it took off and plummeted, nearly always tempting my knees to buckle. Nor was it simply a box attached to cables. With its large size, it nearly qualified as a room.

If it was a little bigger, it would have bordered on being my apartment's size. The elevator sported bright fluorescent lighting, an extremely high ceiling, metal-plated walls that withstood the knocks and scrapes of most any object it swallowed, and an electrical outlet that allowed the worker manning the controls — this elevator serving fifty-five stories had many, many buttons — to listen to the radio. It also had room enough for him to sit in a chair in fan-cooled comfort. Very impressive.

I headed back to Grand Central to catch a subway downtown to my place and then the studio. Striding up Second Avenue, I felt a bit weighed down. By workday's end my courier bag, my bucket of tools, my pole, my window cleaner's belt, and even my squeegee holster usually do feel pretty heavy.

After popping into a deli to take out my usual on-the-go meal of two sesame bagels and a half-dozen bananas, I craned my neck as I walked past the Highpoint at 40th and Second, another new high-rise I worked in occasionally. Its brick and cement don't undulate like the Corinthian's. In-stead, they form a conventional forty-five-story red rectangular box — with ledges that aren't too narrow and don't point downwards. But, like the Co-rinthian, like any building, it has its drawbacks. Whereas the Corinthian's "non-stationary" windows conveniently open in like doors, the Highpoint's equivalent have to be "popped out" of their tracks and brought down onto the apartment's floor to be cleaned. They are ridiculously heavy, unwieldy, and easy to drop, if not to the floor then down to the street. Moreover, many of the apartments feature wall-to-wall carpeting, meaning I typically wrestle these window frames into the bathroom so that I can clean them on the tile floor.

Once, in a bid to save both time and toil in a Highpoint residence, I had availed myself to an absent client's throw rug so that I could clean the windows upon it. Then, upon finishing the job, I realized that I had been using the customer's prayer rug. Oh, boy. Was I going to be smote? But then I figured his Almighty would let me slide since I'd only slightly stained the rug's underside.

The Highpoint, too, had been where I was once accused of stealing a different customer's ring. The man had called Pat and told him that the gold band had been on the table in the living room in the morning when he'd left for work, but had "gone missing" by the time he'd returned. I hadn't taken the ring, and I also knew that the treasured object hadn't been on the table. How? Because after I'd finished that job, I'd killed some time at the apartment, as I had an hour before I had to be at my next job — at the nearby Corinthian. So, I had checked out the table in the living room to see if any of the magazines displayed on it were worth reading. A New Yorker was. And that's all that the table had to show for itself: a few periodicals. Of course Pat couldn't tell the customer this, so he didn't. The client called back the next day to say that the ring had turned up elsewhere in the apartment, but the jerk barely apologized.

Such situations crop up with this occupation. At times, I do know more about a client's apartment than they would like to hear. And, at times, I forget that an apartment does not merely contain a number of windows I have to clean, or is simply a place I spend a few hours with my squeegee; it is someone's home. But this mercenary feeling doesn't crop up too often, and usually only when the client isn't there. It's a case of out of sight, out of mind.

As I chewed my bagel, I rejoiced that I did not have to contend with the Highpoint that afternoon. I could just walk on by. Reaching 42nd Street, I took a left and there, again, took in the Chrysler Building. It wasn't the same from the ground, but I still admired the skyscraper. In fact, from my vantage point on the sidewalk, I could actually see a few of the winged radiator caps that grace the twenty-sixth floor, something I couldn't do from my earlier roost. Now however, I was merely looking up at the building; I wasn't in league with it as when I'd been out on the Corinthian's ledge. I entered the Chrysler's subway entrance.

I now felt lemming-like as I walked ahead, behind, and beside hundreds of fellow riders-to-be, all headed in the same direction. As I approached the stairs that would take me to the platform for the 6 train, I heard the sound of a subway screeching to a halt downstairs as it entered the station. I took the steps quickly and wedged myself into the stainless steel subway car.

Though the train's air conditioning provided immediate and welcome relief from Grand Central's swelter, the collective sweat from the press of passengers quickly overwhelmed the car's ventilation system. Riders glared as they made space for me and my bucket, seeming to regard me as a two-pronged threat. I sensed that those nearest me worried that my clothes might dirty their suits or dresses. And then there was my "22," one end of which just jutted out over the lip of my bucket. Shins and knees certainly did not want to make contact with it.

It's a simple device, my squeegee, possessing a kind of low-tech charm. What you see is what you get: a brass handle to wrap one's fingers around, a brass spanner to slide the rubber blade into, a rubber blade to wipe the window clean, a couple of brass screws to keep the non-rusting tool together. It's not flashy, though its brass does occasionally shine in the sun. My squeegee has allowed me to enter high-profile buildings, but only through the Service Entrance; I am there to do a job after all. By high-profile buildings, by the way, I don't mean the Corinthian or the Highpoint. I'm referring to buildings on the Upper East and Upper West Sides of town.

In this light, I've felt lucky. Otherwise, apartment houses like Central Park West's Century, Majestic, and Eldorado would remain off-limits and unknown. Incidentally, I've always found it appropriate that most of the older Fifth and Park Avenue apartment buildings don't have names, but are simply known for their street addresses. I suppose that the builders and architects simply figured that the street's name was enough. And this tact seems in keeping with the understated outward appearances of such buildings as, say, 912 and 920 Fifth or 755 Park. But, I can say, their interiors are quite ornate.

I peered up at the ads that lined the edge of the train's ceiling; a dermatologist offered a special on chemical peels that promised a new face, if not a new life.

That morning, when I'd thought about coming up with a beat for Michael's new song, I'd wondered what it would be like not having to come up with a cool new beat. The studio hadn't gone that well the night before. One, I was late getting there due to a really time-consuming window job. And, two, I'd dozed off during the session, despite my best efforts. Ten-hour window days wear me down now and then — except that "now and then" had become "often."

I wanted to take the easy out and figure that squeegeeing was tiring me out more readily than it used to; that my drifting off in the studio was simply a sign of my needing more sleep. But I had my doubts. I mean, I hadn't been tired when I wasn't thinking about coming up with beats. And to be thinking this now? I mean, here I was off to the recording studio, with a new beat to work on, no less.

Since the thought was in my head, I decided to pursue it. All right then: so, what if I wasn't in a band? Just for the sake of argument, just so I could get the thought out of my head, I decided to play The Scenario Game and come up with all the different possibilities that could follow this potential decision.

What if I didn't have a band? What would I do? What would my life be like? What would *I* be like? In my mind I looked around for possibilities, but couldn't find any. Only blankness. Only nothing.

Then I thought about the band as it was at the moment. What did I see? Only blankness. Only nothing. Huh. Well, at least I had my new beat. And I was going to the recording studio.

As the subway car emptied somewhat on its way south, I placed my bucket on the floor and stood over it, hoping no one would trip over my equivalent of a briefcase; they are about the same size. After a stop or two, a seat opened up and I sat down, glad for even two stops worth of rest. Since, in my rush to depart Sylvia's, I'd apparently left behind my copy of the day's paper, I continued to read the ads that the car offered up, ate my bananas, and dropped their peels into my bucket of squeegees.

TWO

A spacious second-story apartment, a busy side street in the morning, and tilt-in windows in the shade: one of my favorite workday combinations. The low height, passers-by, and easy panes meant I could enjoy some effortless and extended people-watching, with windows that I didn't have to worry about. And, as this apartment overlooked a small corner of the Upper East Side, I did have plenty to check out.

Already that Monday morning, I had seen from the living room windows quite a few financial bigwigs walk out from under their building's front awnings, squeeze into their limos, and be off to Wall Street. Or, perhaps they were lawyers, or bankers, or accountants headed to Midtown. Regardless of who they were, wherever they were going, or whatever apartment house they emerged from, courteous doormen directed the Lincolns, Cadillacs, and the occasional Mercedes into Park Avenue's stop-and-go slipstream below me. The grey, or green, or blue uniforms with matching, brimmed hats smiled, nodded, and laughed, and then turned and did so again for the next departing resident. I knew the feeling of being accommodating, help-ful, and cheerful — even though Christmas tips were half a year away. The customer is meant to be pleased; the customer is always right. Or, more accurately: the customer is never wrong.

The guy whose apartment I was in, however, hadn't yet departed for downtown. He hadn't even come out of the master bedroom. This was just as well, since on the few occasions that I had seen him, he had always struck me as a brusque guy in a dark suit with dark hair whose temper I did not want to test. But odds were that when he left through the front door, he would go unseen.

His wife, however, was up and about, looking slim, tan, and fiftyish in a light-brown designer tracksuit. Her blonde hair, freshly frosted it appeared, accentuated her narrow face as she enjoyed her morning coffee. Phoenix, the family poodle, stood at her side, white, tall, and silent; he had gotten his barking out of the way when I'd rung the kitchen door and the lady of the house had let me and Pat in. Apart from talking about the dog and her recent college-graduate son, my conversations with the lady of the house generally revolved around her seemingly unending need for dental work. I had never really sorted out her mouth's ongoing problems, but then, I didn't really want to know them either.

Fortunately, she wasn't a hoverer — the kind of customer that tails me, checking on my work. So, I could count on such talks being brief and her leaving me and my boss alone with her dirty windows. Pat was one room over, working in the dining room that I always made a point to get a good look at. Though its fabric-lined walls of thin, white and creme stripes weren't my taste, they were impressive nonetheless for their craftsmanship. I'd once heard a contractor complain in another client's place — out of ear-shot of the customer, of course — how difficult such work was: "Do you know how God damn hard it is to get the wall to puff out just right?! But nobody ever thinks about that!" These walls and the rest of this apartment, its mahogany antiques and brass candelabras, its dark red leather chairs and built-in bookcases bespoke a cold, costly elegance. The place seemed more like a showroom than somewhere to live.

With the living room completed, I now stood balanced on a radiator in the den. Having decided to get the window with the air conditioner over with first, I'd turned the machine off and unplugged its chord to prevent my being shocked. As I mopped and squeegeed and chamoised the window's inside pane, I looked down at the sidewalk. A group of girls dressed in their Catholic school's uniform of blue plaid skirts and white blouses strolled below, off to the start of what must have been close to their last week of classes just down the street. I wondered if they would cross Park in time for the first period bell. Men, women, and children who were nearby rushed past, lost in their thoughts as they dashed off to somewhere else. The building's young porter who was sweeping away the dirt he found along the building's edge, however, had certainly taken notice. He'd set his broom aside and leaned against the building, watching the girls. From my angle, I could just make out a smile. He couldn't have been more than a few years older than them, in his late teens or early twenties. But the girls ignored him as they did everyone else, and he went back to his sweeping, passing beneath me.

I watched a large nanny pushing a tiny stroller, but this time I was caught; the kid, blonde and cute and maybe two years old, had been staring up at the trees that lined the street and managed to spy me at work. She waved a little hand and I quickly waved back and then she and her unaware guardian were gone, down the block and likely off to Central Park. I noticed my smile in the clean interior glass.

I then raised the window and everything went wrong.

Instead of a smooth, silent motion, I felt a sudden jerk in the window-pane and heard the grating sound of metal ripping away. An electric chill shot through me as I shut my eyes and clenched my fists, bracing myself for what I knew was to come: the air conditioner detonated on the pavement a moment later.

"Fuck!" I whispered to myself.

The putty-colored rectangular cube now sat on the sidewalk, spewing a bright-green geyser; it looked bigger down there than when it had been right next to me. A breeze blew through the gap in the window frame where the A.C. had been, and I could feel the air conditioner and the window taunting me, besting me. I chamoised the window as much as to give myself something to do as to deny what I had done.

At least no one had been nailed by the air conditioner. No stroller lay crushed beneath it; no dog paws splayed outward from below; no school or building uniform protruded. I suddenly felt giddy in my relief and luck

"Ive!" Pat yelled as he ran into the den. "What the fuck happened?" He was hyperventilating and speaking very quickly. "I heard the crash and I first thought it was a car accident, but then I saw the —"

"I thought," I began, "that —"

"What the hell was that?"

It was the lady of the house striding quickly into the room as well, along with Phoenix. Her coffee had stayed behind.

Since I didn't want to see them, I remained facing the window, pretending to look down at the air conditioner and the small crowd that had begun to gather around it. One or two people pointed up at the open window and me. My eyes were half-closed, opting to stare at a nearby tree limb and its leaves that weren't going anywhere. I began again.

"I thought that it was in place," I said. "There was a bar and everything."

"What are you talking about?" she asked. Her understandable impatience gave her already nasal voice an added edge.

Realizing that I now had to come down, I turned away from the window, jumped down from the radiator, and explained how I had believed that the air conditioner had been secured by a metal bar and not the window frame itself. The bar would have allowed me to raise the window, tilt the frame in, and clean the pane without the A.C. falling; it would have stayed in place. I pointed to the steel span the width of the windowpane, still screwed into place across the bottom edge of the window. But the bar was merely cosmetic. Whoever had installed the air conditioner had only made it *look* safe. Until this morning, Pat had always cleaned this window. He must have told me at some point of the faux safety bar, and I must have forgotten.

As I spoke, the husband walked in and I could hear that my voice was inordinately quiet, even soft. I do that when I'm on the spot; I lower it to keep from being swept away by emotions and the dread possibility of shedding tears. But I think I also simply fear my voice will sound whiny. I wondered as well if it seemed like I was giving a lecture instead of an apology. I realized that I hadn't even said "I'm sorry" yet. I started over, beginning to explain to him what had occurred, but he cut me off.

"Don't bother," he said. His voice was steady and firm, angry but not upset. His hair remained unruffled as well. "I can see the screw-up from here. But look, the important thing is that no one got hurt outside and no one got hurt inside. It is, after all, only a damn air conditioner. But Pat, let me be perfectly clear: you owe me a new one."

I was relieved. I'd been convinced he was going to chew me out. Of course, I could have been the "screw-up" he had referred to.

"No problem, sir," Pat said. "Of course, of course. I'll get you one right away." Pat then turned to me. "But, Ive, Ive. We've got to get rid of it right now."

"Right," I said. But before taking a step, I turned to the customer. "Uh, sir, I just want you to know that I'm very, very sorry for all this."

I tried to put some emotion into the words, but I could hear them sounding flat and detached. I'd try again when we came back up from the street.

"Hey," he said, "these things happen."

As we ran out of the den, through the kitchen, down the back steps, past a few of the building's workers in the cellar, and out the Service Entrance, I knew I'd been granted a reprieve and tried various apologies in my head. "Again, sir, I'm really sorry. I'm truly sorry. I am so sorry." I also wondered if our customers had noticed that Pat's nervous twitch had kicked in. It did so at moments like this and caused the right side of his lip to rise every few seconds. I wondered if Pat knew. I wasn't going to point anything out.

In the time that it took to get to the sidewalk, the air conditioner's geyser had subsided to a dribble. At first, I couldn't believe that pedestrians were simply walking past the A.C. and not stopping to stare. But then they hadn't seen it fall, they hadn't heard it hit. To them, I guessed, the air conditioner appeared to be merely abandoned — not lethal. Perhaps they thought that some lazy workers had just not gotten around to tossing the thing in the dumpster. Pat and I knelt on opposite sides of the behemoth and shook our heads.

Though a customer who worked for the city had once told me that it was against New York City law to have an air conditioner extend beyond a window frame (Building Code Article 9, Section 27/313, "Permissible Projections Beyond Street Lines" states than an air conditioner cannot extend more than ten inches from a window frame when the unit is more than ten feet from the ground; four inches when it is less than ten feet; I looked it up), a stroll down most any street in Manhattan with your head looking up will tell you that it is one of the city's least enforced laws. Looking down at the A.C., I wondered if the building's Super would ban us from the building.

"Okay," Pat said. "Let's get this thing out of sight!"

He was right. Obviously we weren't going to leave it there. Beyond it now being junk littering the sidewalk, I wanted to be rid of the A.C., my emblem of shame. Hester Prinn suddenly came to mind, but my scarlet letters, "A.C.," had a greenish sheen.

"God, we were lucky," Pat said. "It's fucking rush hour!"

"I know, I know, I know," I said. I concentrated on looking at the air conditioner since I didn't want to fixate on his tic. "I can't believe it. I could have killed somebody."

Out of the apartment, I could feel myself returning.

"Man," Pat said, "I heard that sound and I swear, I thought a truck had hit a bus. But then I saw everyone looking toward the building, and then toward the sidewalk. When I saw the A.C. down there, I figured someone up above had lost their air conditioner. And then I thought: Wait! Ivor's in the other room!"

Laughing as Pat and I crouched and worked our hands underneath the A.C., I had to admit to myself that trashing the air conditioner had been kinda cool, if only in a ten-year-old sort of way — like when Lars and I blew a leg off our G.I. Joe by setting a firecracker off in his boot. But trying to raise the air conditioner up from the sidewalk cut short my laughter. The cold metal box was quite heavy. I really could have killed someone. On a count of "One, two, three," we slowly lifted the A.C. The greenish liquid, Freon I believe, made parts of the air conditioner slippery, so we had to take extra care as we struggled to lug it the few feet to the dumpster. As we strained to raise the A.C. above our shoulders to tip it over the container's edge, I joked that it would only be appropriate for the thing to fall on us, or at least myself.

For the second time that morning, the A.C. fell with a thud, but now at least it was supposed to. An old mattress inside the dumpster softened its landing. Glancing back to where the air conditioner had been, I noticed a small dent in the sidewalk. I shook my head but didn't point it out. I felt like we had just disposed of the weapon at the scene of a crime. I didn't want any more evidence to be known about. Looking away, I gazed up at the apartment's open window and knew I could never wash it again without cringing. My greenish letters would stay with me.

"Hey, motherfucker! You nearly killed me!"

Startled, I looked down and found myself facing the building porter, broom still in hand, just a few inches from me: the someone I had come closest to killing. From the apartment, I hadn't noticed his height, but now I could see that though he was a couple of inches shorter than me, he was much broader and stronger. Anger had reddened his round sepia face, and sweat had soaked the front of his grey work shirt. His brown eyes were watery.

I had figured he'd be more relieved than upset. In my mind, the fact that nobody had died made this close-call mean very little. But I guess, in a way, I'd been waiting for this: my comeuppance. After all, I hadn't been the one who'd come very close to dying but ten minutes earlier. "Jose" — his name was stitched across his shirt — pointed a finger at me and shook it. Half-expecting it to become a fist, I took a step back and felt Pat's steadying hand on my shoulder.

"Man, I am so sorry," I said. "I thought the air conditioner was safe. I mean, I had no idea it was gonna drop. I'm totally freaked out, too. But, how are you doing? Are you okay? I feel really bad."

If Jose had decided to whack me with his broom, I wouldn't have blamed him. He didn't, but I wondered what might have happened if he had been off-duty, or if Pat hadn't been standing beside me, if he hadn't been outnumbered.

"Oh yeah?" he asked. "Well, if you feel so bad, then how come you ran right by me? And how come I saw you and your friend here laughing just now?"

"Hey," I said, feeling my face becoming flushed, red. "I didn't see you back there. And the laughing, my boss and I were just feeling lucky that everything was okay. But you're right. We should have come to you first, but we weren't thinking. We just felt we had to chuck the A.C. right away. What can I say? I'm sorry, I'm sorry, I'm sorry."

Walking across Central Park to the West Side en route to the next window job, it was just as well that Pat and I had our own separate appointments to go off to. I needed to be alone for a while. At the park's 79th Street entrance just south of the Met, by the playground with the sleek bronze bear statues, I could still feel myself in a daze. What had happened that morning was never supposed to happen. You just don't drop an air conditioner out a window. I had still not accepted that I had. Okay, so I'd accidentally dropped a few sponges, mops, and even squeegees from ledges over the years. And, okay, so I hadn't hurt anyone then either. But this was worse, exponentially so. Beyond the undeniable threat that an A.C. poses to someone else, I wondered: if I could cause an air conditioner to fall from a ledge, what was next? Me? At times I couldn't believe I had a job this dangerous. That adjective certainly doesn't describe my previous day jobs of posing for art classes and scooping ice cream. Moreover, risking one's own life is one thing, putting someone else in peril is quite another.

At least whenever I'd read about cleaners dangling and even falling from screwed up scaffolding rigs, I knew that could never happen to me because I am not licensed to do that kind of work and have no interest in doing it; despite the much better pay, the work is just too dangerous. But even when I'd hear about window cleaners falling from building ledges, I'd still think: that's them, not me. Window cleaning certainly demands a strong belief in yourself, in believing you'll beat the odds.

I liked these walks across Central Park; I see them not only as a way to save myself a bus fare, but also as a short escape from windows — and on this morning, from air conditioners. I liked the incongruity of carrying a bucket of squeegees on shaded paths and past grassy expanses. If I were running early, I would find a spot beneath some mighty branches where, hidden by the leaves, New York completely disappears. No Fifth Avenue resplendence, no Central Park West Art Deco wonders, no Central Park South hotels. No buildings whatsoever. No panes in sight.

I did, however, always wonder what people did that allowed them to be in the park at midday, be they sitting on benches, jogging by, or simply strolling. How many worked a night-shift? How many were between jobs? How many were tourists? How many were retirees? How many belonged to the leisure class? And, had a few puzzled at a window cleaner pausing under trees?

But I had no time for such ambling at this crossing. No time to stop and admire the stunning surprise of Belvedere Castle looming above its pond or the openness of the Great Lawn's playing fields. I give myself a ten-minute grace period for any job before I consider myself late, but here I was a full hour-and-a-half beyond that. Funny how a dropped A.C. can slow one's day. Fortunately, the maid hadn't been annoyed when I'd called to say that I wouldn't be there when planned. "The windows will still be dirty when you get here," she had joked.

Apart from my intense morning, I'd had a drag of an evening with the band in the studio the night before. Actually, "band" more accurately describes what Michael and I used to be in, used to have. Since our last group, *clear*, had imploded, Michael and I had returned to the recording studio and started over. We had set aside thinking about labels and finding the right people to play with, and simply concentrated on the music. As it was, we hadn't played out in fifteen months, and I didn't see us performing anytime soon either.

Instead, we'd retreated to The Place, a studio in the Meatpacking District at 14th and Ninth, where we'd been laying down demos over the past few years. Because Gary, our friend we had enlisted into this now nameless project, worked as an engineer there, we'd been able to score cheaper studio time. The inevitable catch called for the three of us to be in the studio during off-hours, or in between sessions, invariably late at night. We were lucky to start at 10 o'clock; we'd had only one or two early sessions since my day with Sylvia. While this would usually be fine for Gary (he always seemed to be at the studio) and Michael (he was quite the night owl), I would have to be at work in Windowland early in the day. I regularly dozed off after just a few hours.

The music, too, contributed to my sleepiness. Rather than recording finished songs, we had chosen to explore what we came up with in the studio, consciously turning away from the three-minute tune, the verse-chorus-verse-middle eight approach. This had led to dense drum and keyboard "jams," with just glimpses of guitars. As for vocals, there weren't any yet — and there might not be. They weren't really songs, but then this wasn't really a band either. It was quite a change.

Before, I had figured out drum parts for songs that Michael had written and would demo on his home recording system. I added the veneer of "live" drumming atop the drum machines underneath. But not now. With drum machines truly dominating the rhythm, I would add percussion and only do occasional full-on drumming — like that Stewart Copeland pattern I ripped off.

The night before, we had worked on "Miles," named for three ascending trumpet notes sampled off of Miles Davis' "Sketches of Spain." I enjoyed the piece's subtlety, its small changes in tone and direction. I liked how it swirled, how it hinted. The keyboards mostly bubbled up; the drumming didn't push or shove, but pulsed.

During the playback, however, yearning and listlessness nagged at me: I wanted to do more or I wanted to do nothing. I had accepted Michael's desire to expand the number of works-in-progress from three, to five, to ten. I had kept at bay my need for completeness, for words, for melodies, for endings or even fade-outs to songs. But now I was realizing that with this style, where we were just following the music's path, I wasn't going to get those things. I was bored.

I didn't quite grasp where the songs were going. I felt like a mere observer or listener. I also didn't hear too much of me in any one track. We'd sought to make my drumming, or the drumming we sampled, sound different: natural and yet warped. Be it keyboards, guitars, drum machine, or actual drumset, we wanted them all to sound strikingly "off."

But now I felt that I had been modulated and compressed beyond recognition. I couldn't hear a pattern and be certain it was me. Put another way: I can deal with looking at a baby picture of my twin brother and myself and not know who is who. Though a bit disconcerting, at least both Lars and I are undeniably in the photo. With this music, I wasn't so certain I was in the songs.

I could look past our tune "Walking Backwards" on the *Manifesto* album, even though only the drum machine plays on the song. I was at least in a proper band — one with a name and members and even two record deals to its credit. I had also played the cymbals on the track. Besides, the drum machine just worked well on the song, as the extreme softness of the snare drums appropriately matched the single's plaintive chorus: "I'm walking backwards/Walking backwards all the time." Moreover, the song received a good deal of airplay on the influential radio station, WHFS in D.C. That success eased my being absent on the track as well.

I had crossed the park and stood across the street from the building where I had to be, the Beresford, which dominates the corner of Central Park West and 81st Street. I always liked returning there. My parents had lived in the landmark apartment house for ten years. When they retired, they had sold their fifth-floor two-bedroom "classic six" and moved to the small town of Orient, at the end of Long Island's North Fork. Pat always had a few customers in the building. I used to do my mom and dad's windows there for half-price.

I had read somewhere a description that likened the Emory Roth-designed Beresford to a Russian palace overlooking Central Park. Its three bulbous towers, set-back terraces, and twenty-three floors certainly make for a distinctive silhouette. But majesty doesn't just come to mind, massiveness does, too. Tastefully done massiveness, of course. That's where the marble lobbies with their bronze sconces and stained glass windows came in.

Seeing a sudden gap appear in Central Park West's traffic, I hurried across, my tools bouncing in their bucket. Arriving at the opposite corner, I waved to Yakov, the head doorman at the "211" entrance, my parents' old entrance, and continued walking along West 81st, past the awnings numbered "1" and "3," to the Beresford's Service Entrance. Whereas we used to chat easily while I was "on the job," for the past few years it seemed that Yakov and I had an unspoken agreement to keep our conversations to a minimum — at least when I had my window cleaning equipment with me.

I believe this change was brought about when The New York Times did a profile on me, and I mentioned Yakov. While being interviewed for the story, I had told the About New York columnist of stopping by my parents' place once to kill some time between window cleaning jobs. Because I hadn't gone to the Beresford to clean windows that day, I considered myself off the clock, and so had naturally strolled up to Yakov as he stood below the grey canopy and its elegant "211" in white. I said "Hello" and walked in. Well, tried to walk in. Yakov, a short, squarely built man who liked to play soccer on weekends, took me aside and spoke quietly.

"I'm sorry, Ivor," he said, his Albanian accent softened by his near whisper. "But you have to go around."

I scolded myself for not thinking.

"Of course," I said. "No problem."

"It's just that," Yakov said, "it's during the day and here you are with your bucket."

"That's okay," I said. "Rules are rules."

"Yes," Yakov said, "rules are rules. I'm glad you understand."

I understood that I would have to go around to the Service Entrance, just as Yakov understood that he could lose his job: if an adamant tenant was offended by seeing me, a tradesmen in the lobby, it could happen. The customer, or, in this case, the tenant, is always right.

Ever since that day, whenever Yakov and I spoke to each other, he would almost always make a point of apologizing for sending me around that one time. I think he felt he had humiliated me, or at least slighted me. But I also think that he felt embarrassed to have had to send me around. For that matter, Yakov might have felt I had humiliated him by telling the paper what he had done. I don't know. Ever since, however, I had tried my best to say "Hi" at a distance during business hours, when I had my bucket.

Once I'd been cleared by the back desk, I rode the Service Elevator to the customer's place, pleased that I was off to a "B" line apartment on an upper floor. Unlike my parents' place which had looked out on 82nd Street brownstones, now I would see the Beresford's other side: views of Central Park and the Natural History Museum's Hayden Planetarium. I also appreciated my spell of silence and solitude, as this elevator required no operator — it stopping at floors automatically.

Service Elevators that don't have operators make me think that I am trusted. I know that in the long run, automatic elevators save buildings money since they are more reliable and replace a worker's wage, just as I know that the closed-circuit television cameras many of these elevators feature keep tabs on anyone who rides them. But I like to think that the building has at least a bit of faith in the tradesmen that have been let in — provided, of course, we carry the required one- to two-million dollar liability insurance before we walk through the door, the back door.

The elevator opened and I saw that the rear entrance of the apartment stood ajar, allowing me to enter without delay. I felt welcome. Once I heard the melee inside however, I realized the open door had everything to do with the maid not having to listen for my buzzing or knocking.

"Hey," I called out as I entered the rear hallway. "It's the window cleaner!"

Cheerful, high-pitched screams announced the arrival of a pair of four-feet-high blurs, one blonde, one brunette, that dashed through the kitchen and into the dining room. I guessed they were about seven years old. The maid, a large dark skinned woman, looked up from the sink that she stood before and smiled a "Hello."

I saw that this Beresford kitchen still boasted much of what had been originally installed when the building had been put up in the late 1920s. There were the stainless steel cabinets with glass fronts that my parents' place had; my father thought they gave 5-H a nautical feel. This kitchen, too, had a second sink across from the maid's room, and I quickly filled my bucket in its deep enamel basin. The building always seemed to have great water pressure, no matter what floor.

"I can't believe there are only two of them," I said. The yelling had actually diminished since the kids had apparently moved on to the living room. Their stomping feet and squeals would be back, I was sure.

"That is true," the maid said in a thick Jamaican accent and then laughed. "This is one loud play-date, that's for sure. But they'll quiet down soon enough. I'm going to give them a snack."

"Very shrewd," I said, pulling my heavy bucket up from the sink and bringing it down to the floor. "Where would you like me to start?"

"I was thinking you could start in here," the maid said as she dried a plate, her voice lilting along. She could have been singing a reggae song. "I think that watching you work will keep them occupied."

"That's fine," I said. "I'm happy to be their entertainment — as long as they don't get too close."

My longed-for view would have to wait. The kitchen, like most kitchens in such New York City apartment houses, only looked out on the building's courtyard. Long ago, the Beresford's had apparently been laid out with bushes and trees, stone walkways and a fountain — at least that's what the building's blueprints feature — but plain cement has covered the essentially T-shaped space for decades. I still had plenty to look at though. As in my parents' kitchen, I could see across to the kitchens, dining rooms, and maids' rooms belonging to neighboring apartments. One very early rising guy who lived across from my mom and dad, on the 81st Street side, would prepare his coffee most every morning in the nude. He must have figured no one else would be up at 5 am.

I had always enjoyed the uncluttered view that the Beresford's tall, narrow casement windows with transom panes above them afforded. Once I had started washing windows, I quickly came to appreciate that they also weren't that difficult to clean. Even this apartment's child-guards, that allowed the windows to only open outward a few inches, didn't slow me down too much, just a few screws to remove and put back.

"Okay, you two," the maid called out, "it's time for you to come here 'cause I am going to give you a treat!"

We heard two gleeful yells and then suddenly the kids were silently and politely sitting at the breakfast nook.

"Very good," the maid said, "very good. Now, listen. Do not get in the way of the man cleaning the windows."

"Right," the girl said.

"I'm hungry," the boy said.

I smiled at them and noticed that I had not been referred to as the "young" man doing the windows. That had been happening consistently lately.

The two friends ate their chocolate-chip cookies in outright silence as I explained the mop's role in cleaning a window. After I had wiped down just two panes, they lost interest and went back to a more important matter: the weekend that had just ended.

I gathered that both of their families had second homes. The boy's had had theirs "forever," and I wondered what that actually meant. Since he'd been born? Since he could remember? Perhaps his "brown log cabin in the forest" had been in the family for generations. The girl's home, however, was brand new; her family's "big white box on the ocean" had just been built this past spring. I wondered if her family's place in the city had a scale model of their Hamptons home. I occasionally came across highly detailed set-ups in customers' apartments and figured that they had replaced the model airplanes of youth. Unless, of course, the customer owned an actual plane. A couple of Pat's clients did.

"Outside my house, there are these trails," the boy said as his index finger mapped out a meandering figure eight on the table's wooden surface. "And we go walking on them, and sometimes we see deers!"

"Outside my house, there's the water," the girl countered, opening and closing her hands to form imagined swells. "We always see sea shells and the waves!"

Apparently trumped, the boy called out to me.

"Mister," he said, "Can you tell us about your weekend house?"

"Actually, I can't," I said. I placed my squeegee back in its holster, turned to face them, and sat upon the windowsill.

"Why not?"

"Because I don't have one," I said. "But I do have an apartment of my own not too far from here. Let's think. About seventy blocks south of here, down in the Village. Even though it's small, it does have all my things in one place, kind of like your rooms, kind of like a playroom. I've got my bed and my bike and my stereo and my books. I've even got a refrigerator, and a sink and a stove and a bathroom in there. All in one place. And a couple of windows, too."

"You've got a fridge in your room?" the boy said. "Cool."

"I even have a hole in my bathroom ceiling. A mouse fell through and died when it hit the sink."

"That is really cool!" the boy said, slamming his palm against the table.

"That's gross!" the girl shrieked. "And besides, your room is still here in the city, right?"

Girls do mature faster than boys, don't they.

"Right," I said. "But, luckily, I can go visit my parents at their house and it is right on the water, too, just like yours. That's my weekend house, you could say."

"That's okay," she said. "They're not really our houses either, you know. And, at least you can see the ocean."

"Are there woods there, too?" the boy asked.

"Yes, there are," I said. "I can go walking in a big nature preserve if I go over to Shelter Island."

"Do you see deers there, too?"

"Yes, I do," I said. "I see deer."

I drew my squeegee and returned to the windows, wondering when I'd be able to afford to buy a place of any kind, even a tiny room. Or should I say, "fucking tiny," to quote my sister Ursula after she had sublet my place the previous year; I'd been living with my then-girlfriend at the time. Heck, I could barely afford my rent of $560 a month.

Some years earlier, Pat and I had once, and only once, been in one of the Beresford's tower apartments. We spent an entire afternoon cleaning the five-story place and because the tower's panes were too far gone, we knew we'd never be asked back. Pat had warned the customer not to expect perfection when trying to clean decades worth of dirt off old New York City windows that had not been properly maintained. But the guy had insisted that when he came home that night, he wanted to see his panes looking like new. To neither Pat's nor my surprise, our repeated soaping, scrubbing, and rinsing only caused the glass's baked-in grayness to lighten, but not disappear.

Since we had tackled the 20-odd-foot tower first, we knew our fate pretty early on and so spent the rest of our time there savoring our sole visit to what really was a palace some twenty stories in the sky. The first floor comprised the living room, dining room, kitchen — and a terrace. A spiral staircase led to the second floor, the children's floor. Incidentally, a separate spiral staircase winded up from the kitchen to the maid's room. The young son and daughter each had a bedroom plus a playroom, bigger than my apartment — and a terrace. The third floor could be considered the parents' floor, as it had their bedroom and separate studies for them both — and, yes, a terrace. The fourth floor marked the beginnings of the tower, with an arched floor-to-ceiling arboretum made of glass and brick. The top floor, however, featured the tower's domed ceiling and two ornate oval windows, each about my height. This space had been made into a gym. I found this a shame, considering that I had heard that residents in another of the Beresford's towers used their fifth floor as a ballroom.

With the windows finally done, Pat and I readied ourselves to leave the penthouse just as dusk began to enshroud Manhattan. Though the building's Super had let us stay on later than usual, we didn't want to press his patience — nor did we want to be around when the owner came home. But before departing, I went out on the dining room's terrace. Leaning against the metal railing, I watched the apartment windows that line Central Park light up, as lamps and chandeliers took over from the sun. Within the long and leafy rectangular expanse, trees that not minutes ago stood bright, green, and inviting now seemed nearly menacing, offering neither shade nor solace. Even the serene Great Lawn resembled an ominous moat protecting Belvedere Castle. The cars, taxis, and buses that snaked across the park from the West 81st Street entrance became indistinct splotches of headlights and echoes of horns; colors and noise made mysterious by the encroaching night. I turned and looking up, watched as the gray-black sky began to claim the tower. As the sharp bright lights atop the dome blazed on, pushing back the darkness, I realized the Beresford was not a palace at all, but a fortress.

And it hit me: the people who live here have all of this everyday. I just hoped they appreciated their five floors and spiral staircases, their terraces and tower. Ever since that afternoon, any other apartment in the Beresford (and almost any other apartment in the city) has had to work that much harder to impress me. I had been spoiled.

Having finished the kitchen window, I looked down at the table and noticed that the two seven-year-old blurs had gone. Though, strictly speaking, I should have done the adjoining dining room next, I picked up my bucket and headed to the living room instead. I needed a view before I could get on with the rest of the apartment's windows.

Luckily, I didn't have to wait for the subway, as a C train pulled into the 81st Street stop just as I walked onto the platform. I took my seat in the nearly empty car near the door, appreciating that I could lean back against a wall, in this case a subway system map. I hated being tired and not being able to truly rest because I had to stand or contend with a regular window seat. The Beresford job had taken a lot out of me and I needed to relax. I picked up an abandoned Village Voice next to me and leafed through the music listings.

Though I didn't read the Voice regularly, when I did pick it up or come across an issue, I made a point of checking out the music section. I found doing so occasionally inspiring. Seeing all the venues represented the possibilities, if not a path, that New York City had to offer. From, for instance, C.B.G.B.'s, to the Mercury Lounge, to the Knitting Factory, to Irving Plaza, to the Bowery Ballroom, to Roseland, and so on. I could track where we'd been to where we wanted to be. Unfortunately, *Manifesto* and *clear* had only gotten as far as playing but never headlining places like C.B.'s and the Mercury Lounge.

Now as I flipped through the music pages, I didn't feel exhilarated or challenged. I felt like a sucker, a failure. Despite our best efforts, despite putting up with labels and all the rest, the band, or whatever it was that Michael and Gary and I were up to, was not going to succeed — just like most of the others groups listed. But at least these bands were playing out. I seriously doubted that we would ever take the stage. In my darker moments, I figured we would never finish a song, or get anywhere.

I folded shut the Voice, putting it back down on the bench. Then I picked the paper back up and stared at its title. *The Police* song, "Voices Inside My Head," came to me. It's not a great song from their canon — it's no "Roxanne," "Driven to Tears," or "Message in a Bottle" by any means — but despite being essentially filler off their Zenyatta Mondatta album, I like the fluid hi-hat work Stewart Copeland displays on the track and his extra crisp snare drum sound. I'd occasionally striven for that high-pitched "Crack!" in the studio as well.

"Oh well," I thought to myself as I put the Voice back down and "Voices Inside My Head" took up its residence, "it would have been cool to be the next Stewart Copeland." Then I caught myself. Wait a second. What was that? Would *have* been cool? I'd always thought that it *would* be cool to be the next Stewart Copeland. What's with the past tense?

And then I knew. I knew I had made a decision without even realizing it, like some inner subconscious momentum had finally surfaced. I wasn't striving anymore to be the next Stewart Copeland, or the Ivor Hanson, or the anybody in music. I wasn't up and coming, I was over.

Wow. Was this it? Just like that?

My other bands had ended a bit more formally. Henry had told us he was leaving *S.O.A.* to join *Black Flag* (along with changing his last name from Garfield to Rollins) and since the *Flag* was his favorite band, Michael and I weren't shocked when he agreed to be their lead singer. *Faith* had ended when I'd gone off to college, but we were due for a break-up anyway, as those fabled "personal and musical differences" were beginning to tear at us. In other words, Michael and I saw that one coming to a close as well. That could be said for *Embrace*, too. When Ian MacKaye had announced he was leaving the group, it simply put an eight-month experiment gone awry out of its misery, "p & m" differences once more. With *Manifesto*, it had been different. Michael and I had decided to carry on despite Bert quitting as bass player. Yes, we had changed the band's name to *clear*, but we weren't going to break up; we were simply going to find new players.

But now I was the one departing. And it wasn't because I was off to Vassar, or anywhere. It was because I was tired; tired of waiting for the songs to be finished; tired of the lack of progress and success. "It will happen this year!" had become, "There goes another year." Let's face it: rock careers, like milk, have "sell-by" dates. And my date had expired. But I was also tired of windows.

Tired of being up early and off to Windowland most every morning. When I'd first started working with Pat, he had a policy of working on Saturdays and then being closed Mondays. But as business slowed over the years, we couldn't chance turning away customers, couldn't afford turning away a day's wage, and so Shields Windows started a six-day-a-week work schedule.

Well, at least I had apparently arrived at a decision, and had arrived at it a lot more easily than I'd thought possible. So, did that mean I was really doing it? It would come down to my making it official, come down to my telling Michael and Gary. And that would be a drag. I smiled ruefully as it crossed my mind that perhaps they had been waiting me out. Nah, not so.

Huh. Wild. Quitting the band. Really? Finally. I wondered if this was how it had been for my dad to give up the saxophone and head off to the Naval Academy. When he was a fifteen-year-old scrawny kid, my dad had played sax in a jazz big-band four nights a week — at the Blue Moon Ballroom in 1940s Tucson, Arizona — to help his family get by. Though attending Annapolis certainly meant a welcome step out of Tucson, it also meant a step away from his first dream of performing and singing.

The previous Christmas, I had given my father a recording session as a present. In the studio, I could see and hear his excitement as I watched him through the mixing room window. Before each take of singing over instrumental tapes of such tunes as Cole Porter's "I've Got You Under My Skin" — saloon songs, my dad calls them — he ran through the lyrics, trying out phrasing and sorting out cues as he kept time snapping his fingers or softly tapping his shoes on the wooden floor.

Standing in the middle of the "live" room, its lights dimmed and his eyes closed, my father's baritone voice soared through the room and onto the tape. Upon playback, my dad's smile and his questions — "How'd that go? Did it swing?" — always caused me to look away. I didn't want him to see me blush. But this wasn't embarrassment, it was...pride? Happiness? A mixture of the two. That he enjoyed my gift this much certainly pleased me; here he was, the crooner he'd always been, finally doing what he always thought he could, laying down tracks.

He was still my dad, of course, but he wasn't the Admiral. He wasn't the man who in his career had skippered a minesweeper and a destroyer, commanded a Carrier Battle Group, and had several important tours in the Pentagon, including that of Director of the Joint Staff for the Joint Chiefs of Staff, when he was in charge of the military's most senior admirals and generals.

The recording session had been pleasant time spent with my father, as opposed to, say, a trip to the dump. Beginning in college, my dad and I began holding "summit meetings" and what he refers to as "sit reps," or situation reports (a term left over from his Navy days). These occasional talks first took place over lunch at his office when he was running the National Multiple Sclerosis Society, when I'd be home on break.

Since he'd retired, however, these chats had been taking place in his pick-up truck, on trips to the local landfill to dispose of his and my mom's trash. During these hour-long drives, we would discuss my band's progress (or lack thereof) and invariably, the need for a Plan B in my life. Not surprisingly, I don't enjoy hearing my dad say when I am out at the house, "Feel like a trip to the dump?" or "Simba, it looks like it's time for a run to the dump." I know that these talks stem from concern on my father's part, but they also put me on the spot. A part of me wants to say: "Hey! I'm out of college! I'm an adult! I can do what I want!" But I never have.

Over the years, I know I have feared not measuring up to my dad and mom's expectations, or their accomplishments. Growing up I came to see my parents as depressingly impressive.

As for my mother, by marrying my father she did in her way — as the old recruiting posters put it — "Join the Navy and See the World." And so, shortly after receiving her respective undergraduate and graduate degrees from Wellesley and Radcliffe, she left the sheltered suburbs of Chicago's North Shore behind. She raised five kids in all the places that we'd lived and still managed to make a career for herself in education. She worked for many years at the National Cathedral School in Washington, D.C., capping her experience there by running its middle school. When my parents moved to New York City for my father's civilian career, she worked at the Brearly School, where she eventually became its long-time number two administrator.

I wondered what my parents would think of this decision of mine? I guessed that they'd be happy that I'd finally wised up.

I thought of a customer who lived just down the street from me, whose windows — cut-up switchers with very narrow ledges — I'd cleaned a few years ago. He'd played drums and then stopped, but had never gotten rid of his kit.

Now, his bass drum — the drumset's heart that thuds in time when the drummer beats its back side with the bass drum pedal — lay on its back on the living room floor, its wood grain slightly darker than the carpet's brown shag. This big drum anchored a drumset no longer: no snare drum, floor tom, hi-hat, or cymbals stood arranged around it; no tom-tom drums had been mounted on top. Across the bass drum's round face, a circular plate of clear glass slightly larger than the drum's own foot-and-a-half diameter had been placed. The day's Times, two mugs, and a clay ashtray lay within the glass's smoothed, rounded edges, and now defined the drum's new role as a coffee table. Though I had praised his innovation and resourcefulness, when I looked down at his bass drum, I secretly mourned.

Drumsets can die in many ways. Sometimes drummers destroy their kits in a frenzy of percussion, as when *The Who*'s Keith Moon or *Nirvana*'s Dave Grohl abandoned the beat for rhythmic anarchy and set off explosions of knocked-over drums, cracked cymbals, bent stands, kicked in drum heads and, perhaps, some blood. Through destruction, they created an exhilarating spectacle, one of broken drums and broken rules.

Though tempted, I had never destroyed my drumset. I had taken a different approach, that of ultimately wearing out the kit. My first set lasted thirteen years. My parents had bought the navy blue Premier kit for me in seventh grade — once Gil, my drum teacher at the Navy School of Music, had told them I had enough talent and was practicing enough to make spending four-hundred dollars on a mid-range kit a worthwhile purchase. The day I got the set, I placed a Navy sticker on the bass drum's curved side and never took it off; I'm sure that at punk shows I played, the eagle and anchors got a few looks. But I didn't care. The sticker reminded me of learning to play, and the Premier five-piece symbolized responsibility and recognition. I couldn't destroy that.

When I stood over that customer's coffee table, it had occurred to me that the customer's drumset had been essentially stuffed and mounted on the wall — for here it was, dead and on display. The client then told me that, having decided to convert his floor-tom into a bedside table, he now just needed to figure out what to do with his tom-toms. I didn't ask about his snare drum or his cymbals. But right then I knew that should I ever stop playing drums, I would keep my drums alive by giving them away to a band that would use them.

Who would I give my drumset to? I had no idea. Or was it that I didn't want to come up with a likely candidate, that I didn't want to take such an undeniable step? I cut myself some slack, gave myself some time. I had only been living with my decision to stop playing since 81st Street, just eight subway stops. I didn't have to know the answer yet.

I closed my eyes and everything vanished except for the question: So, now what?

Maybe I could just go about getting in a different band, one with different people. But no, being in a band that didn't have Michael had never felt right. I'd been in a few groups in college, and while they had allowed me to play, I had never liked those groups' songs as much. They weren't as catchy. As for being a studio musician, well, I didn't think that I was good enough to do that. But also, I don't know, being an essentially anonymous session player had never appealed to me. It wasn't being in a band, it was just showing up to record. It didn't seem that cool.

I hate to admit it, but I guess a part of me has secretly wanted to be a rock star more than a musician, to be in an acclaimed band more than to be an acclaimed drummer. And I know this sounds mean, and chucks aside my whole Stewart Copeland fixation, but, in a way, I guess you could say I've wanted to be the next Ringo. He is good, of course. No, he's great. Just listen to his playing on "Rain." And, as a kid, like many a drummer, I took pride in figuring out his short solo on "The End" from the same record. But as Mr. Starkey once put it — there were plenty of drummers as good as he was, but none of them were as lucky.

One thing I did know for sure. Even though I do mentally drum along to most any song I hear, I had no interest in reducing drumming to being merely a hobby — it had meant a lot more than that. Playing just for the hell of it would only remind me of the success that hadn't happened. As would playing in a cover band, a "wedding band" as I called them. Those weren't possibilities, as they'd just be too depressing. I'd rather not play at all. It would be easier that way. Letting go of drums completely, to not have them around haunting me would be best. Hell, "letting go" was making things easier on myself. It sounded so much better then "giving up." Who was I kidding? This decision could no longer be filed under "surprisingly easy." How about "wrenching?" This felt like flying through turbulence.

My mind wondered along to a hard-to-ignore question: So if I wasn't going to be playing in a band anymore, shouldn't I stop window cleaning? Drumming had been the point in picking up a squeegee in the first place.

I had to face it.

Though window cleaning is a perfectly respectable profession, it certainly doesn't rate high in status. I wasn't a lawyer or a doctor or even a rock star after all. It's a job I feel I must regularly explain.

I could take the approach that Pat, my boss, takes. He feels he doesn't need to justify himself in the least. "Look," he says, "I climb out onto the side of buildings for a living. Don't tell me that's not a real job."

And I do perform my job well. Apart from wanting to keep my job and having Shields Window Cleaning customers continue to call back, there is a point of pride involved: Anything I do, I want to do well. Besides, if I were lazy or sloppy, I risk more than just cracking a window or knocking over a vase; I could lose my life.

The point is that I want to leave my mark on the world. Instead, I've been making sure I don't leave a streak.

I could feel my dad's presence in my head: "So, Simba, what's your Plan B? What have you got in your back pocket?"

My dad had asked this question in his own way the previous Christmas. While I had given my dad his recording session, he had given each of his five kids the same present: attending a five-day, "figure out your life" seminar that an old friend of his ran. Inge, Erica, Lars, Ursula, and I had all laughed later that day. Just what might this gift be saying about how our father regarded the state of his children's lives?

In fact, Inge didn't mind looking beyond running a non-profit that promoted baseball in Harlem. Erica pretty much knew that she was going to stay in the television business in Los Angeles, just as Lars knew he wasn't about to give up acting in New York, and Ursula was quite content being a social worker in Portland. As for me, well, I guess I had put the present in my back pocket. I didn't regard the class as a sign per se, but simply something to do; it couldn't hurt. Well, perhaps now it was time.

I looked at the Voice at my side and knew that at least the voices inside my head spoke of both regret and relief.

THREE

I decided that I couldn't wait for the confession to end before I entered and cleaned the windows. Though I knew I had been standing on the off-white hallway's tan carpeting for ten minutes, I glanced at my watch anyway for confirmation. He had said forty-five minutes ago that they would be finished by now, but they weren't. In the name of money, clean glass, and not falling behind schedule, I knocked at the door, turned the stainless steel knob, and pushed.

"Excuse me," I began before I could even see the counselor's face at his desk and the back of the confessor's head sitting before him. "I'm sorry for interrupting. But you're my last window here and I'm running late."

The man behind the grey steel desk glanced up, adjusting his gold and blue striped tie to disguise his being startled. He looked to be in his forties, slim and tall with close-cropped curly black hair. His narrow, cocoa-brown face sported wire-rim glasses, a strong chin, and a moustache as neat as his desk. The man sitting in the chair opposite lowered his head further, so that I could barely see his own short black afro. He stared at the floor, his hands folded in his lap. Despite his clean white pressed shirt, he looked crumpled.

"That's okay, come on in," the counselor said in a quiet and smooth voice. "We're just about done here. Sorry about the delay."

I entered with my bucket and closed the door behind me with my hip. Though I regarded the Budget & Credit Counseling Services job as one of my favorites, these moments were not. I did my best to work my window cleaning around these appointments by darting from empty office to empty office and keeping track of where I had been. But as I ran out of windows and time, I inevitably crossed paths with at least one BuCCS client.

I walked across the stark room in silence, doing my best to concentrate on yet more off-white walls and light-brown carpet, seemingly designed to keep the focus on whatever transpired at the desk. As I approached the windows, I appreciated that this counselor at least kept his windowsill clear of office clutter. No plants, coffee mugs, or files to move; no plaques, family photos, or "Hang In There, It's Almost Friday" bulletin boards to put back. Though I tried my best not to look, when I passed the desk, I did notice that the two men had been going over a "Bankruptcy Progress Chart."

I jumped up onto the sill and began to mop down the huge rectangular single-pane belt window, the top and lower panes each nearly five feet tall and seven feet wide. As usual in this circumstance, while I mopped I could feel my presence growing more awkward in the room. I didn't want to be here. Mr. Crumpled didn't want me here. I remained silent and even kept my "mop, squeegee, chamois" noise to a minimum, forgoing my regular "tap, tap" of the squeegee blade on the glass after each swipe to remove excess water.

Even with my back to them both, I could sense their stillness: No calculator being tapped, no pencil scribbling, no paper sorting, no coffee stirring, barely any creaking of chairs. Crumpled's financial confession had completely stopped. Finally, I heard a cleared throat and some mumbled words, followed by the counselor's reply in a now quiet but firm voice.

"Well, yes, Dean," he said, "he does have to be here. This gentleman has a job to do."

Did the remark infer that Dean Crumpled didn't have a job or hadn't done the job he was supposed to, or wasn't a gentleman? Probably not. Hopefully not. But he did have that chart to contend with. Without turning to face them, I spoke up.

"I'll be outside in just a moment," I said flatly, in an attempt to simply impart information. I didn't want to be a person to be compared with, I didn't want to be a "gentleman with a job to do." I just wanted to be out on the thirteenth floor's reassuringly wide ledge. A moment later I was.

For a building likely put up in the 1920s or 1930s, 55 Fifth Avenue's windows were in pretty good shape. Their wooden frames lifted and dropped easily, their ballasts and metal chains still worked, their belt hooks remained tight and secure. The windows' glass, alas, had not been so lucky. Though the thick robust panes had endured the pollution of the past seventy or eighty years, they had not been able to withstand a recent acid wash to 55's exterior. Apparently through either contractor sloppiness, the wind, or both, chemicals had rained down on the glass, burning white and grey splotches and streaks into the panes; I'm glad I wasn't cleaning windows nearby then. But because these patterns made a perfect cleaning job impossible, they did make my job easier — the acid damage easily outshone any streaks. I just feared this damage would hasten the replacement of these windows. I would miss their pureness and their ancient ingrained ripples. Belt-hook single-panes with wide ledges give me joy. Then again, most any window in August does that. When BuCCS had rung, Pat and I had welcomed the call. It was a slow month, with many customers away on vacation. Only January brings less business.

With these preferred windows, instead of leaning into the frame in a wary crouch, I can lean back, knowing my belt and the building's hooks will hold me. Instead of small, cut-up panes that check my pace, I have a large glass expanse to work with, reminding me of canvas. Sweeping the mop and the squeegee across the glass plane gives me a sense of accomplishment and freedom. Doing so dangling one-hundred feet or so off the ground only enhances this feeling.

Over the years, I have thought I was experiencing my death-fall, only to realize it was almost caused by something as minor as needing new shoes. And yet, I can't quite shake the ledge's allure. While the risk I encounter daily could certainly kill me, the thrill it provides makes up for the fact that I am, ultimately, just cleaning a window.

It's about self-reliance and risk in a way, just as it's about knowing when to walk away from a job that's not worth the exhilaration. Some folks climb mountains because they're there, and spend lots of money to do so. I climb out on a ledge because some windows are dirty. And I get paid to do so. Not enough, but I do get paid.

Though I have never painted, in a way, window cleaning seems like its reverse in that I am removing instead of applying. I am working backwards to emptiness, nothingness.

Out on 55 Fifth's ledge, I concentrated on the window more than usual to reduce my chances of making eye contact with Dean Crumpled. The glass wasn't that damaged, just the top left corner of the upper pane resembled a see-through Rorschach test. The acid's splash and dribbles reminded me of a dragon spouting flames.

Glancing at Dean, I saw that he had unfolded his arms and now leaned upon his elbows on the desk. The counselor pointed to a line on his chart. Was Crumpled keeping his head down so he didn't have to see me?

I wondered how much debt this guy had incurred, how much he paid BuCCS a month to handle his creditors, and how far along he was in the typical four-year pay-back program. Was he sorting out the possibility of new shoes for his kids? School was starting again soon. Would BuCCS be able to, in their words, "rehabilitate" this debtor "so that a financially healthy consumer is returned to the credit market." Out of curiosity, I had once taken a brochure of theirs home. And how had Crumpled gotten into debt in the first place?

Though I'd finished the window, I mopped, squeegeed, and chamoised the pane once more since I didn't want to interrupt a second time. Besides, if I were a "gentleman with a job to do," what example would I set by lounging out on the ledge? But after cleaning the window and deciding that instead of a dragon, the pattern actually appeared to be a spaceship, I leaned back nonetheless, and looked down.

I have always found it ironic that the headquarters of BuCCS lies directly across the street from the headquarters of Forbes Magazine. I doubted that anyone who worked in the somber granite building would soon be making a visit here. I know that plenty of people go into debt, plenty of people can't resist the credit card offers that arrive in the mail, plenty of people, it seems, have to max out the plastic just to get by. But I figured that if anyone across the way needed to fill out a Bankruptcy Progress Chart, they would do so at more upscale equivalents.

I also liked that two churches were within two blocks of BuCCS. Though neither was Catholic — one was Presbyterian and the other was Episcopal — perhaps their spires were what had prompted me to regard these BuCCS sessions as confessionals. I had once spotted a woman whose session I had also intruded upon walk quickly across the street and enter one of these houses of worship after she'd departed from the building. Even from this high up, the bright-red bonnet she'd been wearing in the office had easily caught my eye.

Looking northward, I could spy the lower edge of Central Park by the green haze hovering just off the ground. Rockefeller Center's limestone grandeur I could also just make out. The Empire State Building just twenty blocks up the avenue and soaring above its neighbors was impossible to miss. Thinking of the fallen woman from the 1940s splayed out on the car, I felt the need to check the window's belt hooks just to be sure. I wanted to remain a part of the skyline, not become a part of the sidewalk. I also wished we charged more than ten dollars per belt window. I was starting to feel that my life was worth a bit more.

Looking south, Washington Square Park declared the end of Fifth Avenue. And though the white-marbled triumphal arch dominated its surroundings, it nonetheless looked short and small from my vantage point. New York City has plenty of monuments, but they can't really compete with the city's buildings. A few blocks down Fifth was what Pat and I called a "Christo" building — when a building undergoing extensive exterior work gets wrapped in plastic, just as Christo, the artist, has done to such buildings as Berlin's Reichstag.

Looking back at the window, I noticed the confessor looking up at me. When our eyes met and he looked away, back at his chart and other papers on the desk, I wondered: Why wasn't I sitting in his place? As a window washer, after all, I don't make that much money.

I get paid by the window, not by the hour. So, the more windows I clean, the more money I make. It's my version of piecework, my variation on the equation, time equals money. Of course, the six, or seven, or ten I charge per window doesn't all end up in my pocket, except for the occasional "off the books" cash job. But, truly, almost all of my income does get reported. That means I set aside 28% of whatever I make in a savings account devoted to paying my federal, state, and city taxes, social security — and my tax preparer; I stopped doing my own taxes the moment I left the 1040EZ form behind.

And Pat takes his cut. As owner of Shield Windows, he gets 35% of what I do. Other window cleaning companies take 45% or even 50%, but Pat figures that if he pays his employees more, they will be that much better workers.

Essentially, then, though I take home less than half of what I walk into — $37 on a $100 job — the $28 I have earmarked for taxes will more than pay what the IRS, New York State, and New York City expect from me. This means that by the time I send them my checks on April 15th, I typically have a couple thousand left over, my stand-in for a refund.

I know my financial standing well because not having money forces me to; not having money means it's always on my mind. Because I don't have a set annual salary — no set pay check every two weeks to plan by, no end of the year bonus to look forward to — I must plan ahead. So, during window cleaning's busy times in the fall and spring, I set aside as much future rent money and spending money as I can for the slow times.

Pat generally shuts down his business for the month of January, and February is pretty dead as well. Though I welcome this two-month break, I do my best to set aside enough money to get by until the spring thaw. I like to have saved at least three months rent and have $3,000 in the bank to cover the sluggish summer and winter seasons.

It's simple: My head's just above water, and I don't want to sink.

This dog paddling has made me hate spending money. I go to movies and catch bands, but I choose what I'll see carefully. I also buy CDs at discount shops like Disc-O-Rama or Sounds and used or reviewer's books at the Strand. I am like most New Yorkers in that I like bargains, and that I get by.

The most I've ever made in a year is $30,000. That, I must say, meant a lot of dirty windows; I was very tired that year. Generally, I earn somewhere in the mid twenties. Fortunately, along with my low salary, I have low rent. My room on 13th Street is cheap. I lucked out in the rent stabilization sweepstakes by landing the place through a broker a while ago and have held onto it. Though the apartment is tiny, it's well worth it.

Financial discipline, low expenses, and small cash reserves, however, only explain so much about my frugality. I realize that in many circles, having plenty of material objects represents success, if not the norm. It's the American way after all. What do those tee shirts and bumper stickers say? "Whoever dies with the most stuff wins."

My years of near-daily proximity to things exquisite, expensive, even priceless have benefitted me in an unexpected way. I know now that simply experiencing an object matters more than actually possessing it. Of course, the objects in customers' places aren't mine. But being in the presence of esteemed paintings, classic furnishings, raw silk drapes, by having them be a part of my life, they can be mine without my desiring to own them. My practical side also recognizes that I can appreciate an object's worth without having to pay for it, or ever being able to buy such things, at least not as a window cleaner. I regard such objects as I do a window's view, as something you "have" but isn't really yours.

That morning, just before the BuCCS job, I had been at a place where I doubt the three of us — me, the counselor, and the confessor — could ever afford to shop: an art dealing customer's apartment on the Upper East Side. Her Madison Avenue living room occasionally doubles as a viewing room.

"Got anything on sale?" I had joked as I had set down my water-filled bucket and decided which oversized, time-consuming belt window to clean first; each one sported 32 cut-up panes of glass.

"Well, Ivor," she replied, pausing a moment to allow for a smile. "Feel like a Degas?"

Moments later, I found myself moving not a ballerina portrait, nor an in-the-wings view of a ballet performance, nor a glimpse of jockeys on horseback in the homestretch of a race, but a landscape away — far, far away — from my bucket.

Usually though, paintings aren't for sale in someone's apartment, nor are they so pointedly displayed as they are in the stores in which they're sold. The objects aren't kept behind glass, or behind the counter, or supervised by a salesperson. Instead, the objects, once home, ideally work in a low-key, even informal way to be part of the place, part of the room. And because I am in the room for a while, the objects more easily become a part of my experience. I don't need to have them, just behold them briefly and be around them for a bit.

Of course, I have seen some other noteworthy things in customer's living rooms.

At one place on the West Side, a guy has the set list John Lennon wrote out for his album, "Rock and Roll Music," a record of cover tunes he did in the mid Seventies.

The customer was a lawyer for Lennon at the time the rock 'n' roll legend was sorting out the record and happened to be sitting next to Lennon when he had simply jotted down the list. Afterwards, this guy asked Lennon if he could keep the list, and Lennon had said sure. Now it's framed and hangs in his living room.

At an apartment on the East Side, a client has an inscribed black and white photo of Roy Cohn taken in the mid Sixties at some banquet that also featured William F. Buckley, Jr.

Another customer, who has lived in the same Greenwich Village rent-controlled one-bedroom apartment for the past forty years, has on her living room wall the photo she took in 1977 of Bianca Jagger riding a white horse at Studio 54. When I saw it, I'd remarked that '77 was quite a time to be there, to which the customer had replied: "That was the only time to be there."

Then there's the doctor on Park Avenue who has a few Picassos in his living room and a de Kooning in his dining room. I admire these paintings every time I visit, for beyond their beauty and genius, they reveal to me why people collect art. He can view these paintings at six in the morning in his bathrobe, coffee in hand. How amazing that must be.

But not if they're tchatches. I'd been working in one of Fifth Avenue's modern, even flashy, early 1960s apartment houses, one with picture windows so wide and numerous they nearly qualified as glass walls. Unfortunately, the customer had fallen into the trap of thinking that because she had a large space — her apartment took up the entire floor — she needed to fill it. Accordingly, she had crammed nearly all her window sills with tchatches. Her delicate, garish, ceramic doodads simply took up all the space, making the expansive, open living room look cramped and cluttered. Though I had removed the curios from the front of the room, the boisterous wind that day decided to go after a small table covered with baubles on the far end. Even with my head and shoulders out the window so that I could better negotiate the breeze and a squeegee that threatened to slip off a pole, I could hear the crash as the table fell to the ground with perfect timing: just as the lady of the house entered the room. We both dashed to the spot where the ceramics lay. There I witnessed a near-miracle. All of them had survived but one. "I actually liked that one!" the customer said.

No tchatches for me, thank you. I have no money, no space, no need for unnecessary things.

I'm pretty sure that if I were confined to an office job day-in and day-out, I wouldn't have the variety and proximity of fine objects I've grown accustomed to having in my life. I wouldn't enjoy the very good odds of seeing something rare, beautiful, and striking that morning or afternoon. Sometimes I do wonder what it would be like to have a Degas hanging on my wall. I also wonder, should I find myself in that office job one day, my squeegee days behind me, will I view objects differently? Will I covet them? I hope I'll just miss them.

Movement from inside the office window caused me to notice the BuCCS counselor rise from his chair. I watched his narrow back and shoulders walk around his desk and approach the confessor, who now stood as well. Heads nodded and smiled. The counselor then pointed towards the door and the two walked out of the room, shaking hands in the hallway. The client then disappeared from view, taking a left and heading for the exit. The counselor took a right and disappeared as well.

I raised the window and let myself in, slowly lowering my body from standing on the ledge, to sitting on the sill, to standing on the office floor. With Crumpled's file now put away, the desk was neat once more. I patted my wallet inside my pants pocket and walked out, closing the door behind me.

In the hallway, I passed BuCCS' distinctive ashtray stands. The upright rectangular bases made of see-through acrylic are filled with the shards of cut-up credit cards that once, presumably, belonged to BuCCS clients. The resourceful bass drum-coffee table maker would be proud. I dumped my bucket's dirty water in a back hallway slop sink, picked up the check from the Finance Department, and headed uptown once more.

Since the 6 train didn't offer up any seats, instead of reading the paper, I stood and found myself scanning the ads on the car walls. After glancing at a poster for a technical institute that would give one's life some needed direction, I started mulling over the sort-out-your-life seminar I'd taken a few weeks earlier. Actually, the company calls the programs it offers "Life Planning." And even though that term is accurate, it nonetheless brings to my mind last wills and testaments, insurance policies, and funeral services. The class itself had been pretty instructive, however.

The seven of us in the group had gone about trying to put together thorough self-portraits that reflected our interests, values, and goals. We did so by answering such questions as: Who do I hold in high regard and why? How would I spend a hypothetical ten million dollars on myself? To whom would I give away the same amount of money?

Regarding a role model, I wrote down James Bond, insofar as I have always admired his effortless élan, his British cool, his directness, his grace under pressure — and his theme music.

I decided that I would spend my pretend money on a Soho loft and a sailboat. As for a donation, I would give the bucks to GDS, my liberal, laid-back high school. It was a private school, but you didn't wear a uniform and you called your teachers by their first name.

By recalling important experiences in our lives, we sought out clues that could point us towards new directions, or reinforce hunches we already had. I was stuck. The only hint that I could take from the experience of hearing a *Manifesto* song on the BBC was that I liked being in a band. I had gone into the class knowing that it was time to put the ol' college degree to use. Having been an English major meant, therefore, that I should write. But write what? More English papers? No, I didn't picture myself doing that, or becoming an English teacher for that matter: too many papers to grade. At the end of the five all-day sessions, the question, "So, now what?" still hovered about. A fellow seminar attendee swatted at the question: "Ivor, I see it so clearly. Even if you're not playing in a band, you can still think like a musician. So, write about music, write about bands."

As it turned out, my personal visionary had gone to Columbia's journalism school and was a reporter; she wanted to sort out how she could reconcile being a reporter with wanting to windsurf. She raved about the school, saying how great it would be if I went there and then set out to "cover" music. I had to admit that I found the idea alluring. I'd be back in school; I wouldn't be squeegeeing; I would have a Master's degree; I'd eventually be writing and getting paid for it. I considered myself just the kind of "out of left field" applicant Columbia would like; I figured at the very least I had a good story, even if my application did end up in the oddball pile. I'd decided to apply.

But to cover music, to cover anything, to "get the story," that sounded so...responsible. But isn't that the difference between a day job and a real job? And, wouldn't it be nice to have one's job and career be one and the same? Along with this practical take, a part of me also liked that at the very least, the process would define the next two years of my life: one to apply, the next to — hopefully — attend; Columbia's journalism school program did only last two semesters, albeit jam-packed. Which was just as well since I couldn't afford to go for longer than that.

Then, degree in hand, I would...well, be a writer of course. Oh right, a journalist. Granted, going from playing music to writing about music did make sense. But I couldn't really picture myself as a writer. To try and ease into this new me, a few days after my Life Planning seminar ended, I had signed up for an expository writing class at the New School which would start in just over a month, in mid September. I had a plan: my writing class and my application. And I had an escape hatch: getting into Columbia didn't mean I had to go. Of course, who knew if I would get in?

Seeing that a seat had opened up, I sat down, resting my feet atop my bucket's edge. I wondered how my I'm-quitting-the-band presents for Michael and Gary had gone over. Not that they knew why I had shown up at the studio a few weeks earlier laden with bootleg recordings of the Stones (for Gary) and the Beatles (for Michael) and sleek designer ashtrays from the Soho store Moss. I had planned to make an announcement of my intentions, but just couldn't. Instead, I'd said something about how I'd seen these things and thought of them, that I was celebrating how well the songs were coming along. I might have even said they were given simply in friendship, but I don't really know. I've done my best to block that night out. Despite Michael leaving messages for me about two or three sessions since then, I had not walked the few blocks to the studio.

I hadn't had the directness to simply say "I quit." What a hypocrite I was. I had been pretty mad when Bert had quit the band without truly saying so. Now I had proved I was just as good at it.

Plus, now that window cleaning was the only thing I was doing, my day job had become, well, my real job? Had become...me? Man, I hoped not. But it had sure begun to feel that way. Once I picked up my Columbia application, it would fill my time. I would have essays to write and letters of recommendations to sort and forms to fill out. Still, it wasn't playing in a band.

I closed my eyes and tried to think of something else, tried to fill my head with a song.

Though both the doorman and the Service Entrance porter had assured me downstairs that no one was home, I knocked loudly anyway just to be certain. Never enter a customer's apartment unannounced. I had once and happened upon a couple in bed. A lunchtime assignation? I wasn't about to ask. But I do know they've found someone else to clean their windows, since neither Pat nor I have ever been asked back to their place. Beyond the possibility of surprising people in such a way, entering without making some sort of proclamation also seems suspicious. What if a neighbor were to look out their door's peephole and see me silently entering? So after waiting a few seconds, I knocked again, then unlocked the door and stepped inside.

"Hello! Hey there! Anybody home? It's the window cleaner!"

My words met only welcoming silence. Now, then: Time to find the check. I put down my bucket, exited the foyer and headed straight for the living room window. Ignoring for the moment the 18th-floor view of the Upper East Side that beckoned, I looked instead at the barren windowsill. Pat had instructed the client to leave a check there, but no envelope with "Shields Windows" written across the front awaited me.

I returned to the foyer and scanned its bureau, but saw no envelope, or check, or cash, or note amongst the magazines and old mail strewn there. Bad sign. After inspecting the kitchen counter and breakfast table, I concluded that they'd forgotten.

This was the risk of agreeing to key-permission jobs, when a customer is not at home but has promised to leave a check. Since they hadn't, I now faced a dilemma: Do I go against company policy and clean the windows anyway? Or, do I walk away, leaving the dirty windows behind — along with a note explaining why.

If I chose the latter, I risked at the very least an irate customer. Perhaps a big deal dinner party that night would be marred. Worse, they might drop us for other window cleaners. Still, if I stayed and did the windows, they might well forget the check the next time, too.

I filled my bucket. Actually, the windows made my decision for me. They were too easy to blow off: big picture windows that opened inward like a door, framed by narrow side panes. As I saw it, since the job had already been scheduled, why should I kill time till the next job if I could make some money instead, albeit deferred. Plus, the clients were theoretically good for the money, and they were our customers. The family that lived here was perfectly nice — a husband, wife, and their teenage son. They'd been home at least once or twice when I'd cleaned there before. I didn't want to disappoint them.

I lugged my bucket into the living room and then, once I had dusted off my work clothes, settled into a fluffy flower-print sofa to leaf through a bit of the day's Times and sip a glass of cold water. Especially since I wasn't going to be paid right away, I would make a point to enjoy the benefits of a key-permission job: no customers. I took my time reading a bit of the paper's Arts section. Then, I took advantage of another aspect of key-permission apartments. I looked around.

There was the black, red, and blue Kandinsky print on the living room wall. There was the Stickley Mission Style dining room table and chairs one room over. It's kind of like in "Curious George Takes a Job," when the little monkey becomes a window cleaner: The doorman tells George as he hands him a squeegee, mop, and bucket to clean the windows and not look at what the people in the apartments are doing. But, of course, Curious George can't resist.

I do, however, draw a line. I don't rifle through a customer's closets; I don't rummage through their drawers. I am there, after all, to do the windows, not to learn whether the lady of the house wears garter belts. I am not a digger or a thief. I see what people leave out and about, not what they hide.

But if what I see reflects on my customers, well...so be it. While on the job, I have read love letters left on display in a kitchen, come across pot and cocaine on some apartments' coffee and bedside tables, and, in others, copies of books on how to tell your kids not to do drugs even if you did. I have seen presidential cufflinks from the Reagan White House in someone else's dressing room.

At a Fifth Avenue apartment belonging to a very proper couple, I came across tons of porn. Magazines and tapes were strewn across their bed, but I studiously ignored them as I went to work. Reflected in the glass I was cleaning, however, I could see the lady of the house tiptoe in, throw the comforter over the stash, then sneak out. She never asked me back.

Apart from satisfying curiosity, such gleaning also helps to make up for the sunup-to-sundown drudgery of "mop, squeegee, chamois," "mop, squeegee, chamois." Similarly, I only play CDs readily on view.

Now that I was about to clean, I no longer desired silence. I walked over to the stereo set in the large wooden bookcase that spanned a living room wall and looked through the musical offerings. Hmm, mostly Broadway show tunes, but no *Jesus Christ Superstar*. Then I noticed "The Best of *Bread*," David Gates' Seventies soft-rock band best known for such hits as "Guitar Man," "Baby I'm-A Want You," and "If." I had always liked "Diary" myself, a tune which tells of a husband who secretly reads his wife's journal and comes to regret it. The love she writes of in the pages turns out to be for someone else. Lesson learned? Voyeurism can hurt you.

I decided it was better to survey what the kid's CD collection had to offer. I'd learned from previous cleanings that he was a punk rock fan. Indeed, the kid had a poster of *The Beastie Boys* taped to his wall.

At some point, I had mentioned to the son that I used to be friends with NYC's own superstar rock-rappers. I told him that I'd hung out with Michael Diamond a lot during his one semester at Vassar our freshman year, and how he had left school to pursue *The Beasties* as their single, "Cookie Puss," began to get them noticed. I told him about running into the band in London where we gate-crashed an exclusive club and I actually met Paul Simonon of *The Clash*.

As expected, the kid couldn't believe that his mom's window cleaner could ever have "been down" with Mike D, Ad Rock, and MCA.

Afterwards, I wondered why I had said anything at all. I knew that I had mostly opened my mouth to surprise the kid, just as I also knew I'd engaged in some silly name-dropping. Part of it was that he seemed kind of like I had been back then: into punk but not punked out. No spiked hair, no bondage gear, not even a sneer. Still, a part of me wanted this teen to regard me as something other than just a window washer. Even a baffling, oddball window cleaner would be better.

I'd done a variation on this at another Upper East Side residence, one where the upper crust client had been consistently indifferent to me, if not haughty. Then I spotted a directory to the Century Club in his den and mentioned that my father was also a member. The chap was suddenly quite chatty.

Kneeling below the image of Mike D and his bandmates fighting for their right to party, I flipped through the discs and was pleased. *The Beasties* were there, of course, as were *Bad Brains*, *The Clash*, *The Damned*, *The Sex Pistols* — so far, his taste matched a lot of my favorite punk bands. There was also a "Best Of" collection for the *Ruts*, an underappreciated English punk band whose drummer, Dave Ruffy, I counted as one of my favorites. At some point, I had urged the kid to get some of their music and was now happy to see that he had.

Was it incongruous to find such records in this upscale East Side apartment? I don't know. How incongruous was it for me to play in the bands I did? It seemed that most every kid involved in D.C.'s punk scene came from middle class backgrounds if not higher, with parents who worked as lawyers, bankers, government officials, professors, writers, and the like. *Faith* had practiced in Michael's basement in Georgetown. His father was a university professor and his mother was a psychologist. The point is that, despite what our parents did or who they were or where they lived, we were still teenagers, and we still felt frustration, alienation, and the need to be ourselves.

I quickly took to Washington's punk scene. Shows offered more than just an opportunity to play before an audience. They convened our community of straight edge punks. "Straight edge" bands — a term Ian Mackaye had coined while in his band *Minor Threat*; he'd also co-founded the Dischord label — disavowed drugs and alcohol while relishing harsh guitars, raucous drumming, and youth's rebelliousness. As a teen, Ian had looked around and seen other teens getting fucked up and wanted nothing to do with that.

We weren't outcasts necessarily, just people different from the rest; we didn't do drugs or drink alcohol, viewing them as crutches; we didn't like rock 'n' roll, seeing it as tired. Our music and our outlook were new and unexpected: visceral but intelligent, as well as slightly threatening. We relied on ourselves and did so without apology, espousing the Do It Yourself punk ethic.

The scene had its own record label, the aforementioned, resolutely independent Dischord Records. And, since the local clubs didn't particularly like that most of the crowd wasn't buying drinks — either by choice or because they were too young — the punks convinced them to stage all-ages shows held on weekend afternoons; "hardcore matinees," as they were called.

Slam dancing, while a bit dangerous, we regarded as a small riot among friends. When the father of my high-school girlfriend attended one of our shows, he wept at the sight of the kids hurling themselves in the air and swirling about in the pit. He thought we were wasting our energy on anger. But he didn't get it: anger was part it. Plus, we were just letting go.

Though I committed myself to my band, I still couldn't quite commit to the scene entirely. I didn't acquire punk's accoutrements: the spiked hair or shaved head, combat boots and leather jacket. Instead, I wanted to be — or at least, felt the need to be — myself: pleasant, presentable Ivor. Indeed, the essay I wrote for my college applications that fall told of my being in a punk band but not quite being a punk. At some level, I suppose, I wanted to assure the schools I applied to that I wouldn't burn down their campuses once I arrived. Even so, a month into my freshman year at Vassar, I was nailed for spraying graffiti on the cafeteria's doors alongside the-soon-to-be-leaving and soon-to-be-famous Michael Diamond.

I hadn't regarded drumming in my first band, S.O.A. (short for *State of Alert*), as an act of rebellion or as a life-changing event. At first, it was simply being in a band. Michael and I went to the same high school, and since he had seen me perform a drum solo at a GDS talent show the previous spring, he knew I could play. As it turned out, the band's first drummer had to quit so he could attend summer school. When Michael asked me to join, I told him I'd think about it.

S.O.A. already had a record out, the "No Policy" e.p., which crammed ten songs onto a seven-inch disc made of green vinyl. Michael gave me a copy to take home and check out. I knew they were a punk band, but I had never gone to see them or any of the other D.C. punk bands perform. When I played the record that night on the stereo, I first thought I had set the turntable at the wrong speed. The songs were quick and short; some clocked in at just over a minute. They blared a tangled insurgent mess of jagged guitars and punchy bass, shouted unintelligible vocals and an insistent, aggressive drum beat: Boom-bap! Boom-bap! Boom-bap! Crash! Boom-bap! Boom-bap! Boom-bap! Crash!

My response was a question: I'm supposed to play this fast? Though I couldn't understand the words on most of the songs, I did understand the point. This exhilarating, liberating music possessed an appealing energetic anger.

"Public Defender," one of the slower songs and my favorite, railed against police brutality while boasting a discernible and melodic chorus: "He doesn't care a fucking bit/He's gonna hit you with a stick!/Man in Blue comes for you/Siren's red, you're gonna be dead!"

This was far different from the last band I had performed in, a group thrown together for an eighth grade talent show. I backed two flutes and two trumpets, and we performed "The Sound of Silence" and "The Hustle." *S.O.A.*'s music deliberately staked out the edge. The next day, I told Michael I'd join.

The day of our first practice, when Michael, Wendell, and Henry appeared at the gates of the U.S. Naval Observatory — my family had quarters there at the time — the Secret Service called and asked that I escort the boys to the house. The agent regarded his request as being merely "prudent and precautionary," in light of the Vice President being our neighbor on the grounds, and the fact that he couldn't believe that these "characters" with shaved heads and tattered clothes could be friends of mine.

It turned out that I only played one show with *S.O.A.*, since Henry Rollins had made his decision to ditch us in favor of *Black Flag* not too long after I'd joined. In fact, for what turned out to be *S.O.A.*'s last show, we opened for the *Flag* and Henry sang a few numbers with his new bandmates, allowing the audience to literally witness Henry take another step towards becoming a punk icon. That gig also featured a riot, courtesy of some Philly white trash not appreciating out-of-town punks in their neighborhood. The locals paid their admission, slashed a few slam dancers inside the Starlight Ballroom, and then ran out. Punks charged after them into a setup: a vacant lot filled with more white trash wielding baseball bats. Quite a first show.

Faith, like *S.O.A.*, had been part of Washington D.C.'s straight edge hardcore punk scene, or "harDCore" as one poster for a show cleverly pointed out. It was the band that Michael and I had gone on to form with Alec and Chris, the band where I snuck in my admiration for *The Police*'s Stewart Copeland pop-reggae-rock sensibility on one song by hitting my drumsticks against the snare drum's rim to produce a clacking sound, like on "Regatta de Blanc" and "Walking on the Moon."

Faith was a straight-ahead, super-fast punk band. Our songs were such that, though I spent most of my time keeping the beat going in a blitzkrieg of half-beats (Boom-bap! Boom-bap! Boom-bap!), my drumset nonetheless included a splash cymbal. It was kind of silly. I didn't hit it that often and when I did, it was probably never heard. But at least I had it, and at least I played it. It was another salute to Stewart Copeland.

At a *Police* concert, after the band had finished playing, Steward Copeland had turned and tossed one of his splash cymbals back up at us in the crowd. The cymbal sailed through the air, and I leapt for it. I had never been a baseball fan, but right then I understood why people bring mitts to the bleachers. You see the ball coming and you just have to have it. I wanted that cymbal. It was mine. And as I leapt up to catch it, I just knew I would have it. I saw my upstreched arm reaching and reaching and I saw the cymbal heading right towards where my hand would meet it. Then the cymbal's brass met my fingers' flesh — and slipped away. Instead of catching the splash, I merely stopped its forward motion. And so instead of landing in my hand, the splash dropped into the hands of a short young kid — maybe five feet tall, maybe ten years old — standing right next to me. He hadn't even tried to jump because he knew it wouldn't make a difference. He clasped that cymbal and ran off yelling, "Mom! Mom! Look what I got! Look!"

Chris, Michael, and I went on to form *Embrace* after *Faith* had ended, with Ian Mackaye as frontman. That group had been an instance of an apparently good idea not matching up with reality. Though we had admired each other's previous bands, our time together turned out to be a very long ten months. We just didn't gel. As it turned out, Michael's songs demanded a voice that could really sing; Chris' personal problems and erratic bass playing didn't make things any easier; Ian wanted a band as musically tight as his previous band, *Minor Threat*; and I...I just wanted the band to work. It hadn't.

Despite our problems, I still think our posthumous record sounds pretty good. Ian's adamant vocals and Michael's intricate guitars do at times contrast sharply, but the slowed pace lets the music be heard more readily and marks the band as one of the earliest examples of "emo-core" or simply "emo" — punk rock with a range of emotions and not just anger and frustration at its center.

At a record store many years after our record was released, I came across the *Embrace* record in its own section (as opposed to filed under the generic "E"), and the staff of the store had declared the group "Godfathers of Emo."

A year after *Embrace*'s break-up, Ian Mackaye formed *Fugazi*, the acclaimed, successful, respected punk band that embodied punk's D.I.Y. philosophy. The band puts out their own records, and have sold copies in the hundreds of thousands. They tour the world and charge only five bucks (or thereabouts) for their shows. They dictate their own terms. *Fugazi*, the band I had once hoped to be in.

I had "jammed" with Ian (on guitar) and Joe (on bass) the summer before my senior year of college, the summer before Ian and Joe decided on a final line-up. The two had played with a couple of drummers and were sorting things out. I had been quite taken with their songs and felt they were onto something not just viable, but important. Joe's fluid but charged bass lines melted into reggae inflections, while Ian's harsh guitar chords underpinned his hoarse truths, combining two of my favorite aspects of D.C.'s music scene: seriousness and distortion.

One song called "Waiting Room" epitomized Ian's approach. Playing in Dischord House's sweltering basement with my earplugs snugly in place, I could barely make out his words, but they felt familiar.

Though I didn't ask Ian, the lyrics certainly reminded me of conversations he and I had when we'd played in *Embrace*. I know I never used the words "waiting room," but I do remember saying how it seemed at times that I was waiting for my life to begin. In the basement that summer, playing with Ian and Joe, I felt like it was.

At the end of August, I took Ian and Joe out to dinner and tried to persuade them to wait for me to finish college. I told them I would come down from Vassar on weekends, spend vacations in Washington, do whatever it took. But I had to finish college. I had already taken two years off (the first to play in *Faith*, the second to play in *Embrace*) and if I left once more, I'd likely never go back. I couldn't do that to my parents. Give me nine months, I had said, and then you'll have me for life. But Ian didn't want to wait that long. I also recall him joking that he didn't want to deal with the Admiral. More to the point, he and Joe had been playing with me in part because Brendan, another drummer from D.C. punk bands, had been out of town.

Brendan had played with Eddie and Mike and Guy in *Rites of Spring*, another of Washington's "emo" bands. But they, like *Embrace*, had also broken up following a scene-rejuvenating "Revolution Summer."

Ian said that they would see how things went with Brendan — and Guy for that matter: since Brendan and Guy had always been a musical team, perhaps Guy would join as well — and let me know. But I knew "my" version of *Fugazi* was over as the waiter cleared away the fortune cookies. That hunch became official six weeks later at *Fugazi*'s second show. I had gone down to D.C. for October Break, gone to see them, and even ended up onstage accompanying the band on tambourine to "Waiting Room." As I looked down at my freshly blistered palms, Ian thanked me for playing with them the summer before.

During Christmas Break, Michael and I started planning another band, what became *Manifesto*. We recorded one album that was barely known in America, and our label dropped us from our contract just eight weeks after the record was released to stores.

The next band Michael and I formed was *clear*, who essentially imploded during a four-show, ten-day visit to London. We'd tried to entice a label or two in us, but nothing had panned out. To compensate for not landing a deal, our last night in town Michael and I had decided to splurge on an expensive meal. Over samosas, vegetables done vindaloo style, and nan bread, we'd agreed that once we got back to New York, we would cut ties with the guitarist and bassist we had been playing with and brought along on the trip.

Over the years, while *Fugazi*'s fortunes grew and *Manifesto*'s did not, I occasionally found myself wishing that they'd break up and Ian, now in need of a drummer, would give me a call. Sometimes I'd just wish that *Fugazi* would break up. I have played the pathetic "if only" game, as in: if only I hadn't felt so compelled to finish school and had joined the band instead. Indeed, after my mom once read about *Fugazi* in the Times, she remarked that perhaps I should have dropped out. I told her she was reading my mind.

Then I wised up: Leaving school wouldn't have changed a thing. Ian had made his decision. I had to live with it. I mean, I truly doubt Ian has ever wondered what his band would have been like with me. Over the years, though, I have reminded myself that Ian and Guy together bring more to one band than if they each had been in their own groups.

Ideally, such longing leads to inspiration. But it has occasionally made me wish I'd been in other bands, ones more successful.

Picking up a *Fugazi* CD in the boy's bedroom, I flipped it over and saw "Waiting Room" listed as a track. I'd learned a couple of years earlier that once when the band had played at Vassar, Ian had introduced the song by saying that it was about a friend who had gone there.

I looked about the room I was in: at *The Beasties* poster on the wall, at the CDs before me, at the one in my hand, and at the dirty panes. Not being in a band and not being in school, it hit me that I was in a waiting room once more. I placed the disc back, and returned to my bucket and the picture window in the living room awaiting me. I put *Bread* on the stereo and then pulled my squeegee from my holster and got to work.

FOUR

Though only early September, the afternoon had a cold bite at its edges, the sign that I had to start wearing a second layer of black tee shirts. The shortening days and the lowering temperatures had put a bit more pep in the steps of passers-by, making that fabled New York energy all the more apparent. I also liked to think that this sense of renewal and purpose could be attributed to the leaves changing colors.

Most every tree in the city seemed a fireworks display that burst into red, orange, and yellow before the spent sparklers fell to the ground. My views of Central Park were now all the more special. But that uptown spectacle lay a good two-and-a-half miles to the north and one job away. I was, instead, downtown in Greenwich Village looking for a walk-up and enjoying the show put on by the trees of Perry Street.

This time of year, whenever September snuck up, whenever the leaves began to turn, I had always felt that I should be back in school. "Academic Weather" was stricking once more, and it seemed that I should be studying in a library, taking classes — thinking. At least my course at the New School had just begun, and after I'd finished the day's jobs, I was going to head up to Columbia to pick up my application.

Man, was I beholden to "name schools," a sucker for the Ivy League and its "Seven Sisters." But at least I knew where that feeling came from: The Naval Academy and Oxford, Wellesley and Radcliffe. As well as my sister Inge's going to Yale undergrad, my sister Erica's going to Brown undergrad, my brother Lars' going to Yale's drama school, my sister Ursula's going to Columbia's social work school. I needed my own Ivy degree, didn't I? Just as I needed $18,500 in debt? But wasn't that a small price to pay for a good cause? (And I don't mean journalism, but myself.)

I did my best to ignore that I could barely afford the $400 hit I took so that I could enroll in my New School class. It wasn't anything like being in school full-time, but at least I was wading back in. We'd met for one class, and while the classroom in the bunker-like building at 14th and Fifth was a bit dreary itself — it was windowless save for a few narrow, vertical, rectangular panes that looked out on the hallway — Candy, the teacher, was cool. She knew what she was talking about in terms of writing, the whole "show don't tell" thing and emphasizing that we work hard to reveal something new and unusual in our weekly four-page pieces. She really seemed to look forward to reading what we'd written.

I was working on an essay about Lars and me visiting "Twin's Day," the annual national gathering of twins in — no kidding — Twinsburg, Ohio. By the end of our afternoon there, Lars and I had been chided for not wearing identical clothes, but we'd also come away as something of twin snobs ourselves, believing that fraternal twins were just wannabe twins.

For better or worse, my New School class was reminding me how hard writing is. What was I doing applying to journalism school?

Seeing that townhouses lined most of the block, I was expecting to clean a tiny flat. It turned out, however, that the red brick building I had sought out was bigger by far, a true apartment building dating from the 1930s. This relieved me, as it considerably lowered the odds of the residence being extremely cramped, one with the bed shoved up against a window and the windowsill serving as the sole bookcase.

No doorman greeted me or sent me around back. Nor did the place have a front door that locked; when I tentatively pushed the handle, it easily opened. I then noticed an apparently ignored note taped to an entryway mirror that implored residents to securely close the door behind them. I walked into the dark and slightly shabby lobby that made spotting the details in its deep-green marble floors and walls more of a challenge. But they were there: black speckles and spindly veins — along with the echoes of my footfalls. I noted that the lobby windows still had their original wooden frames that perfectly matched the hall's dark green. Nice touch. But no elevator. Not so nice a detail. I took the stairs to the sixth floor two steps at a time. Moments later, I knocked at an ancient wooden door also painted hunter green.

"Come in," a slightly harsh and gravelly voice called from behind it. "The door's open."

I let myself in. The apartment, like the lobby, was dark, but marble walls and green paint couldn't be held responsible. Instead, only layout and location could be blamed. I'd stepped into a back apartment, one that faced the rear of the building. Its white walls strained to bring out as much light as possible. These apartments are a classic New York City trade-off: not much sun, but not much noise. Appropriately, a low-key Ella Fitzgerald sang from the apartment's stereo at a discrete volume.

From the doorway, I saw a small thin woman in her fifties, with pale white skin. The faded yellow sundress she wore looked to be an ill-fitting holdover from the summer; it seemed too large for her. She sat at a small chrome and red Formica breakfast table placed in the middle of this, the main room, smoking a cigarette. Her grey hair matched the smoke rising from the ashtray. A bedroom and a bathroom adjoined the living room at the far end. Not too big a place, not too bad a job, not too many windows. I guessed it would be a minimum, forty-two dollars.

"So glad you could make it," she croaked. "My windows are a mess."

"That's what I'm here for," I said. I smiled as I walked over and shook her small soft hand. "Hi, I'm Ivor."

I put my bucket down near the sink and removed my tools, placing them and my courier bag in their usual pile against the wall. Next, I began to fill my bucket with a slow trickle of water from the ancient faucet.

"What kind of a name is Ivor?" she asked, her rough voice making her seem more blunt and humorless than I hoped she actually was. "It's a bit different."

I smiled as I used some of the sink's water to rinse my chamois. I could handle this one.

"I did look it up when I was kid," I said. "It means 'military archer,' or 'one who carries the bow.' So, either I'm a warrior or a caddy for one."

I took her rough-edged laughter as a good sign.

"Okay," she said, "and how in the world did you get into this line of work?"

I told her how I'd played in bands and needed a job. I did my best not to make my answer sound like a spiel, even though it really was. I had answered the question so many times. Now, at least, I had something to add, by saying how I was applying to grad school. When I told a client this bit of news, it sometimes seemed to make up for the fact that I was squeegeeing. This time though, it felt like I was just having a conversation.

"And what about you?" I asked. "What sort of work do you do?"

"I'm a nurse," she said. "Been one for a while. I work just around the corner. It's my day off." Her voice seemed smoother the more she spoke.

"That's nice," I said. "Must be hard at times."

"Yes," she said. "But I love it."

My bucket was now full; it was time to clean. The place only had six windows: three new easy replacement tilt-ins in the living room, whose green frames didn't match the building as well as the three old switchers in the bedroom and bathroom. While I usually get the harder ones out of the way first, since these three tilt-ins were right there, I decided to knock them out. Besides, she could start enjoying her clean windows sooner, and I could more readily hear Ella sing. As I walked across the room's creaking wood floor, bucket in hand, she lit up a fresh cigarette. These windows weren't going to be so easy to clean after all — and they wouldn't stay smoke-free for very long.

"I once had a conversation with a nurse I'll never forget," I said upon reaching the window, kneeling, and wetting my mop. "I used to manage an ice cream store, and once, while I was biking to the bank with the weekend money, I got hit by a car. The ambulance took me to the hospital, and the nurse there scraped the asphalt out of my arms."

As I squeezed out the long mop, I looked down at my left forearm and could still easily make out the white patches where the asphalt had been.

"To keep my mind off that," I continued, "she started talking to me, asking me questions. I remember telling her about the accident, about losing control of the steering when the handlebar had brushed against the car's door, and about how busy the ice cream store had been that weekend, how we'd had a line out the door. And then she told me that the emergency room had also been really busy over the weekend and that they'd had a line out the door, too. I remember thinking that was not quite the same thing."

"In its own way it is," the nurse said and smiled.

"Have you lived in the building a while?" I asked.

"I've lived here forever," she said. "I certainly couldn't afford this neighborhood otherwise."

I lifted my mop and started wetting down the windows. The water immediately turned a yellowish brown; the inside panes had a thick veneer of caked-on smoke. Though I scrubbed the windows thoroughly, the mop continued to hesitate across the glass. I could feel it sticking. The panes weren't ready for the squeegee yet. I sprinkled some Soilax into my bucket. It's a degreaser designed for walls and floors, but Pat and I use it for troublesome windows. Because it has no phosphates, it's safe for the environment and the glass, but I'm not so certain about my hands. Sometimes after using it, they feel unnaturally dry.

The Soilax, however, made a noticeable difference. The windows came clean with a bit more mopping. I squeegeed them a couple of times to be certain the crud was all off. Since the outsides were also very dirty, I wouldn't be able to gauge what I'd done on the insides until I'd cleaned both sides of the glass. Luckily, the ballasts were in good shape, the windows tilted in easily and didn't threaten to shoot up and out of their tracks.

While I cleaned the three windows' interiors and exteriors, the nurse returned to reading her paper, Ella sang softly in the background, and the water in my bucket turned black. I would need to replace it before doing the other three. After I finished off the living room, I went back to the sink and dumped the old water, grateful my slop didn't stain. I then refilled my bucket with fresh water. I rinsed out my squeegee, mop, and chamois as well. It would take a while before I could declare the back windows clean.

"You know," I said as I put my squeegee back in its holster and the chamois back on its loop that hung at my waist, "it's funny. But whenever I meet a nurse, or a cop, or someone in the military — anyone who wears a uniform — and they're *not* in their uniform, it sort of throws me. It's almost like I expect them to be dressed up all the time. Do you know what I mean?"

"I know exactly what you mean," the nurse said and chuckled. "You are what you wear." She blew a ring of smoke into the air.

Of course, the black clothes I wore all the time could be a uniform of sorts for many New Yorkers. But I like picturing those striving for that arty, severe look — including myself — as chimney sweeps, stagehands, and original cast members of *Zoom*, the '70s kids show on PBS.

I certainly couldn't sport that look when I was interning at the Senate during some time off while I was in *Embrace*. I did this in part because I was interested in government, but also, to please my dad. Mostly to please my dad. As if to say, "Hey, I know I am playing in this punk band, but don't worry. I can still do something you relate to."

Since my father was an old friend of Rhode Island's Senator Chafee — my dad worked with him when Chafee was the Secretary of the Navy — getting a job at the Senate was easy. Actually working there, however, was not. Though Chafee was a moderate Republican, due to his seniority, he ran the Senate Republican Conference, essentially an in-house public relations firm for Republican Senators.

Not surprisingly, I was the only liberal Democrat on the staff. While there, I occasionally irked my colleagues by telling them that then-President Reagan was out of his mind, or at least an idiot. Of course they returned the favor when, after watching a videotape of my band perform, they told me they didn't consider *Embrace*'s songs music. But that's what happens when you work with people you can't relate to.

While I didn't sabotage the Conference's workings, I certainly did not always do my job with a spring in my step. I took my time to do anything for Senator Helms' office, for instance. And, while I did wear a tie to work, I resisted wearing a coat. Instead, I donned an old leather flight jacket of my father's. He had given it to me when I'd paid him back $1,500 he had generously lent me. While at the Senate, I was also once chided for being "disrespectful" of Chafee, by being too casual with him. I apologized to the Conference's staff director by explaining that I couldn't help but consider Chafee more as an old family friend than as a Senator.

Obviously, that Senate job was not for me, even if I had worn the correct uniform.

I lifted my bucket out of the sink and started to lug it to the bathroom. The floor creaked in this direction as well.

"Sometimes I'm a nurse," my customer said, "and sometimes I'm a patient. I'm expecting a call from my doctor."

"Oh," I said, putting down my bucket.

"Yes," she said, "I have cancer. I've had it a while, and I've had lots of treatments. But it's been pretty stubborn. Of course, I've been pretty stubborn, too."

At this, she tapped her ashes into their tray.

It seemed like she was reeling off a spiel — like she'd said this many times before — but I didn't begrudge her that. I had my own spiels after all.

"Anyway, I'm waiting to hear some results," she continued.

"I hope it's good news," I said, lifting my bucket once more.

As I entered the bathroom, the phone rang. She let it ring twice, then picked up the black plastic receiver. I took a step inside the bathroom but didn't quite close the door.

"Hello? Oh, hi, Doc. Yeah, it's me."

She paused, listening to the voice on the other end speak briefly.

"Oh. Really. Yes, that's not good.... No, I understand.... No, no, I told you to call me, regardless.... I don't know, I'll have to check.... Actually, can I call you back about scheduling all that later? I just can't think right now.... Thanks. I'll talk to you soon."

She put down the phone and sat quietly. Ella sang. After a few moments, she wiped away a tear from one cheek and then the other. I opened the bathroom door and walked as softly as I could across the squeaky room. In a few strides I stood next to her and put my hand on her shoulder nearest to me.

"This is not good," she whispered.

I continued to stand and lightly squeeze her shoulder.

"I'm a professional," she said. But she wasn't talking to me. "I can...."

She didn't finish her sentence. Instead, she broke down, tears and sobs at the kitchen table.

"I'm so sorry," I said. "I'm so sorry." It was all I could say.

I took my holster off and placed it and my squeegee and chamois on the floor at my feet. I pulled the red Naugahyde chair opposite us over and sat next to her, putting my hand back on her shoulder. After a minute or so, I realized that Ella had stopped singing and that we were therefore sitting in silence. Neither of us moved, or said a word. Even our breathing seemed hushed. I considered putting the record back on but decided not to. This wasn't my house. This wasn't my news.

I thought of a customer that had died of cancer who'd lived north of the Village, on the Upper West Side, on Amsterdam and the low 80s. It had been a long, drawn-out illness in her case as well, and years of treatment had not been able to conquer the disease. When Pat and I came to clean her windows that last time, we knew we would never see her again.

"Can you be sure to clean the bathroom window this time?" she had asked, her head topped with a white terry cloth turban. "I know we never clean it, what with its frosted glass, but I really want as much light as possible right now. Pure light."

Sitting at the kitchen table on Perry Street, I wished that the sun would come out, that this apartment could bask in its rays, that this place had a skylight. But the two of us continued to sit in what now seemed like near-darkness.

She lit a cigarette and then waved the match dramatically to extinguish its flame.

"I guess it doesn't really matter now," she said and smiled wryly. The grin that was supposed to stop the tears only brought on more. She didn't bother to wipe them away.

I stared at her Marlboro Light. Its burning end flickered and slowly grew in length before being tapped into the tray. I managed a smile myself, but sadness underpinned my effort. I patted her shoulder, then squeezed it once more, letting my hand rest there. We sat in silence. Finally I stood.

"Ma'am," I said quietly, guiltily, "I have to go finish the windows."

She smiled once more, and this time wiped a tear away.

I put my tools back on and returned to the bathroom. The window there and the two in the bedroom were all that remained to be cleaned. They were incredibly dirty, both inside and out. Even after cleaning them not much more sunlight entered the apartment. I knew that even when the many leaves providing shade fell to the ground, their absence wouldn't make too much of a difference either. This back apartment would never be that bright.

I took my time rinsing out my tools and placing them back in my bucket. I wanted to stay, but had to get to the next job; I was running late as it was.

She wrote out a check for the forty-two bucks she owed me and gave me a ten-dollar tip. I thanked her and made my way to the door. She rose from her chair and followed me; pallid skin wrapped in a sallow dress.

"Take care," I told her. "And good luck."

"No," she said. "You're the one who should take care. I'm not the one hanging off the sides of buildings. I can handle this."

I smiled and closed the door behind me. I heard it lock as I kneeled and retied my shoelaces. I began walking down the steps. At the landing I heard Ella singing once more.

Back on the street, I looked up at her building's windows.

I tried putting myself in the nurse's position, and then was glad I wasn't her. I looked away.

Jesus, how could I be thinking about myself after what I'd just seen up there?

It's like that line that Bono sang so long ago in the Band Aid song, "Do They Know It's Christmas?": "And tonight thank God it's them instead of you."

I've always found the lyric extremely disconcerting — how charitable a response is that to people starving in Africa? — but it's also pretty honest. You think about how lucky you are and how different your life is.

What was I doing cleaning windows? And why had I quit drumming? And why was I applying to graduate school? What was the fun in that?

Still, for whatever reason, I had come away with a reinforced feeling: Why go back to school if it wasn't a good one? For that matter, why be in a band if it wasn't going to make a point?

I'd known for a long time that I was a music snob. I think most musicians are, in their own way. And, of course, being in bands on Dischord Records, too, had given me a high standard; I'd been in good bands that made an impression and promoted clear-headed, if not hard-headed, self-reliance.

But this school thing was something else. A part of me knew that at some level, I was enamored of such a name school being on my resumé, and not just by the challenge it represented. At Vassar, I'd done well in some classes, mostly my English courses. But in history and Spanish, I would routinely get B's and even the occasional C. I'd also outright failed two classes, Intro Anthropology and Intro Economics. But Anthro had too many bones to memorize, and Econ had too much math to deal with.

Was I even in school? Was I even in a band?

I began making my way over to the A,C, and E subway stop at Eighth Avenue. Not just the nurse's block, but all of the Village's honeycomb of streets were quiet for the moment, and pretty much empty of people, even Bleecker and West Fourth. I wondered when she would next leave her apartment and what that outing would be like.

Though I couldn't really avoid walking past Thirteenth Street, I purposefully avoided looking down my block. I never like being that close to home and not being able to go there. My bucket suddenly felt heavier.

As I approached the subway, a tall tan man with long black hair, a long thin face, and a pierced ear caught my eye as he crossed Thirteenth. For a moment, I wondered if I should call out to him or not.

"John!" I yelled. "John!"

He stopped and glanced about. He looked the same as he had years earlier, when he had wooed my band, *Manifesto,* to sign a deal with the label he had worked at then, East-West Records. East-West was itself a division of Atlantic Records, which, in turn, was part of Warner-Elektra-Atlantic, making us part of a major label. It's kinda convoluted, but that's part of the record business.

John was wearing his New York look, a black varsity jacket of wool and leather, black jeans, and black high-tops. Not what I suspected he wore down in Florida, where he'd lived for the past few years. He looked right at me. To preempt an awkward moment, I called out once more.

"John! It's Ivor Hanson."

"Ivor! Wow! What's going on with you?" John said, his voice seemingly caught between sincerity and slickness; just as I remembered it. If he hadn't recalled my name, he certainly didn't let on.

I told him how Michael and I had retreated to the studio with Gary, and how I had essentially walked away when I saw how our — their — songs were never getting finished. I made a point, however, of not bringing up East-West since the label had dropped John at the same time it had dropped us; a bit cruel, but that's also part of the record business. The band had figured that we would follow John to the next label he landed at, but that didn't happen: John decided to split from the music biz after twenty-odd years, move to the Sunshine State, and teach children with learning disabilities. While I was pleased for John's sake at this change — if not turn-around — in his life, his timing certainly didn't help us. But, I had joked, one doesn't usually schedule getting a conscience.

Seeing either John or Dave, the A&R guys that handled us at, respectively, East-West and Fire, always reminded me of running into my old girlfriends (or old bandmates for that matter): We'd been attracted to each other, we'd made an agreement not to see (or play) with anyone else, we'd been together...but it hadn't worked out. Since the afterglow of shared memories burns bright for only so long, I don't necessarily like to revisit them. Besides, these embers inevitably remind me of whatever did us in. Why reminisce over what was ultimately a failure?

How much do you mention? How much do you studiously ignore? I pick and choose. With Dave, I reminisced on biting down hard on the recording contract the band had just signed with his label. Leaving my teeth marks on the document seemed the appropriate way to commemorate entering into a multi-album deal with a small independent label that paid only okay royalties and coughed up only puny advances. I certainly felt like an indentured servant. I can also bring up with Dave the memory of Michael being arrested in London while *Manifesto* was over there promoting our record. Michael and a friend spent a night in jail for "interfering with a vehicle," when really, they were just drunk and tapping the side-view mirrors of cars they stumbled by. I liked reminding Dave that, fast-thinking record exec that he was, he called the music papers before he called the label's lawyer.

I don't, however, bring up Fire's behind-our-backs scheming that landed us at East-West with less clout — and less money — than originally planned. Even though John and East-West were set to sign only *Manifesto* to a U.S. deal, Fire went ahead and agreed to sign a blanket agreement that included *all* of Fire's artists with another Atlantic label. Instead of a coveted single act, we became just part of a tossed-off litter, possibly the runt. As for Dave, he bolted from Fire shortly thereafter and moved up to a "boutique" label backed by a major. At least the two of us have reached the point where I can joke to him that he ruined my musical career. Dave knows I'm only half-kidding.

As for John, I was never quite sure when he was kidding. As it became apparent that *Manifesto* and John were about to be "let go" — he and the label's head were not getting along; our single, "Pattern 26," had not zoomed up the appropriate radio charts; and other East-West staff who had also championed us had already left — John had looked out his Mid-town office window and surveyed his career: "From *Pink Floyd*, to Dylan, to *Midnight Oil*, to you guys." Michael, Bert, and I — and John — had all laughed, but he was also right. Call it gallows humor.

Since I hadn't really kept up with John after he'd left East-West and New York, I'd never had the chance to selectively bring up "the old times" with him. Now that I was unexpectedly standing before him on a Manhattan sidewalk, I realized I didn't really want to remember the shows we had hung out at, or the occasional meetings we had had in that office of his at "Rockerfeller Center" — how East-West's address had been spelled on the back cover of the *Manifesto* album. I'd always hoped it was a semi-clever intentional typo. But I was never entirely convinced. Being at East-West's office had usually left me feeling very uncool (and very un-rock star). It wasn't simply because one of the radio staff had taken to calling us "slugs." At East-West, I felt shuffled about and a low priority, despite John's enthusiasm and his position of Senior Vice President. I also felt very self-conscious of my bucket of squeegees — the band usually had to go see John between my window cleaning jobs.

"Ivor, I'm disappointed," John said. His ready smile skillfully undercut the edge of his words.

I wasn't sure what he meant. Then I stopped looking at his perfect white teeth and saw that his intense brown eyes weren't focused on me, but my bucket.

"What?" I said as I stepped over my tools and stood in front of my bucket. "I don't know what you're talking about."

John laughed. "So," he said, "you're still cleaning windows?"

"Hey," I said, "you're not the only one who's disappointed. You can add me to that list!"

This wasn't the plan after all: to wield a squeegee for years on end. I thought about mentioning Columbia, but I didn't want to go into all that. Even so, I was surprised at how willing I felt to name-drop the school.

"I always thought you did a good job at my place," John said. "And I always liked that *Manifesto* record."

In the year that John and *Manifesto* had worked together, I had added him to my list of customers. Though it felt a bit laughable — there I was, cleaning the windows of the guy who, if everything worked out right, would help make it possible for me to never clean windows again — a buck is a buck. In his case, close to eighty: eight belt windows with sturdy hooks but rather narrow ledges. I cleaned the windows of his Lower Broadway loft a couple of times, particularly just before he sold the place. By then, East-West was done with us, and John wanted to get out of town. Though John rightly viewed teaching kids as a second chance, I bet he regarded the classroom as a second choice. I knew I would.

I thanked John and then we both realized we had run out of things to say. Recounting the incident with the nurse didn't really seem appropriate, as it hardly qualified as small talk. More relevantly, unlike Dave, who had left us behind to continue on in the music business, John's career had ended with us. Why talk about that?

"I should be on my way," John said, "I'm running late to see my son. Can't believe he's at NYU now."

"Really? Cool," I said. "Yeah, I'm running late, too. But guess where I'm going? To the Dakota! And, I will tell you, I am not disappointed by that."

I wasn't. The Dakota is one of my favorite buildings, one of my favorite jobs. After saying goodbye to John, I kicked a few leaves into the gutter and headed down into the subway.

On the train, I found myself wondering what John would be like as a dad. At the very least, he wouldn't have minded his son having earrings. I smiled to myself as the C train rumbled uptown.

Taking the year off to play in *Embrace* marked the first time I was really living on my own. I was scooping ice cream to pay rent on a basement apartment. To mark this bit of independence, I not only bleached my hair, but decided to pierce my left ear — twice: since the store refused to pierce one ear for half-price, I wanted my money's worth. Unfortunately, as I don't have much earlobe to speak of, the second earring had pierced some cartilage, causing my ear to be inflamed. But, so be it; I had chosen to do it. I also regarded this personal act in keeping with the D.C. punk scene's call for a "Revolution Summer" — a time to recommit to its musical and activist endeavors, like staging "Punk Percussion Protests" against apartheid in front of the South African Embassy.

When I'd returned to New York for a family reunion dinner a week after I'd pierced my ear, however, my peroxide head and the yellow and blue studs came as a shock. My siblings and my mother couldn't believe what I'd done.

"You look like an albino with a red ear," Ursula had told me in true younger sister fashion.

"Just wait till your father gets home," my mom had warned. "Thor will hit the roof."

When my father walked in from work a half-hour later, he did just that.

"Now look, Ivor!" my dad had yelled after I'd tried telling him that an earring wasn't a big deal and pointed out that I was nearly 22 years old. "I am ordering you, ordering you, to take those out right now! Before dinner! Do you understand me? Right now! No son of mine will have a pierced ear!"

"Yes," I said, and then it just slipped out: "Sir."

I retreated to Ursula's bathroom, where my eyes burned and my ear pounded. I sat for what seemed a while but what could have been a few minutes. Or it could have been the other way around. I wasn't sure. I hadn't cared. I couldn't believe it: my father had never pulled rank on me this hard before. But then, I had never tried to mutiny before. After yanking out the two studs, I tossed the earrings down the toilet.

I then took my place at the round dining room table and nibbled at dinner. When someone asked about Washington, the ice cream store, or the band, I answered them. No one, however, mentioned the earrings or the blood dripping onto the collar of the nice white shirt I'd especially worn for the occasion. The next day, my dad apologized for losing his temper, and I told him to forget about it, that the earrings weren't a big deal. So much for my "Revolution Summer."

The pierced ear episode aside, the Hanson household resembled neither the taut and fearful Marine Corp family in Pat Conroy's *The Great Santini*, nor the cartoonish spit-and-polish of *The Sound of Music*'s Captain Von Trapp.

Actually, both my father and mother are Democrats — a rarity in the armed forces and my mom's childhood home of Winnetka, Illinois. And in regards to what we would do when we "grew up," Inge, Erica, Lars, Ursula, and I had grown up with our parents telling us: "Do what you want; we'll support you. Just not financially." Such flexibility was hard to argue with or rebel against.

Emerging from the station at 72nd and Central Park West, I looked to the trees seemingly ablaze in Central Park. Then, I searched for but didn't find a pile of leaves to throw myself into. Too early in the season I guessed, or perhaps the piles had already been raked up. Next, I took in the dense eight-story yellow brick building that has been variously described as "Brewery Gothic Eclectic," "Middle-European Post Office," and "the Dowager Queen Mother of apartment houses." But I simply consider it cool. Does any other building in New York really have the same cache?

The Dakota is, after all, the city's first luxury apartment house and has been called home by the likes of Rudolph Nureyev, Lauren Bacall, and Leonard Bernstein. It served as the setting for *Rosemary's Baby* and, of course, was where John Lennon lived and was gunned down. History, celebrity, and tragedy all ensconced in an architecturally cluttered chateau.

I looked up at the steeply pitched slate roof embellished with pointed gables of brownstone and terra cotta, copper cresting, dormers, widow's walks, and chimneys. My eyes then moved downward, taking in assorted balconies, some recessed, some projecting, and, of course, the windows: bay windows, arched windows, large windows, small windows. Many looked out on Central Park, some on 72nd, some on 73rd. I had come to do a dozen or so that looked over the back of the building from the seventh floor. And though I do consider windows a source of light and cheer, I'd always considered the Dakota's windows a tad ominous. Did they seem to scowl in 1884 when the place opened?

Before heading around the corner to the Service Entrance, I searched the nooks and crannies of the building's exterior for an Indian head or arrowhead I hadn't noticed before. Late 19th century wags inspired the ornamentation when, during construction, they compared the apartment house's then-remote location to being in the Dakota Territory; an unfinished Central Park and the shacks of squatters had provided the view for the first tenants. The developer, Edward S. Clark, took the mockers in stride by making their gibe the building's namesake.

I have no idea what prompted the Dakota's waterless moat or the recurring busts of Zeus and his attending sea monsters that bite into the moat's iron railing, but I tapped the heads of one set as I walked by — my way of thanking the supreme Greek god and his pointy-eared, scaly companions for standing guard along this fence.

Inside the Dakota's dimly lit basement, just past the soda machines, the worker on duty at the fenced-in check-in desk wrote down my name, "Shields Windows," the date, my entry time, and the apartment I was off to in the log — a large book documenting all the contractors doing business in the building on any given day. Unlike most other buildings, once he had called upstairs to confirm with the apartment that I was okay to be sent up, he then issued me an identity sticker.

Beneath the words "The Dakota" printed across the top, he wrote within the blue borders all of the log's information as well. I silently swore I would try once more to smuggle out the sticker as a memento when I left; on all my previous visits, the attendants had always demanded the piece of paper back. Rules are rules. The Dakota is a very thorough place. For a building with such prestige, I've never felt that the Dakota's workers have a corresponding attitude. Some guys on Fifth, Park, and Central Park West really do let the address where they work go to their heads. They apparently forget that the building isn't actually theirs. Obviously they have more of a claim to the apartment building than I do, but they ignore that we all are ultimately working for the same person: the resident.

For my part, however, I try my best to ignore that a hierarchy does exist in buildings, and that contractors usually don't rank very high on that totem pole. Maybe I cut the Dakota's workers a bit of slack because I am so starstruck by the place. I like to think the workers there figure that everybody who enters the Dakota — for any reason — knows it is a special building, knows it is a privilege to be there, and there's no need to flaunt it. At least that's my hope.

I stuck the badge where it wouldn't be in my way while working, on my shirt sleeve, and headed over to the Service Elevator shoe-horned between piping, brickwork, and an iron spiral staircase. I pushed the button marked "Seven" and rode the ancient box up.

Since the customer was off at work, the maid answered the door, a young Hispanic woman with a ready smile, who wore a work smock and blue jeans. Unlike maids in other places I've worked, I was glad that she didn't have to wear an outright maid's uniform, the standard grey, or pink, or black dress with white trim. They've always seemed a bit too much of a throwback, a hierarchical cliché from an earlier time.

Those outfits always remind me of a window customer's Upper East Side duplex where the maid had to wear that traditional uniform. I remember her once remarking to me when she had finished dusting the lady of the house's vanity, crammed with perfume bottles: "All these, for one person." Our smiles reflected both disbelief and acceptance.

At the Dakota, the maid's smile was one of welcome as she let me in, said "Hi," and returned to her dusting. I think she'd been around when I was there before. Though I ordinarily scheduled this job early in the morning, it hadn't worked out today, which was a shame. Usually when I arrived at 8 am, I get to hear a little bit about the client's world of advertising. She's a bigwig exec at an agency with offices in the Chrysler Building. Imagine that: living in one New York City icon and working in another. I hear how product packaging, market surveys, zinger catch phrases, and all the rest each contributed to the latest ad campaign for this product or that, be it breath mints or heart medicine. I like that she had helped come up with the Peace Corp's slogan, "It's the toughest job you'll ever love." I also like the photo of her with David Bowie, circa Ziggy Stardust.

I could have charged her $130 for her thirteen windows, but I never asked for more than $100. Though I'm sure she wouldn't have quibbled with the higher number, I did this for a few reasons: she was a friend of a friend, and I like to give such referrals a price break; because this was a "personal" job and I didn't have to give Pat a cut, I could afford the discount; and, I really did feel honored to be in the Dakota. Though it didn't make too much financial sense, I didn't care. Thirty bucks to spend a morning in the Dakota? Why not. Small wonder the company's not named "Ivor's Window Cleaning."

Before I stepped out onto the kitchen window ledge, I took in the view. This being another rear apartment, most of its windows looked out over the back of the Dakota, meaning I had no view of the park.

At the kitchen window I might.

From my vantage point, I could see the back windows of the "front" apartments, those that faced Central Park, and, if I was lucky, a clear shot through to Central Park's trees. But not today. Most of the neighboring windows, especially the small dormers that dotted the remaining upper floors of the Dakota's roof, had their blinds lowered or curtains drawn.

Since this window looked out over the building's immaculate, swept courtyard, I found myself not inside looking out, but inside looking inside. Being surrounded by the courtyard's four brown brick walls, having them be so immediate, made the Dakota appear even more like a large-scale gingerbread house. I looked down and saw a man in a grey suit walk from a far corner in the courtyard to the two-story arched entryway. I wondered if he was "somebody" — i.e. famous — until I saw him put his cap on and realized I'd been watching a doorman return to his post.

The sound of a flag flapping in a sudden breeze prompted me to look up, away from the doorman. I spied a half-dozen workers standing on the Dakota's widow's walk, below the flagpole that topped the roof's pyramid-like center point. When I saw one of the guys point east into the park and the others look, I guessed that they were enjoying their own view. Girl watching, perhaps? Some models on a shoot?

From "my" kitchen window, I faced mostly other kitchen windows and dining rooms that similarly looked down on the courtyard. I spotted one maid doing dishes and another vacuuming across the way.

Once I had gone out and washed the large kitchen window, I squatted on the ledge and ran my hand along the turquoise-colored copper drain-pipe. Nearly hot from a day's worth of sunlight, my fingers and palm appreciated the warmth. Fall was really kicking in. I then reached up and spread my hand across a smooth, thin, rectangular section of grey slate. It, too, felt warm to the touch, even soothing.

Coming in off the ledge, I noticed the oversized box of Dristan atop the kitchen cabinets — left over from a promotional campaign. I jumped back down to the floor and moved on to the maid's room. Following that window, I entered the dining room. Along with featuring two large court-yard windows, the nearly 19-foot by 24-foot room served as the home of a gigantic pool table. Very cool. From there, I knocked out the six windows among the three bedrooms.

Aside from not wanting to disrupt the maid's work, I found washing these panes quickly quite easy since they looked out on the neighboring Mayfair Towers. This 37-story, white brick monstrosity with hideous mus-tard-colored balconies dwarfs the Dakota. My customer's privacy notwith-standing — remember: if you can see out, someone can see in — I wasn't surprised that she kept most of her curtains drawn. There was nothing worthwhile to see, and nothing to slow me down.

While out on the ledge of the library however, I did check the gutter. On a previous cleaning, I came across some pornographic playing cards there that had, I guessed, fallen out of someone's windows from above and ended up scattered about the roof's edge. That was a first. Usually gutters only offer up leaves or crud. Once, though, while cleaning the windows of the Polo/Ralph Lauren building, I found the skeleton of an apparently long-dead pigeon in a gutter there. Quite a contrast to the designer clothes displayed inside the former Rhinelander Mansion.

While returning from the pantry's slop sink to dump my dirty water, I stopped in the hallway to admire the large painting hanging on the wall. It was a Botero portrait and characteristically featured a plump, bulbous person, in this case a young girl, walking down the street. The people in Botero's works strike me as silent, introspective folk who look about the world wisely while going about whatever they are doing.

At another West Side apartment, the customer had been a bit obnoxious to me once; on that day at least, she came off as one of those people who feels superior to others, or at least to a window cleaner. Anyway, she had a Botero, too. In a stab at diluting her exclusivity, I told her it seemed that I'd been seeing a lot of Boteros lately in customers' apartments. But she had her riposte at the ready: she had bought her Botero years ago. Touché. If this exchange had occurred a few cleanings later, I could have topped her by telling of a new window cleaning customer, one on the East Side, who had commissioned Botero to paint a portrait of his wife. Though the woman is slender in real life, in "her" painting, she has the requisite puffy cheeks, if not a nearly inflated face.

Despite having only three Dakota windows left, I filled my bucket with fresh water. I regarded these windows — the extra tall one in the narrow hallway outside the living room and the two windows in the living room itself — as the most important, as they let in the most light. Like the nurse's place, this apartment was also dark. In addition to its location, the mahogany and oak trim didn't brighten things, and even the 12- to 15-foot ceilings only seemed to provide space for more darkness. But hey, it was the Dakota. I wasn't about to hold a lack of natural light against this apartment house. I cut this building a lot of slack.

It was odd. The nurse's windows I had cleaned for *her*. I hoped that sunlight, pure light, could help her in some way. But these windows, I knew, I cleaned in part for the Dakota itself. Obviously, I wielded my squeegee for my customer, too; they were her windows after all, and she wanted them clean — and her name appeared on the check, not the building's.

Still, I liked to focus on the address that appeared below her name: 1 West 72nd. On the check, the Dakota was as much the customer as she was. That's how I am with "celebrity buildings," buildings known for themselves, apart from whoever lives inside them. Fortunately for me, between Shields Windows and my own customers on the side, I'd been able to work in many of New York City's celebrated apartment buildings.

In addition to Central Park West's Dakota, Beresford, and the previously mentioned Century, Majestic, and Eldorado, I have cleaned windows in the San Remo, 88 CPW, and 55 CPW (a.k.a. the *Ghostbusters* building), among others. I've also worked in the West Side's Apthorp, Belnord, and Ansonia, Chelsea's London Terrace, and even a top floor studio in the Chelsea Hotel; its rickety belt hooks always scare me. On the Upper East Side, I've worked in 912 Fifth, 920 Fifth, and 755 Park, but I've also been in 45 East 66th, 944 Fifth, 1001 Park, 1185 Park, and 895 Park.

I admit it: a part of me does want a bit of the Dakota's "status" to rub off onto me through association. But I also readily concede that I've only been able to set foot in these buildings as a hired hand, as a servant of sorts to the customer. To make up for this, I've tried my best to bond with the buildings themselves. By cleaning the windows of the Dakota, I am, therefore, doing my part for historic preservation. Yes, I know it's a stretch, so call it a rationalization, call it transcending the Service Entrance and Service Elevator — and my squeegee for that matter — in whatever way I can. But at the very least, call me lucky for being out on the building's ledge at all.

I ignored the ornate fireplace and its elaborate and original brass fittings, the grand piano covered with family photographs, and the delicate antique couch upholstered in bright-red fabric; I'd admired them all on previous cleanings. I wanted to be out on the day's last ledge. The second living room window not only looked out over 72nd Street, but boasted a small, narrow terrace as well. It was actually just a very wide ledge, maybe four feet, with a decorative wrought iron railing. Regardless, I unbuckled my window cleaner's belt and let it fall to the Oriental rug. I would break a rule of my own and not use the window's belt hooks.

I mopped, squeegeed, and chamoised the window's insides, pleased that the afternoon sun showed off the care I had taken. I then raised the window and stepped outside. Granted, at just seven floors up, I wasn't high off the ground compared to the Beresford's tower apartment balcony, but at the moment that twenty-something-story view seemed lofty, even remote. This height made the sights and sounds from the street, avenue, and park undeniably, delectably close. The taxis and buses on 72nd revved distinctly but not obnoxiously; the passers-by walking, jogging, and rollerblading below me were still people, not specks; Central Park's leaves blazed just down the block, some near my own height. The city was alive and nearby.

It's funny. When I am inside cleaning a window, I hope to be seen by passers-by, people in tour buses as they drive below when I'm in the Eldorado or the Beresford or the Century — or any building.

Once I am out on the ledge, I'm usually too concerned with hanging on to care if anyone sees me or not. I do like being spotted by people down on the sidewalk looking up — as long as they are not idiots who yell "Jump!" It happens. I clean apartments in a building at Madison and East 75th Street, across from the Whitney Museum of American Art, and quite regularly visitors waiting outside catch sight of me and come up with such witticisms.

I leaned my shoulder into the Dakota's brown brick exterior and braced my feet as well. I knew I was foolish for not hooking in, but I know the difference between pushing my limits and getting what I deserve.

Looking down at the sidewalk and seeing a mother or nanny pushing an old-fashioned perambulator toward the park reminded me of the movie poster for *Rosemary's Baby:* a stark, haunting green and black photograph of a similar baby carriage alone on a desolate outcrop of rocks. In the film, the woman first selected to give birth to Satan's child falls to her death at the Dakota; she's a young lady who pays the ultimate price for apparently not wanting to go all the way with Lucifer. Her killers — the charming, elderly devil-worshiping couple she'd been living with — do their best to explain away her plummeting to the sidewalk. I'd always liked their cover story: she must have slipped while cleaning an apartment window. So what if it was at night. I've done windows at night.

Having cleaned my last pane, I put my squeegee back in its holster, looked a last time at Central Park's arboreal fireworks, and stepped back inside. With my window cleaner's belt in my left hand and my bucket in my right, I began making my way back to the pantry's slop sink and a glass of cold water. But in the living room's anteroom, I stopped, put down my bucket and belt, and went in search of the maid. I found her in the kitchen, just as she was preparing to leave. Having changed into her own clothes, she now wore a pink cotton sweater and an oversized tan leather jacket.

"Hi," I said as I selected a pint-sized glass from the cupboard. "Busy day?"

"It was okay," she said in a high, light voice. Her ready smile had returned — along with questioning eyes. "I'm just glad it's over."

"I know what you mean," I said. I paused and then smiled broadly, hoping my grin would put her at ease. Still, odds were good she was about to consider me a freak. "I was wondering," I said, pausing again and smiling once more, hoping that she would sense I was about to ask her something fun and silly — or at least something she would consider silly. "Would you mind if I rang the doorbell and you let me in through the front door? You know, just to see what it's like?"

The ready smile became a loud laugh.

"It'll only take a second," I added hurriedly. "I promise."

"You really mean it," she said, her voice a bit higher. "You're not kidding?"

"Uh, no," I said. "I just want to try it."

"Well," she said. "Okay."

"Great," I said. "Thanks."

The two of us left the kitchen through the pantry, then walked through the pool room to the hallway, to the anteroom. I hadn't really considered the place a maze until then.

"I look at it this way," I said as I led the way. "I always use the back door, but here I just want to try the front. I mean, it's the Dakota."

The "Uh-huh" I heard from behind me didn't sound convinced. We'd reached the door. I found the massive, thick, dark slab of oak more reassuring than menacing; the small panes of etched glass bordering the door lightened its demeanor slightly.

I turned the large brass handle and pushed open the door, hoping it would creak. It didn't. As I crossed the threshold into the hallway, the door shut behind me with a secure thud. I looked around. The closed, deeply stained wooden doors of the passenger elevator were just steps away, as was the marble staircase. Diagonally from where I stood, a curved window built into the corner of the building looked out onto the roof's slate and copper, the wall's gingerbread bricks, and the momentarily empty courtyard.

I looked back at the door. Though the doorbell was nestled in its frame, I opted to knock. It seemed more appropriate. Besides, a client down the street at the Century had a doorbell that chimed "hava nagila," and I didn't want to risk such a distracting incongruity here. I rapped three times. My knuckles might as well have been striking a Mosler safe. The door opened to the maid's ready smile. Over her shoulder, I could see into the library and my eyes went immediately to the window in view. The panes shimmered. Since I didn't know the maid, I wasn't about to pretend she lived in the apartment and improvise a scene exploring the premise. Instead, I smiled as well.

"Thanks," I said as I stepped across the threshold. "You can knock and I'll let you in if you like."

"No, no," she said. "That's okay."

Now I knew she regarded me as weird.

On our way back to the kitchen, though it was longer, I chose to skip the pool table shortcut and walk through the hallway instead. The route allowed me to pass the Botero painting once more. I said goodbye to the maid, thanked her again, shut the back door behind her, and then emptied my bucket. After I had tidied my equipment, I peeled the sticker off my shirt sleeve and put it in my pocket. Once I'd taken the Service Elevator back down and maneuvered around the cellar's obstacles, I approached the attendant nonchalantly.

"Hey, buddy," the voice for the log said. "I need the sticker."

Damn.

Despite the now-gone sticker, I nonetheless emerged from the Dakota's Service Entrance with a grin, as I always did. Since I was walking directly below the nine windows I'd just done along the back wall, I looked up at the seventh floor and managed to see my handiwork. Taking a left to head back up the alley to the street, I admired the windows I'd done along that wall as well.

Once I was back on 72nd, I knew that I should have taken a right and walked over to Broadway to catch the uptown local to Columbia, but I didn't. Instead, I took a left towards Central Park West. Apart from wanting to enjoy both the avenue's stretch of buildings and Central Park, I also wanted to put off picking up the J-school application since I knew that once I did, I would feel bound to the essays it demanded. I would instead walk down CPW to Columbus Circle and catch the subway there.

Looking up, I spied the small balcony I had just stood on overhead. Moving along, I waved to the doorman as I walked past his sentry-like outpost and peeked at the Dakota's courtyard through the entryway's arch. Back on the outside again.

I liked that the most famous building on Central Park West didn't even have a Central Park West address. I looked uptown. Nine blocks north were the Beresford's three rounded towers, another nine blocks beyond were the Eldorado's two stark towers. Just blocks away loomed the two opulent towers of the San Remo. Looking down the avenue, directly across the street, stood the aptly named Majestic, its two towers emanating a 1930s Moderne sophistication. Farther down a good ten blocks, I could see its sister building, the Century — and her pair of Art Deco towers. I headed for them, taking in Central Park's leaves along the way, especially as I passed 80 CPW, a post-war plain box of a high-rise at the corner of 68th Street, the only ugly building on Central Park West. No need to give it a glance. I noticed once that a resident had placed in front of their living room's picture window a set of rice-paper Japanese screens. Since they seemed to be made-to-measure, the entire glass — their whole view — was covered over, I guess, pretty much full-time. How could they? I just didn't get it.

In addition to my bagels and bananas, I decided to splurge on some overpriced Tropicana orange juice from the Gristede's located in the street level floor of the Century.

The sound of industrial grade plastic scraping along the linoleum floor caused me to look up, a bit baffled. That's the sound I make, I thought to myself. But I hadn't pushed my bucket at all, I hadn't even moved. Then I saw the person I'd been standing behind not only had a sandwich from the deli tucked into a bucket, but a variety of squeegees: a fellow window washer. He was a short man dressed in a grubby turquoise work shirt and matching trousers. A dark-blue Yankees baseball cap covered his head. Though not fat, the thick grey beard that rolled down his face gave him the look of Santa Claus on hard times. And while I guessed him to be in his fifties, the years he had apparently weathered on the ledge may have simply made him look that old.

"How's it goin'?" he asked. His voice was as gruff as I thought it would be.

"It's going all right," I said. "The fall rush is keeping me busy, but not too busy."

Unless Pat has said he needs extra help, I never tell other window cleaners that I am swamped with work since they may want to glom onto our jobs.

"Where you been working?" he asked.

"Up and down the West Side today," I said, tapping my bucket forward with my shoe. "Nothing special."

Similarly, I don't say what specific buildings I clean in since it may inspire a window cleaner to try and swing the building's Super his way. Though New York City has enough dirty panes for all, I'd prefer to hang on to the windows I've already got.

"What about you?" I asked. "September treating you all right?"

"Oh, yeah," he said, pushing his bucket ahead once more. Our buckets sounded like a pair of sandpaper shoes. "I've got plenty to do here and there. Always do."

He was keeping things pleasantly vague, too. But I understood.

"Hey, buddy," the window cleaner in front of me said in a low whisper, "you want some speed?"

"Huh?" I said. "Oh, no thanks." I wondered if I sounded surprised to be speaking to Santa, the pusherman.

"It's on the house," the man said, his eyes twinkling. If he had had a belly, I guess it would have been full of...illegal substances? "It's what keeps me up there."

"No, no, that's okay," I said. "That's cool. Thanks though."

I saw that my polite refusal brought only silence. Had I insulted him? When I saw the big grey beard start to devour his sandwich, it occurred to me that perhaps Santa simply had the munchies. To each his own. I just hoped I wouldn't be cleaning windows at his age.

Up at Columbia, I walked through the wrought iron gates at the 116th Street Entrance half-expecting the guard there to send me around to some Service Entrance. But he paid no attention to me or the bucket in my hand, and I strode onto the campus that felt so grand, so immense, and so mighty. Was this the power of Corinthian columns at work? These buildings bordered on being daunting, like some ancient temple, reassuring and strong. In other words, the place reeked of scholarship, study, and yeah, prestige.

Leaves of gold, orange, red, and brown bedecked the trees lining the cobblestoned road that bordered the Graduate School of Journalism Building. "Academic Weather" was in full bloom. Come January, when I would return to Columbia to take the J-school's writing exam, it would be cold, harsh winter. In preparation for the test's current events section, I decided I would study-up on the A section of the Times until the day of the test. I wanted to keep track of the news they would be quizzing me on: 25 questions to be answered in 25 minutes.

Fortunately, this ordeal was far away, months away. I put it aside, preferring to consider my present moment: attuning myself to Columbia, its campus, its quad, its J-school, absorbing all I could of its aura. Then I noticed a flyer taped to the Journalism Building's granite wall, and all that absorbing abruptly stopped.

What caught my eye was not a band's name for an upcoming show, but an image, an icon of Soviet propaganda art, that of a hammering man. Man, I hadn't thought of him in a while — but what was he doing on somebody else's flyer?

Early on, my old band *Manifesto* had used Hammering Man as our symbol. He's an outline that is quite powerful, strong, even threatening. He's got a huge hammer in his hand. Actually, he has three hammers and three heads to convey the sense of him, first, raising the hammer back over his head, second, bringing the hammer forward, and third, crashing the hammer down in front of him. Soviet Russia's equivalent to our John Henry, you could say.

Being a trio, Michael, Bert, and I felt that Hammering Man's three heads and three hammers encompassed the three of us. In the first couple months of the band, we all agreed to get Hammering Man tattoos. I first pictured him on my right bicep, but then decided to put him on my left shoulder blade. A tattooed friend told me that since that skin isn't exposed to the sun, the color wouldn't fade as readily, and since that skin doesn't change much over time, the tattoo's shape would be less threatened. Still, a part of me wanted it on my arm, perhaps even my forearm, somewhere it would be seen. It's not like my dad could order me to remove Hammering Man before dinner!

But none of us in the band ever got the tattoo. I forget if we just never got around to it, or if we chickened out. Probably the latter influencing the former. Apart from flyers, we ended up featuring Hammering Man on the back cover of our first single, "Burn." But the closest Hammering Man ever got to my skin was whenever I wore one of the *Manifesto* tee shirts we had made. Three red Hammering Mans grace the black shirt's left-hand sleeve.

Then again, maybe my dad wouldn't have been so upset with the Hammering Man.

I remember being out at my parents' house one summer just a few years ago. I was on the back porch reading in between stretches of looking out at Long Island Sound. On the other side of the porch, Sverker, an old college friend of one of my sisters, was reading as well, as was my father.

"Admiral," Sverker said, interrupting the silence. "I am wondering. Seeing as you are a long-time Navy man, have you ever gotten a tattoo? Isn't that what Navy men are supposed to do?"

My father laughed, and I looked out at and then away from the water.

"No, Sverker," my father said. "I did not."

I waited for the he-would-never-do-such-a-thing line, if not the comparison to having an earring. I didn't think he would mention my earring episode; even so, I braced myself.

"But you are right," my father continued. "Plenty of sailors do get tattoos. And, you know, in some ways, I regret that I never did."

And that was that. Sverker, apparently satisfied with this answer, went back to his reading. My father returned to his book as well. I'd wanted to know more. But, obviously, my dad was done with the subject. I looked back out at the Sound.

Looking at the flyer, I did feel a bit.... I wasn't sure. Betrayed? No, not really. It wasn't like Hammering Man had chosen to be on the flyer. Ripped off? He was our symbol — despite it being eight years since we'd used him; despite the band being over. Of course, we had appropriated Hammering Man for our own purposes, ripping him off from his original place. The odds were good, too, that some other band or bands before us had used him for their own posters. Now it was *Steelcut*'s turn. I walked on, turning the corner and making my way round to the J-school's entrance.

Inside, before I approached the Journalism school's receptionist to pick up my application booklet, I did my best to silently hide my bucket, window cleaner's belt, and pole in a corner of the building's marble echo chamber of a lobby. Though I knew I would be stressing my window cleaning in my application essays, I didn't want to be seen with my mops and squeegees up on campus.

FIVE
PICTURE WINDOWS

At my dripping mop's insistence, I looked away from the Dakota across from me on the park's far side, and turned my attention back to the narrow ledge I was standing on — and the picture window I was cleaning. From a 'celebrity building' to a celebrity's apartment: in this case, Tom Hanks' penthouse.

Lots of white made the duplex a very pleasant and very bright place. Clean windows made it all brighter, even on a grey day like this one. Perhaps Hanks and his family were opting for Manhattan instead of L.A. this Thanksgiving? Turkey Day was just a few weeks away.

Having positioned myself half-in, half-out — my left foot in on the sill, my right foot out on the ledge — I reasserted my left hand's grasp on the chilled window frame, glad that this was my last to hold onto in the place; Pat was finishing the upstairs. I then slowly raised the extended mop-topped metal pole in my right hand and began to quickly wet down the exterior of the expansive pane of glass with short back-and-forth strokes.

Despite my speed, I took extra care in trying not to drip water. Usually I didn't care that much if water splashed down onto someone else's windows. These things happen after all, and it is only water. But a few stories down lived another client, Mrs. S. It was through her that we had been able to land the Hanks job, as well as other building residents. That should have been reason enough to be painstaking. But a short conversation a few weeks earlier had guaranteed that I would be forever prudent when mopping down a pane that lay above her place.

While I cleaned her windows, Mrs. S. had, as usual, asked me how I was and what I was up to. Unlike our typical customer who gets their windows done once or twice a year, Mrs. S. had her living room windows done every other month. She figured that since she had such an amazing view, it might as well be clean. In other words, I saw her pretty regularly.

When I'd told her that I'd applied to Columbia's journalism school, Mrs. S. had not only told me that its Dean was one of her best friends, but that she, Mrs. S., would write me a letter of recommendation.

Who cared that I'd already lined up my three official recommenders: an English professor from college, my band's lawyer, and an old family friend who was a retired admiral. I liked the variety. One more certainly couldn't hurt. I was, after all, only applying to one school.

My mop now rested on the ledge, a slice of the window was wet, and I was in a crouch. I relished the brief pause the weather afforded. If it were the summer, I would have had to race against the sun's evaporating rays. If it were winter, I would have to compete with temperatures low enough to freeze the water on the glass. Instead, I could take my time when pulling in the pole and replacing the mop with a squeegee: up to a minute instead of, say, a few seconds. And, unlike during June, July, and August, when I wore only tee shirts, now the sleeve of my tattered wool sweater served as an appreciated layer between my skin and the pole. I started to squeegee dry the picture window's wet sections.

Hanks' living room has two picture windows. One of them I like, one of them I don't. In fact, nearly all the residents in the building have the same arrangement. When they replaced the original cut-up belt windows with the pictures windows, the different sizes of the two spaces resulted in two different kinds of windows. The living rooms have a standard picture window: a large pane framed by two narrow windows. Both of these side windows open to allow for easy cleaning. The master bedrooms, one room over from the living room and also facing the park, however, received an *almost* standard picture window: a picture window the same size as its twin, but framed by only one side window. Hence the pole in my hand that allowed me to reach the distance of the picture window from the opened side window. Actually, Hanks, like other residents in the building — like Mrs. S., for instance — had torn down the bedroom wall to create a very spacious living room. In other apartments, this meant deeming one of the rear-facing rooms as the master bedroom. But Hanks' sleeping quarters were on the second floor — overlooking the park, of course. Though I generally don't like East Side apartment buildings, I could see being quite happy in this one.

That's the thing with window cleaning. I can find myself having inane thoughts, strange debates, like: Could I deal with living on staid Fifth Avenue but have a view of Central Park West's incredible buildings? Or, would I prefer to live in one of C.P.W.'s classic edifices and make do with a comparatively boring view of Fifth Avenue. Will I ever actually face that choice? Of course not. But I always side with Central Park West anyway, specifically a two-bedroom apartment in the south tower of the Eldorado. There, I could look down on Central Park's reservoir — not just a "prk vu," but a "wtr vu" — as well as the Beresford and the San Remo; unfortunately, I believe the latter building blocks out the Majestic and the Century. And, though the Eldorado does have cut-up casement windows, I could live with the hassle of cleaning them in my own place. Or I would live at the other end of Central Park West, down on 62nd, in the Century, in an apartment with a wraparound corner terrace. In that pad, even the master bathroom has its own balcony. Decadent. There I could appreciate how Central Park keeps Midtown's high-rises at bay. Plus, no cut-up window panes! Of course, there's always the Dakota.

Would I really turn down any apartment on Central Park West? Or Fifth Avenue? But such thoughts do help to pass the time.

Just as I had done a moment earlier when the mop had been attached to the pole's tip, I pressed the near-end of this slender piece of metal along the crook of my elbow while simultaneously pressing my wrist down on the pole's midsection. Although painful — but not as painful as when I wear only short sleeves — doing so afforded just the right touch: enough pressure to control whatever tool was atop the pole. The squeegee glided across the pane. I lowered the pole to the next wet patch of glass.

Unfortunately, apart from hurting my arm, attaching a mop, squeegee, and chamois to a telescoping shaft of metal also makes for awkward window washing. The act of cleaning becomes indirect: I feel apart from my tools — and the glass. It's why I don't like wearing Glacier Gloves. Indeed, I only resort to donning those frogman-like rubber gloves when the squeegee's brass handle, the pole's shaft, the wet mop, and the frigid air prove to be too much for my callused hands to bear. But it's not just a point of pride that keeps the Glacier Gloves in my bag until absolutely necessary. Wearing them, I've learned from experience, greatly increases the odds of dropping my tools. I'm not truly holding them after all.

With the first section of the window squeegeed and chamoised, I wetted down the next dirty stretch of glass with the pole's help and contended with the usual gusts of wind that blew up against the window. This bit of the East Side seemed prone to such blasts more than others; just ask the tchatche woman from down the street. I wished I was wearing my leather jacket. But I stayed put on the ledge. In fact, I wasn't even tempted to leave: I believe in the window washer's superstition of never going back out on any window twice during a job. And so my jacket remained in the kitchen, beneath my pile of tools.

Squeegeeing the second section of Hanks' picture window proved easier and less painful since the glass was closer. I still had to worry, however, about the squeegee slipping off the tip of the pole since neither Pat nor I had gotten around to replacing its stripped head. We really did need to visit Racenstein's — a window cleaning supply company located in the West 30s. I enjoyed seeing the latest in window cleaning equipment there, though doing so tended to make me feel a bit too close to my job. I mean, I never stopped by music stores to behold the latest drumsets. On the third and last section of the glass, I didn't have to use the pole at all, so I carefully put it back inside, glad that I could grasp my tools with my hands once more. My work suddenly seemed quite easy.

Once I'd finished the window, I freed up my hands by leaning my left shoulder into the window frame and wrung out my mop. Watching the beads of dirty water fall earthward, I was pleased to see that they avoided

Mrs. S.'s windows. Even with that promised letter, better they hit her panes than drip inside on these floors. I stepped completely back inside and after tucking the now merely damp mop alongside the pole, I first squatted and then sat on the windowsill. My shoes dangled just a few inches above the living room floor. I hoped Hanks' assistant would catch a glimpse of this tease, but she had her back to me, on the phone busy scribbling something down in her notebook. I leaned over and reached past the pole and the mop for the matching lengths of white cotton I'd also left on the sill. Grabbing the two, I returned to sitting upright. It was a very nice floor — and the assistant aimed to keep it that way. I fitted the pair of surgical booties over my Adidas.

I had no clue what kind of wood comprised Hanks' living room floor, but the nearly black-brown planks were apparently quite delicate. Water could stain them, the assistant had told us — warned us, really — just as sneakers could scuff them. Wearing the booties, then, was essential. Or, as that binocular-using Corinthian customer had suggested to me: Pat and I could work in our socks. We chose the booties. Though I found the dark floors striking, they certainly contrasted with everything else, jarringly so. But at least the room didn't have pickled floors, a process that drains all color from the wood leaving a blanched — if not sickly — look. Water does stain those floors. I've accidentally dripped on some of them and been nailed a few times for doing so. It seems even if you wipe away the drops within minutes, they still leave behind telltale spots. Having white floors in New York City is like having, well, white carpeting. Why willingly bring on an extra aggravation? I draw the line at white couches. Even though the white sofa in my parents' apartment had to be regularly cleaned when they lived in the city, the thing really did brighten up their living room. It also made up for their other couch, an antique opium bed that really wasn't that comfortable.

Wearing the booties, I certainly didn't feel like a surgeon with an operating room boasting a view of Central Park, but I didn't quite feel like a window cleaner either. The equivalent of wearing Glacier Gloves on my feet, perhaps? At least Hanks' assistant had readily agreed that we didn't have to wear the booties out on the ledge. Pat and I did what we had to do for the windows, but by slipping on the booties, we also did what we had to for the floor.

Cleaning the windows of famous people is a bit odd in that way — I'm even more willing to oblige. If the Famous Customer is around, I guess I hope that a bit of their celebrity will rub off on me. Of course, I don't want to encroach and run the risk of a celebrity brush-off. I never ask for their autograph, in other words. The best tact, not surprisingly, is to simply leave them alone. Still, I like to try and engage them in a bit of conversation. Since I do this with my non-celebrity clients, I simply pretend that the Famous Customer is just regular folk. Regular folk, that is, I happen to be in awe of. I have told Sigourney Weaver, Frances McDormand, and the film-making Coen brothers that I admire their work. My only defense: I really do admire their work. And, I sometimes choose to forget that just because I am seeing them in person in their homes, that doesn't automatically allow me a bit of informality. By that I don't mean calling them by their first name — Fran, you were great in *Fargo*!; Sigourney, loved you in *Year of Living Dangerously*! — but I do mean being able to at least say something. After all, I'm not experiencing these people second-hand by flipping through a photo spread of their places in Architectural Digest or In Style magazine — I am in their homes with them. But I guess I also choose to forget that I am there to simply clean the windows.

This didn't stop me, however, from being tongue-tied (and, I believe, blushing) the first time I met the Coen brothers. I told the two that I not only loved all their movies but had actually seen an advance screening of their first film, *Blood Simple*, since my oldest sister's boyfriend at the time had been friends with one of the movie's producers. I needed a connection and credibility no matter how tenuous! Pathetic. I also told them that I'd been in search of the soundtrack to *Blood Simple* ever since, but had learned that it was out of print. A part of me, I admit, hoped that they would whip out an extra CD from some drawer. Instead, they agreed that the music was indeed hard to find.

Meeting another Famous Customer had been a bit different. The guy had stopped me on the street one afternoon in late fall while I headed for home at the end of a busy work day. Spying my bucket of tools, he'd asked if I could do his windows. We discussed the kind he had and then we agreed on a price. As for when, he wanted them done right then if possible. I had wanted to get back to my apartment — I was tired and my hands were cold — but the prospect of $100 proved too strong, as it nearly always does. Besides, I knew that this guy was somebody, I just didn't know who. Despite his low-key blue jeans, green down vest, and black watchman's cap, there was something distinguished about him. His deep voice and his assured bearing were somehow familiar, as were his deep, dark eyes and his thin, narrow face. But I couldn't place him. Along with the money, I wanted to learn who he was. Once I began cleaning his Greenwich Village belt-hook windows, I asked him what he did. He smiled and told me he was involved in the crazy world of theater and cinema. But even with this clue, nothing clicked. Instead, I could only tell him that Lars was an actor. He was genuinely enthused, yelling out to his wife: "Honey, did you hear that? The window cleaner's twin brother is an actor!" Only when I studied a small portrait of him hanging in his den did it hit me.

I then walked into the kitchen and told F. Murray Abraham that I had figured out who he was and that I was a big fan — I'd certainly loved his Oscar-winning portrayal of Salieri in *Amadeus*. I also told him that I did feel a bit foolish for not recognizing him earlier. I had, after all, even asked him what he did for a living. Mr. Abraham had laughed.

"I've been found out," he had said, looking up from his snack of orange slices. "But, you know, I'm lucky. I don't have a handsome face. Instead, I have an actor's face. I have a face that doesn't get in the way. The characters I play aren't threatened by my looks." He had laughed again, and then continued. "People come up to me and say, 'Don't I know you? Weren't you my butcher?' I smile and tell them, 'No, that must have been somebody else.'"

Once I had made my way to the Abrahams' television room, I took down the curtains from the windows and draped them on the bookshelves built into the walls. And then I saw him: Oscar. He wasn't set apart, or highlighted; indeed, the figurine seemed almost ignored, tucked away. He was just there — and even needed dusting.

I looked toward the other end of the apartment and listened. The conversation Mr. Abraham and his wife were having sounded stationary, sounded like they weren't about to move into this room. So I set the length of curtain aside and stood before the award. I put my hand out, but stopped. Picking it up seemed like a violation somehow. It wasn't mine after all; I hadn't won it. But then I quickly wrapped my right hand around Oscar's chest and lifted him.

Holding Oscar was cool — literally. His bronze skin was cold. He also felt heavy, his black base being made of something solid, or maybe it was Oscar himself. I cradled him and noticed that while Oscar's head and legs had remained golden, his torso had been rubbed down to a dullish silver. I wondered how many other people had done this as well. I then raised Oscar in exultation over my head. I thought of the Oscar shows I'd watched, and the actors hearing their names being announced, and their thank-you speeches. Then I thought of Lars — he's the actor after all — and felt rather silly.

It's funny. When it comes to celebrities whose windows I have cleaned, I can think of who they are and what windows they have, but not much more. It's not just reluctance on my part to divulge, though that's part of it. Because, of course, it is their home — and their windows for that matter. It's their private place, and, ultimately, just another apartment window I clean.

Still, I'm not totally above a bit of celebrity "wash 'n' tell." In my head, I break them down this way:

Tom Hanks' apartment: challenging picture window and easy replacement cut-ups in an old building on the East Side — plus those surgical booties for the sake of his living room floor. Have never met him, and likely never will.

Sigourney Weaver's apartment: replacement tilt-ins in an old building on the Upper East Side. Liked that when I moved away a side table to clean a bedroom window, I came across her American Express card and a prop from her movie *Dave*, a campaign button that featured her movie husband, Kevin Kline. Also liked that her dining room featured a jukebox that played vintage Blue Note jazz singles and that their record covers were displayed on wall racks originally intended for plates. No wonder Pat and I had been called in advance of an Italian design magazine that had decided to photograph the place. Met her once. I told her that Lars, too, was a Yale drama school grad and that she should check my twin out as a bank teller on the season premiere of *Law and Order* the following week. Lars corrected me later that afternoon: "I play a loan officer, not a bank teller!" I offered to call Sigourney back to make the distinction clear.

Joel Coen and Frances McDormand's apartment: replacement tilt-ins in an old building on the Upper West Side. Met her once. Very cool place, very cool people. They're not "Hollywood" at all.

The Coen brothers' office: original cut-ups on the Upper West Side. At first, I thought that the apartment filled with props and stills from their movies belonged to an obsessed fan. But then Pat told me where we were. During a subsequent cleaning, the raw footage of their latest movie showed up. Now they could begin editing something called *Fargo*. Their assistant told us that Joel and Ethan had returned to their roots on this one, in which a kidnapping goes horribly wrong.

Cameron Macintosh's duplex apartment: easy one-over-one single pane belt windows in an ornate Midtown building contrasted with heavy pain-in-the-butt, sound-dampening interior storm windows. Have never met him. Have never seen *Les Miserables* or anything else he's produced on Broadway either. When I admired the apartment's circular foyer walls painted to depict fields being harvested, his assistant told me the scene matches the actual view Mr. Macintosh enjoys at his house in the south of France.

F. Murray Abraham's apartment: vintage cut-up belt windows in Greenwich Village.

Christy Turlington's townhouse: vintage cut-up switchers in Greenwich Village. Have never met her. Nearly fell from a second-story window's extremely narrow ledge. Liked that her gymnasium took up the entire top floor.

Tuli Kupferberg: co-founder of the seminal political and poetic rock 'n' roll band, *The Fugs*. His ramshackle Greenwich Village apartment has ancient switchers and storm windows. A really time-consuming job. He told me about New York City in the '60s, as well as the problems he was having with his legs.

In regards to any fame or real success that my bands had attained, Michael and I had needed to work on our timing: Henry's next band had been *Black Flag*, after all, and Ian's was *Fugazi*. And, in terms of any celebrity, well, whenever that spotlight had been pointed directly at Michael, Bert, and I, we hadn't fared very well.

The band's clothing choices had not helped us at our photo shoot for the East-West album artwork. At one point, someone involved in the shoot said, "Is anyone coming from wardrobe, or is this what they're wearing?" I considered this a snide remark until I didn't hear anyone laugh in response. Perhaps it had been an honest question. Regardless, I ignored it. I was enjoying myself. I didn't end up liking my picture though. The photographer had used a special effect to stretch my torso and arms, making me appear to be an elongated tree with spindly branches wearing a grey turtleneck sweater. I look through the *Manifesto* booklet less often than I listen to the CD.

With Hanks' windows now officially done, the time had come for Pat and me to be paid. Fortunately, Hanks' assistant usually took care of this then and there, meaning we didn't have to wait for a check to arrive from the Los Angeles office. I adjusted the booties to be certain that no part of my shoe would touch the all-important wood. I then stood and lifted my bucket off the towel it had been placed on and padded across Hanks' living room floor. In this case, Pat and I had agreed to dump our dirty water down on the street. Hanks' assistant didn't want to risk staining the sink either.

Downstairs, while I leaned against the building's back wall, the freshly emptied buckets at our feet, Pat flipped through his November calendar to the day's schedule.

"I know the next job's uptown," he said, running his index finger across his scrawled handwriting. "I just don't remember where. Here it is: 1660 Madison."

"When were we due there?" I asked. I liked to rib Pat about his routine tardiness.

"We are due there in twenty minutes," Pat said. "Plenty of time. Let's say we walk?"

"Very funny," I said. "Let's take the bus. Besides, it's too cold."

I didn't feel like walking forty blocks. I did feel like being on time. And I wasn't really sure if Pat was kidding or not.

1660 Madison Avenue meant upper Madison Avenue: Harlem. Pat and I didn't usually go that far north. Our customers lived, for the most part, on the Upper West Side and the Upper East Side — with a smattering of clients in Greenwich Village, Tribeca, and Soho. And while Harlem had been experiencing another renaissance of sorts along 125th Street with a new shopping center and rising property values — plenty of poverty remained in this section of the city.

In other words, despite the Madison Avenue address, we weren't about to visit a palace in the sky along the lines of, say, the place where the woman with the Degas lived. No, the northbound M1 bus we'd catch over on Madison would leave that behind after twenty blocks or so. Rather, we were off to an apartment in a city-owned building. We were headed for the projects. Pat and I didn't believe this was a set-up — when window cleaners are sent to an address in a questionable neighborhood so that they can be robbed once they arrive. That happens every so often. A few years ago a rash of such thievery took place in Chinatown. But this job sounded legit: Mrs. Jones, the lady who'd called, was very adamant about needing her windows cleaned and how she expected us to be on time. Besides, with both Pat and I going there, there were two of us — just in case. The bottom line, however, was we weren't going to turn down money if we didn't have a reason to.

So we took the job. November is a busy month, but not really until just before Thanksgiving. Then it seems that for a week or so Pat and I live on Central Park West. Buildings from the Beresford at 81st on down all look over marchers, floats, and balloons in the Macy's Thanksgiving Day parade. Until then, the month can be slow. A buck is a buck. As we walked towards Madison, we passed an apartment building and its doorman called out to us from the lobby.

"Hey guys, how's business?" the voice asked, deep and brusque, but playful. "Not bad, boss," Pat said, without slowing our pace. "Things are picking up."

"Sounds good, my man," the voice replied. "And at least you aren't carpet cleaners!" A loud laugh followed.

Pat and I looked at each other.

"I didn't know there was a hierarchy," I said.

"Neither did I," said Pat.

We obviously ranked far below Upper East Side doormen.

Pat and I got off the bus at 112th Street. Though Fifth Avenue and the tip of Central Park lay just blocks away, that wealthy part of Manhattan seemed very distant. Doorman buildings had ceased, and a stretch of bodegas and high-rise public housing had begun. As we walked into the hulking building — cement and cinder block at its most brutally efficient, with no adornments save the graffiti — we passed two silent black teenagers coming out of the elevator. Pat and I smiled and nodded our heads at the pair who both wore oversized blue jeans, black puffy down jackets, and quizzical expressions.

I wondered if they, too, felt baffled by Pat's and my presence. The encounter hadn't felt threatening or charged, it was just an odd moment of recognition — two worlds colliding in a scuffed-up lobby.

On the ride upstairs, I read some of what had been scratched into the elevator's dark red doors and kicked-in walls. "LB + JM," "Cypress Hill," and "HOT WATER NOW!" spoke of love, music, and frustration, respectively. The doors opened at the sixth floor to a dimly lit hallway. The smell of greasy hamburgers from somebody's apartment stove mixed with the sharp scent of ammonia; the hall's cracked and worn linoleum floor had just been mopped.

Unfortunately, Pat and I couldn't escape this combination of aromas right away. Since not all of the apartment doors were numbered, we had to spend a few frustrating (and very long) minutes wandering up and down the hall before we could make an educated guess as to which door we wanted. Pat knocked, hoping we would find our customer behind Door Number One. Almost immediately, the door opened to reveal a rotund, elderly black woman in a dark-blue housecoat whose wide oval face grimaced below greying hair.

"You two gentlemen are fifteen minutes late," she said sternly, while leaning against the doorway. "When I say two o'clock, I mean two o'clock. I was just walking over to the phone to call your office and see what the problem was."

Mrs. Jones, I presumed. Pat and I both apologized for our delay, and I began to wonder if we should begin regretting coming up all this way. If the lady was this miffed about our being slightly delayed — with my ten-minute grace period, I only considered us to be five minutes late — how might she be about her windows? The odds were good she would check for the slightest streaks and any stray water, the little clusters that collect in the corners and edges of windows.

I thought of a customer, a widow on the West Side, who has always felt compelled to look for these flaws whenever I do her windows. She says she has no choice in the matter since she approaches everything in life this way, as had her husband. This means I touch up her windows with my chamois cloth at least twice, even though I know they were fine the first time.

I think her desire for control — to show who was the boss — outweighed her need for a clean window. Not surprisingly, when I'd gently suggested to that customer that she concentrate on enjoying her view of the Hudson River instead of inspecting her windows, she told me I was trying to get out of doing a good job. When I'd tried to explain that you can easily find imperfection in most anything, especially a window, she'd said that her panes were perfectly fine. When I'd told her to try and look out the window, and not at the window, she didn't seem to understand the difference. I will always feel sorry for that lady.

Standing before Mrs. Jones in her doorway, I wondered if she was an uptown equivalent. We were in her living room, a long and narrow rectangle with one wall featuring a picture window. Mrs. Jones limped slightly in her turquoise slippers as she started to escort us toward the glass, then thought better of this. Once she'd closed the door behind us, she leaned against its frame.

"Those are why I called you," she said, pointing at the four window panes. "I want all the windows in the place cleaned, but these are the ones that matter. They're my view."

I didn't look out the windows, but instead looked at them. They were indeed dirty, but not depressingly so. Rather, they just hadn't been cleaned well. Streaks and patches of dirt sullied the outside glass in nearly semi-circular patterns.

"Obviously the man from the building didn't know what he was doing," Mrs. Jones said. "But then that's why I opened the phone book and called you. You're professionals. Right?"

"Yes, we'll certainly do better," Pat said.

"You know you're the only company I called who was willing to come up this far," Mrs. Jones said.

"It's a pleasure to be here, ma'am," Pat said.

In at least one way it was: the sun had already passed over Madison Avenue and Mrs. Jones' building, on its way to the West Side before setting by the Statue of Liberty; we wouldn't be working in its glare, the prime cause of streaks. Even so, this seemed a small consolation as Pat and I approached the windows. These hadn't been cleaned well for a reason: the child-guards.

Damn. There were thin metal gates attached to the interior of the window frames that prevented the windows from being entirely opened. No wonder the windows were poorly washed: the guy couldn't get past them. This meant the guards were probably mounted with irreversible screws. Beyond being an extra thing to do, such screws also take a lot of time to remove. I have to clamp my pliers onto the head of the screw, hope that it takes, and then slowly twist the screw out. So much for this only being a two-bedroom job; so much for our next appointment being a leisurely three hours away.

I also noticed in front of the panes a waist-high wooden pole, nearly the length of the window, that resembled a dancer's bar. I couldn't, though, picture Mrs. Jones doing a plié on it. I guessed that it served as a secondary homemade child-guard. Or, perhaps a daughter had danced? At least whoever had installed the bar hadn't used irreversible screws. It would have to be removed as well.

Apart from the dirt, the windows themselves looked in okay shape. They were sliders — big, long window panes that slide from side to side in grooves, and pop up and out of the grooves in order to be cleaned.

I looked out the windows and checked the ledge: pretty narrow, but just wide enough for my foot. I then checked the size of the windows. They weren't so wide that I would need to use my pole to clean the center of the pane. I could probably get by with stretching my arm out pretty far, a reasonable amount of risk. I looked around the room, checking to see if I'd have to move anything more than the rust colored throw-rugs. I was also, of course, curious. A book shelf that covered an entire wall perpendicular to the windows held a huge television set, books, CDs, and curios. I noticed that the small African art figurines matched the large masks hanging on the opposite wall. Next to the stereo rested a small bust of Martin Luther King, Jr. Cloudy plastic covers had been fitted over the modular furniture, a brown leatherette couch with matching chairs. Only the old stand-up piano near the window would have to be shoved a few feet — just to be safe — and the lamp on top if it would have to be put on the floor in case of wind or, yes, my squeegee. As I walked over to the piano, I noticed the lamp's base, a shiny porcelain sculpture of two elephants fucking. Wild.

"Can you believe my daughter paid good money for that?" Mrs. Jones said dismissively. "I just wish she took it with her when she got married."

I turned and smiled. But as I looked back to the lamp, my smile disappeared. So, she'd been watching me. Seeing Mrs. Jones' reflection in the elephants continue to watch me confirmed my fear: Mrs Jones hovered. Every little thing I'd do would be scrutinized. Great. I walked across the room with my bucket, over to the kitchen sink. While I waited for my bucket to fill with water, I piled my tools and my beat-up leather jacket on the floor, out of the way.

"You know," Mrs. Jones said, still supported by the door. "If you want your business to prosper, you have got to be punctual. There's just no way around that."

"I'm sorry, ma'am," Pat said by the piano. "It won't happen again."

I decided to change the subject. "You have a very nice place," I said as I lifted my full bucket from the sink.

"Oh, thank you," Mrs. Jones said and smiled. "I've lived here a good while now, ever since I got my job with the Port Authority. I've put in a lot of time getting this place to look nice. A lot of dusting and cleaning and mopping. But now I'm getting ready to leave. Gettin' set to retire and move back to North Carolina."

I walked across the room with my bucket to the picture windows and joined Pat at work on the dancer's bar. Once I'd put my bucket down, I knelt to pick my Phillips screwdriver up off the floor — and marvel at the elephant lamp once more.

"I got that bar put in after my injury," Mrs. Jones said. She had moved to a large black vinyl recliner arranged so that it directly faced the windows. "I can't stand up for too long now and it lets me look out. Except that I can't hang on for too long either."

"What happened?" I asked as Pat and I began to unscrew the bar's handles at opposite ends.

"Believe it or not, I got hit by a bus," Mrs. Jones said, leaning back into cushions that seemed to exhale. "Mercy, it was horrible. One moment I'm crossing the street to my home, the next I'm smack on the street — out cold. I only woke up when the paramedics got there. I don't really know what happened. But I do know that the good Lord saw me through it."

"I'm glad you're okay," Pat said, looking up from his screwdriver.

A moment later, the bar came down without too much trouble, apart from being unwieldy. The child-guards, however, proved worse than we'd feared. The irreversible screws had rusted in place. More time and more bother. I would need more than my pliers. Landlords love irreversibles since they provide a "set it and forget it" solution: No more liability, no more hassles, no more maintenance. The windows are not their problem anymore. But they are mine. I returned to our pile of tools and brought back a pair of pliers, crowbars, and rubber mallets.

"We're going to be doing a little pounding now," I said. "But we won't be able to clean your windows otherwise."

"You do what you've got to do," Mrs. Jones replied. "I just want my view back."

I thought of another customer of ours, another elderly widow on the West Side actually, who lived on a relatively high floor in an old building on

West End Avenue. After I'd finished cleaning her somewhat treacherous cut-up belt windows — the hooks were a bit loose and the window frames themselves were deteriorating, with paint flaking off and wood slivers falling away — we talked over some afternoon tea she had prepared for us. After I learned that she had lived in her place for fifty years, I asked what had been the biggest change in the neighborhood. The woman had looked down at the cup in her hands for a moment before looking back up at me and answering.

"The day they finished filming *West Side Story* across the street was one of the saddest days of my life. Everyone here knew that an entire neighborhood of lovely, old brownstones was about to come down and be replaced by *that*."

She pointed out the window at Lincoln Towers, eight high-rises comprising over 3,800 apartments. Before, my customer told me, she would spend hours at her windows, just looking out and seeing what was going on. Being above the roof line had been one of the reasons why she'd taken this apartment in the first place.

"But, honestly," she said. "I feel like I've been in mourning ever since. I really haven't been able to bring myself to look out my windows. How can I when I have that blight right in my face? I might as well be living in an air shaft."

The thing was that while Lincoln Towers really is an eyesore, the buildings weren't right across from her window. They stood down the street, past a half-block of one-story buildings. So some space did exist between her and it. But then compared to low-level (and charming) brownstones, her view really was gone.

Pat and I banged away at the screws in Mrs. Jones' child-guards.

Though the mallet hits themselves were quiet, the sounds of the metal screwdrivers striking the metal screws and metal window frames were not. Slowly, we forced out the screws. A few came quite readily. Most had to be pried loose, and the heads of some of these screws broke off in the process, requiring replacements. This always pleased me, since it not only pointed out the stupidity of irreversibles being used for this purpose — spanner head screws make much more sense, despite the special screwdriver required of them: at least the windows can be easily cleaned — it also gave the Super another chore. Finally, the last screw came off.

I looked at my watch. The hands read nearly three, and we hadn't even wetted down a single window pane in the apartment yet. Plus, all the guards and the bar had to be put back in place. At this rate we wouldn't be making the five o'clock job by five o'clock — or ten after.

"Oh, don't worry about the time," Mrs. Jones said. "I'm not going anywhere."

I smiled. No, I thought to myself, and neither are we. I suggested to Pat that he call the next job to tell them that we were running late, but he nixed this, deciding to wait until later. The next customer, Pat pointed out, if given enough lead time, just tended to reschedule. If at all possible, Pat wanted to make that money today. If that meant keeping the customer in the dark, or even cleaning their windows in the dark, then so be it.

Pat and I began to mop down the picture widow's inside pane. The glass began sudsing up on us, the sign that someone had sprayed Windex on them, the bane of window cleaners everywhere. While such products do indeed remove dirt, because they contain soap, they always leave a slick soapy film behind. This means we have to wash the windows twice: first to get the Windex off and then to make sure the windows are actually clean.

"I regularly wash those myself," Mrs. Jones said. "That's why they're so nice."

"Thanks," I lied. "We always appreciate that." The customer is always right.

After finally finishing the insides and then chamoising the edges once more — I figured that she would have asked me to do them again anyway — we could open the windows. But they barely budged when we tried to slide them along their tracks. Another hint of trouble.

Since Mrs. Jones' windows had difficulty sliding, it was no surprise that they did not pop out of the groove when Pat and I tried lifting them. The windows were either warped, or a lot of crud had accumulated in the grooves. Regardless, we'd have to use a crowbar to pop the windows out. More time-consuming fun.

"Those windows are hard to even open," Mrs. Jones said, who was beginning to remind me of a Greek chorus. "But there's ten dollars for each of you when you're finished. I don't mind rewarding hard work for a job well done."

While I appreciated the impending tip, I wouldn't have it in hand anytime soon: the crowbar wasn't working. The casings for the wheels that roll the windows along the groove had worn out, meaning that the window couldn't clear the lip of the groove, meaning we couldn't clean the windows. Window cleaning has a lot of "cause and effect" situations, though at times it feels like the Domino Theory.

Popping the window out would require sheering off the casings — along with their wheels — making the window even harder to open. But, rather than explain all this to Mrs. Jones, I lifted the window up as high as it could go within the groove, and Pat jabbed the casing with the crowbar until it broke free of the window frame. She wanted her view back, and we wanted to give it to her. We weren't about to concede defeat. After we'd hacked off the eighth and last casing, the four "removable" windows could finally be removed and cleaned.

We pried them out with our crowbars, then carefully leaned two against the bookcase and two against the wall. Though we usually clean these windows immediately, Pat and I each opted to wash the outside of a stationary window, the picture window. At that moment at least, we regarded being on the ledge our reward. We straddled our bodies over the window frame, one half-in the apartment, the other half-out, our wetted-down mops in hand. After the hassle of the child-guards, the bar, and the windows themselves, this had become the easiest and most enjoyable part of the job. The risk seemed almost a relief.

While we worked, we heard a knock at the door and then two young women let themselves into the apartment. The first teenager, short and slightly heavyset with a round face, wore dark blue jeans, a striped blue and orange New York Knicks jacket, and carried a sleeping baby in her arms. The second, taller and thinner, wore a long navy blue skirt, a white blouse, and black loafers. Instead of a child, she held a piece of paper. They strode into the living room and sat on the couch. Its plastic covering squeaked.

"Mrs. Jones, when are you going to get rid of these?" the first one asked as she rubbed the covering. "They are so uncomfortable, and worse, they're tacky!"

The two laughed, causing the couch to squeak again, and even Mrs. Jones cracked a smile. But she quickly recovered.

"We're not here to talk about my furniture, Trish," she said. "We are here to talk about you and your son."

"Yes, ma'am," Trish said and looked down at her baby. The white blanket wrapped around him set off his light-brown skin and dark, curly hair.

He could only have been a couple of months old.

"Now then," Mrs. Jones said and paused. I appreciated that this apparent chiding would be directed at someone else for a change. "I hope you fed your child something more than Cheerios today. I saw in the paper that the C-Town has some baby food on sale right now."

"I'll go over there later," said Trish.

She looked once more at her child and kissed him on the forehead.

"You'll go over there after you leave here," Mrs. Jones said, evidently unimpressed. "Have you read to Jamal yet today?"

"Yes, ma'am," Trish said and smiled, "I read to him this morning. Just before his nap."

"Well, good," Mrs. Jones said, her voice slightly softening. "Be sure to take a few books from my Tracy's room before you go."

"Yes, ma'am," Trish said. "Thank you, Mrs. J."

Mrs. Jones nodded her head and then moved on to the second girl.

"Natalie," she said and paused once more.

I wondered what it felt like to have those eyes focused on you like that.

"I hope you've got your resumé together," Mrs. Jones declared. "No spelling mistakes, no punctuation mistakes, no mistakes at all."

"I got it right here, Mrs. Jones," Natalie said in a voice both assured and tentative; Mrs. J. might as well have been her prospective employer.

"I brought you a copy just like you asked."

"Let me take a look at that," Mrs. Jones said.

Her large hand took the piece of paper and then those eyes hovered over it. After a few minutes, she gave it back and smiled.

"That looks good, child," she said. "Good work. Now when's the application due at Macy's? Monday afternoon, right?"

"Yes, ma'am," Natalie said, allowing herself a tiny grin. "I'll bring that by tomorrow so you can look it over one last time. I'm planning on wearing this outfit when I drop it off."

"You look very nice," Mrs. Jones said, "very appropriate. But be sure to bring that application by here tomorrow morning. Now then, Natalie, what's that no-good Marcus up to?"

"I don't know," Natalie said, her grin now gone. "We're not talking right now."

"I've said this before," Mrs. Jones said. "Why not just forget about that boy? Get yourself a real boyfriend, or don't bother!"

"Yes, ma'am," Natalie said.

I wondered if Natalie would heed this advice and whether Jamal's father was around. I wondered what advice Mrs. Jones would have for me.

"Okay, we're done," Mrs. Jones said, moving her hands from the chair's armrests and placing them in her lap. "I've got my windows to tend to."

"Thank you, Mrs. Jones," Natalie said. "I'll see you tomorrow morning."

"Thanks, Mrs. J.," Trish said. "I'll go get those books now."

The two girls and the baby rose from the squeaky couch. While Natalie stood and looked over her resumé once more, Trish and Jamal left the living room. They returned a few moments later with three slim volumes in her previously free arm. I recognized the orange, white, and turquoise striped cover of "Go, Dog, Go!"

"Bye-bye," Trish and Natalie said as they closed the door behind them.

"Somebody's got to keep them straight," Mrs Jones said, looking at the door. Then she looked back at the windows. "Hey, they're starting to look all right."

Leaving Pat to finish the outsides of the removable panes, I went to take care of the other rooms. Both of the bedrooms were stark, neat, and orderly. The daughter's looked as if she still lived at home, with dolls and drawings from her childhood decorating the walls. A small wooden bookshelf contained many more books for Trish. In Mrs. Jones' room, the clothes that weren't yet put away had been neatly folded and placed on the bed, above which hung a simple wooden cross.

Was it seeing those two girls? I suddenly felt like such a dilettante. I felt like I wasn't making the most of my advantages. Here I was, a college-educated guy who was simply cleaning windows. I wondered what advice Mrs. Jones would give me.

I guessed that my application essays were getting to me. In them, I'd been detailing my mantra of sorts: I am now making the essential leap from playing music to writing about music. Of course, my drafts did not include my feelings toward most music writers. They were rock star wannabes who never truly "got" the band since they were too busy trying to conveniently pigeonhole the music. Instead, I'd written that I possessed the requisite experience for real insight. I hope so. Sounded good, at any rate.

Speaking of music, I'd heard from Michael that he and Gary continued to record in the studio. I pictured them leapfrogging from one track to another, never quite completing a song, but didn't say so. I just wished I could hear what they were up to.

In each room, I removed my shoes and then folded back the beds' comforters and sheets so I could stand on the mattresses and get at the windows. The panes were small, narrow rectangles placed high up near the ceiling, barely providing light, let alone a view. They only needed bars to look straight out of a prison. These windows, too, were hard to slide and pop out, but I was grateful they didn't have child-guards and that I didn't need the crowbar.

Being old and poorly made windows, cracked seals had let moisture, dirt, and air in between the panes, leaving a telltale permanent grayish haze on the glass. Even when I'd cleaned the dirt off, the window didn't look clean and never would. Still, they were cleaner than before, and they weren't really going to be looked out of. I finished up quickly. As with the casings, I decided I wouldn't mention the cracked seals to Mrs. Jones either. If she called to complain, we could tell her over the phone.

I returned to the living room and helped Pat re-install the wooden bar and place the child-guards back into their slots in the window frame's grooves. Nicely enough, since most of the screws were shot, we didn't have to deal with securing it back into place, meaning that this took just a few minutes.

"Be sure to call your Super about getting some new irreversibles," Pat said once we'd finished.

"I'll go see him first thing in the morning," Mrs. Jones said. "But that can wait. Finally, I can enjoy my view."

She slowly raised herself up from her recliner and then carefully walked over to the windows and us. Once Mrs. J. reached the bar, her strong hands grabbed onto the wooden pole, and she pulled herself to the center of her picture window. The panes glistened, reflecting our images even as they allowed us to see what was outside.

As it was nearly dusk, Madison's streetlights had come on. They illuminated not just a deli and a store for religious items, but a vacant lot overgrown with weeds, and the torched shell of an abandoned car. Lights lit up apartments in neighboring buildings, as did flickering televisions. Underneath one lamppost about a block away, a half-dozen kids did their best to look nonchalant. A few wore only track-suits, most wore coats. A boom box played, but not too loudly. A couple of them appeared to be rapping along to the song, but the rest just sat tight.

Suddenly, a silver Nissan Sentra pulled up, and everyone crowded around the sedan. One by one, each of the young men spoke to the driver as he sat at the wheel. The car pealed off after just a minute or so. A drug deal had just gone down. The lot belonged to the weeds and the burned-out car once again.

In the apartment, no one said a word. Instead, I started looking for streaks and water clusters that didn't exist, while Pat excused himself to telephone the next customer and try to convince them that we should still come. I moved the piano back into place, along with the elephant lamp. Mrs. Jones just kept looking out her window.

SIX

LITTLE MATCH GIRL

Wishing my hands were warm did not make them so, just as my pretending that the moon was the sun didn't make a difference. The fake snow on the other side of the pane didn't help either, nor did seeing my breath. Three hours after starting work, the novelty of overnight window cleaning had officially worn off. Even with the Glacier Gloves on, my palms and fingers were cold, bordering on numb. I tend to forget that this outer gear isn't designed to keep the extremities toasty, just dry. Regardless, the constant stream of water that had been soaking the gloves was putting that feature to the test, courtesy of the leak in the Tucker's mixing chamber that I held in my hands. At least my watchman's cap kept my head warm.

The Tucker is a specially designed scrub brush attached to a telescoping brass pole. A rubber hose runs through the length of the pole to a spray jet built into the scrub brush head. Though Pat and I were only doing second-story work, we had to extend the pole a good ten feet longer than the typical twenty, since the building's awning didn't retract. This prevented us from standing as close to the building as we would have liked, close enough so that a steeper angle on the pole would have made the Tucker's fifty-pound weight more manageable. Now, with the pole extended, the brass tubes flexed like bamboo, causing the tool to become pretty unwieldy. Cleaning with a Tucker, while at times dangerous, is always arduous.

First, Pat wets down the window — or the occasional greenhouse, marble exterior of the Bryant Park Hotel, or other surfaces the two of us have cleaned with the Tucker — and scrubs. Then, I adjust the mixing chamber's two levers to add soap to the water stream, and Pat scrubs once more. Another lever switch on my part allows Pat to rinse the soapy water away with just plain water — and then he scrubs once again. Ideally, the spray jet's "sheeting action" will leave no streaks or smudges behind. But Pat scrubs and sheets a final time for good measure, and then figures we've done as much as we can to clean the window. We do switch places every couple of panes so that I get my own workout. Though named after its inventor, I've come to think that this specialized scrub brush got its name from leaving window cleaners tuckered out.

Did Racenstein's sell Glacier Boots? Since my shoes and socks had absorbed some of the Tucker's leaking water, my now wet and numb feet demanded an answer. At least the Santa mannequin on display in the now clean window, wearing a shiny silver winter parka, could be more readily seen than before. Moreover, at least Pat and I were nearly done with the hassle of the Polo/Sport job. Next would be the welcoming one-over-one belt windows that Polo/Ralph Lauren's flagship store since 1986 — a.k.a. "The Mansion" — featured across the street.

A case of doing the hard work first and rewarding ourselves with the easy job second? Not quite. Pat and I had to wash Polo/Sport first since cleaning that building's 19 picture windows required our drenching the sidewalk, and we didn't want to wet down any pedestrians, nor be sued by one should they trip on the water hose. Doing the job in the middle of the night kept their numbers to a minimum. Despite New York being called "the city that never sleeps," I'm still surprised at how many people I've had to shoo off that stretch of Madison Avenue sidewalk at 72nd Street between 2 am and 6 am — usually a couple dozen or so. We clean Polo/Sport on Saturday nights and The Mansion on Sundays since the stores are closed then; no customers or Polo workers to get in our way. And window cleaners at work during their business hours just wouldn't do; we would get in their way. I'm sure in that place we would look a bit declasse.

While Pat did his job of rinsing down the last pane, I did mine by holding onto the Tucker's mixing chamber and the hose attached to it. I had to keep them clear of Pat's feet as I trailed behind him while he worked the scrub brush across and down the windowpane. In an effort to take my mind off my hands and feet and my bladder and bowels — the Cokes I had drank at midnight for the sake of caffeine had made their presence known, as had my midnight snack of, yes, bagels and bananas — I concentrated on The Mansion reflected in the Polo/Sport store's street level windows.

The firm of Kimball & Thompson really knew what they were doing when they designed the Gertude Rhinelander Waldo House as a Renaissance Revival chateau back in 1898. The place simply reeks of fin-de-siècle ostentation. But then with half a million dollars to spend, it should have. Apparently, cramming in as many windows as possible was a part of that look. I was always amazed being in there.

Just as I help to maintain the daydream of Ralph's vision of the American aristocracy, I have also partaken in the illusion. Once, when I was standing before one of the curved windows in the second floor's main room, whose antique glass ripples slight imperfections across the pane, I looked out over the corner of 72nd and Madison Avenue. I not only sensed that I belonged in these elite surroundings, but that this mansion belonged to me. I could feel a kind of snobbishness bubbling up. Not my music snobbery. No, this had everything to do with class. I wasn't looking down on other music, but other people. Fortunately, my having to crowbar open a window that some workman had painted shut broke this spell.

Now my head was sopping wet.

I'd managed to line myself up with a Tucker-caused waterfall coming off the blue awning's edge. At least it wasn't windy. I'd then be suffering iced ears and a frozen scalp. Then again, it wouldn't be as bad as the cold blasts in apartments that overlook the Hudson. Forget tchatches, those gusts imperil paintings, vases, and chandeliers — not to mention freezing the just-applied water on the windowpanes. Seeing that Pat was now temporarily stationary as he worked on the sheeting action rinse, I placed the mixing chamber at my feet and squeezed out what water I could from my cap's black wool. Then I looked back at The Mansion, up at the fourth-floor balcony.

Even though the Rhinelanders apparently never actually moved in, I have always wondered what it would've been like to have lived there back then. To have that overlook above Madison. But when I've tried picturing well-to-do scions out there, it didn't seem likely. The balcony is small, most likely merely decorative. Besides, as it doesn't have a proper door for access, venturing out would have required raising a window, crouching down, and stepping out over the sill. Wouldn't that have qualified as undignified? Perhaps a rebel Rhinelander would have sneaked smokes or kisses, or whatever wasn't allowed indoors. They probably would have left that space to the servants.

I picked the mixing chamber back up and played out some slack in the hose to give Pat some maneuverability. The final scrubbing had arrived.

"Hey, Pat," I said, cocking the mixing chamber just behind my head as I struck a pose, doing my best to be a prepped-out football quarterback about to throw a touchdown in a glossy magazine ad. "Polo."

"Polo," Pat answered back as he looked and smiled. He then responded by striking the best pose he could without losing his balance: treating the Tucker as a fishing pole.

Pretending to be Ralph Lauren models while we cleaned this building was our running joke. My clammy hands, chilled head, and dulled feet, however, cut our fashion show short. Instead of coming up with another pose, say, making the mixing chamber Oric's skull from the Hamlet soliloquy, I focused on Polo/Sport's windows, doing my best to seek out streaks from where I stood by the glow of the streetlights. These large picture windows demand being looked at, despite their Venetian blinds. Unlike The Mansion's panes, when the sun hits these, they really do gleam — just as they show patches of dirt we may have missed. So, I squinted as Pat rinsed the glass, moving my head slightly so I could try and see the window from different angles, increasing the odds of my catching any mistakes that the street lamp might make visible.

I appreciated how once I know a job, at least some jobs, I can kinda tune out from it: not be there mentally while still performing well. So that just now, I'd been keeping the hose clear of Pat's feet (as well as my own) without being consciously aware that I was doing so, just as I'd been giving Pat enough hose so he could do his rinsing, and adjusting the water flow depending on how high he was tuckering. Of course, out on the ledge, I can't allow myself such drifting off, but I do when cleaning the "inside" panes. Apart from countering boredom, I need to have such a distraction since ledge work really does drain me.

A simple thought had begun crowding out all else: Boy, I need to go to the bathroom. I mean, really go.

I did my best to fight against this by looking at The Mansion's reflected first floor.

Since Pat and I don't do The Mansion's first-floor windows — Polo employees clean the panes themselves every day, I've heard — I haven't spent much time on that level. Kind of funny since it really is the store's showplace, where the hand-carved grand main staircase can be seen at best advantage. The main room also features a large wooden table displaying a palette of neckties, a logical place for such an impulse purchase.

The first floor is also where one Sunday morning I came across a rug restorer with his own actual palette of paints. He comes by twice a year or so and paints The Mansion's rugs back into pristine shape, using as his guide a section that lies under the tie table where customer foot traffic doesn't reach. Very impressive. Cleaning windows is one thing, this was quite another — something beyond attention to detail.

Another such instance: in preparation for the Polo/Sport building's opening, Ralph Lauren quite willingly paid a window installer to remove one of the building's picture windows so that a vintage English roadster (from Lauren's own collection, presumably) could be placed inside. Then, just a few weeks later, the window was taken down again to remove the car. Sure, it was undoubtedly written off as a business expense, but I was impressed nonetheless. It must have cost a couple thousand dollars to do, along with the cost of transporting the sports car. But the vehicle certainly made a splash and set the tone for the store and so, I am sure, was worth all the hassle and every penny.

Once during a Christmas vacation in high school, my brother and I made the mistake of being inside the house when my dad was busy doing the bills. Usually my mom, my siblings, and I made a point of clearing out of the house at such times, but Lars and I had remained indoors. Maybe it had been raining, maybe it had been cold, maybe we hadn't realized our dad was downstairs settling the accounts, I don't remember. I also don't remember what Lars and I were doing, if we had been roughhousing or yelling. But whatever we'd been up to had been loud enough for our dad to take notice.

"Simba! Parlo!" he'd called out. "Can you come down here a second? I want to show you something."

Damn! Maybe Lars and I could sneak out the fire escape. But it was too late. So we went downstairs to his den and braced ourselves.

"You know," my dad said, sitting at his desk covered with bills and checks, "I could have bought a car today, a Mustang convertible. But instead I'm sending you both to another semester at GDS. Here, take a look."

Then he showed us the check written out to "Georgetown Day School" for $3,000, the cost of a year's tuition. Now this was a while ago and three thousand bucks was a lot of money to my dad, particularly since Tucson High, the Naval Academy, and Oxford had not cost him (or his parents) a penny in tuition.

Lars and I looked at the check, mumbled some words of thanks and then went back upstairs to our room and spent a chunk of the afternoon studying for the exams we wouldn't be taking for another month.

At the same time, my dad could take his lack of a new car in stride. When my sister was around ten years old, she obsessed about red Cadillac convertibles. Erica would ask us to help her spot them when we were all piled into our '63 VW micro-bus. Usually though, should her favorite car be seen, Lars and I would do our best to cover Erica's eyes so that she couldn't enjoy the view. Once, my dad and my sister put on some nice clothes and drove off to a Cadillac dealership to test-drive a Caddy convertible. But they parked the beat-up VW a block or so away so that the salesman wouldn't see my dad's present wheels and know that he could in no way afford a new car. Some years later, my dad took Lars and me on a similar outing when we test-drove a new Saab — and parked our '74 VW bug a few blocks away.

Cold had smuggled itself into my leather jacket, up through the holes in its sleeves. But I didn't care since we were now done with Polo/Sport. The Tucker's final sheeting action was running down the last bit of the pane. My version of Hans Christian Andersen's *Little Match Girl* could now come to an end. For just as the young match seller had imagined joining her grandmother in heaven as she lit up match after match until she freezes to death amidst a mighty blaze; my version being less dramatic, was I could now actually go inside The Mansion. Which was just as well since now I really, really needed to go to the bathroom. The Cokes, bagels, and bananas were demanding it.

"Pat," I said, my voice more urgent than I expected.

Pat had begun to break down the Tucker in order to hose it down, something I ordinarily helped him do. But not at this moment. I didn't have time.

"Pat, I'll be right back. I've gotta go hit the fifth floor."

I didn't want to say the word "bathroom" since that would make it seem that much closer and give my insides all the more reason to get the better of me.

"Okay," Pat said, "I'll be out here."

Instead of walking across Madison Avenue, I found myself running. This was going to be close. I pressed the doorbell and waited to be buzzed in. But nothing happened. No buzz. No voice from inside. Nothing. So, I knocked and waited and still nothing. The Glacier Gloves muted my knuckles' rapping. I tried again, this time a bit harder. Still, no response. I could feel my bowels becoming anxious and, worse, more impatient.

No, I thought, addressing them. No, don't.

I pounded at the door, and involuntarily began hopping a bit to keep my insides distracted. My window cleaning had kept all this at bay, but now that was done with. Not good.

"Come on, come on, come on," I whispered as my fist hit the door. "Open the God damn door, open it! Come on!"

I pounded a few more times as I hopped, but still nothing. Just silence and stillness. My bowels continued their rebelling. It'll be okay, I told them. It'll be okay. Just hang in there. Please, hang in there. I ran across the street, but considerably slower in an effort to remain in control.

"You think he's asleep?" Pat asked.

My knocks must have been louder than I'd thought.

"Yeah, I don't know. I've just gotta get out of here and find a bathroom."

"Good luck, Ive," Pat said as he returned to wrapping the hose into a circle.

I barely heard him since I had already begun jogging back across Madison and around the corner onto 72nd Street. I doubted anything on Madison would be open, but maybe something near Hunter would be. It was a college after all. Some late-night bar or, at this point, a coffee place about to start its day. Hopefully. Still, I did have to get across Park and over to Lex and then head downtown six blocks. If worst came to worst, at least it was still dark outside, and no one would see me. But I didn't want to think about that, afraid my bowels might take it as permission to let go. I slowed to a combination walk-hop since it was all I could handle.

No, don't. Please, don't.

I sensed myself pulling inward, withdrawing. It wasn't just that I was solely focusing on trying to keep myself dammed-up while looking for a place that looked open. That was all that I could focus on, that was all that I could be aware of, that was all that mattered.

My tunnel-vision propelled me to Park Avenue. Fearing that my bowels might give out at their relief of hitting Lexington, I considered going down Park to 66th, so that its apartment houses and the former Pan Am Building could distract me. But I didn't since I figured that the odds of finding a bathroom on Park were nil compared to Lexington.

No, don't; please, don't; no, don't; please, don't.

As mantras went, this was a bit more ominous than "mop, squeegee, chamois."

I pleaded with my bowels with every step towards Lexington. Once I made it to the avenue, I looked around for neon, for interiors lit up beyond the requisite security lighting, for taxis or limos parked in front of some place for coffee. But nothing caught my eye. I headed south.

I couldn't believe it, nothing was open. The restaurants and cafés I passed were empty and mocking. I could feel my thinking side slipping away, fading. I just wanted a toilet, I just wanted to go. I just wanted relief. Like plenty of other New Yorkers, I wished the city provided public bathrooms. The blocks went by: 71st, 70th, 69th, 68th, 67th. Still no luck.

At 66th Street, I hit Hunter's campus and stopped. There were still no bathrooms to be found. My bowels were pushing at me, demanding action. The darkness that had been shielding me had begun to die off. I was now grateful that no stores were open, that no one was around.

Looking around, I tried to spy a place to retreat to, a place to hide. Then I saw a small space between a long-closed newspaper stand and a row of pay phones along the railing of the 6 train's subway entrance. That would have to be it. My insides weren't going to obey me anymore.

I walked the ten or so paces to my spot, leaned into one of the phone booths and shat in my pants. Warm diarrhea and piss flowed out, first filling my boxers and then running down my pant legs. I could feel the ooze against my skin, but I didn't care. I felt happy that at least the struggle was over.

"Posso it ao baneiro?"

I smiled ruefully at the fourth grade memory, back when we lived in Brazil. In the name of cultural experience, my parents had put four out of five of us kids in a Brazilian school (instead of the American school) so that we could learn Portuguese. By the second year, Lars and I were fluent; our two older sisters had learned much more quickly than we had in part to get boyfriends, Lars and I figured. I had, however, made sure to learn two words in Portuguese right away: "feia" and "gorda." The first means "ugly" and the second means "fat." I used them on my sisters immediately.

One day at school, though, during my first year there, I really needed to go to the bathroom. Then, as just now, my bladder got the better of me so that in my anxiety, I couldn't remember how to ask the teacher in Portuguese if I could go. Now, I should have just left the room, gone to the bathroom and come back, telling her once I could think clearly where I had just been. But I didn't. Because I wasn't thinking at all, because my need to urinate overwhelmed all else. I peed in my pants.

As with most people when they learn a foreign language, I could understand Portuguese better than I could speak it. But because I didn't speak very often, my classmates figured I didn't know what they were saying. Which was why a kid sitting nearby looked down, saw the puddle of piss at my feet and said quite loudly to the class (in Portuguese of course): "Oh man, look what the weird American did! He peed!"

The teacher then came over and asked me if I needed to go to the bathroom — in English. I told her I did (in English) and then excused myself to the little boys' room and cried. After that day, I never forgot the words I needed to know to get out of the classroom and into the bathroom: Posso it ao baneiro?

I looked around. I was done. My bowels were wonderfully, blessedly empty. The sun was coming up.

To the outside world, I was someone contemplating making a phone call. Or, a homeless person in search of telephone quarters. To the outside world, I wasn't someone whose jeans and boxers were full of shit and piss. But if anyone was looking, if anyone were about to walk or jog or drive by, well, they were about to find out. I had to get my underwear away from me.

As I unbuckled my belt, I realized I still had the Glacier Gloves on. I took them off, placing the pair atop one of the pay phones. I stepped back, out of my own shit, and out of my shoes, doing my best to keep the shit that was on my socks from dripping into my Adidas.

Then, after one quick look for witnesses, I leaned back against the newsstand and carefully pushed my jeans down. I had to do this slowly since I hoped that the shit that was still in my boxers remained there and didn't spill down onto my pants or my legs anymore than it already had. I was only moderately successful. I lay my pants on a clear patch of sidewalk.

Now the moment had come: when I would remove my formerly white boxers and stand naked from the waist down on a public corner of Manhattan's Upper East Side. Unbelievable. But it had to be done.

I took the boxers off gingerly in an effort to smear as little shit on myself as I could. I was amazed at how heavy they were. But, here too, I was only somewhat successful. Once I had my underwear off, I tossed them in the small gap between the back of the newsstand and the apartment building it abutted, and wiped my hands on the building's wall. Standing there half-naked, I tried my best to think of the shit as mud, but its smell wouldn't let me. At least where my thighs and calves and butt were covered in shit, I was a bit warmer. And though I wished I could have tossed my jeans back there with my boxers, I, of course, could not.

Though it seemed inherently wrong, I put my shit-stained jeans back on over my shit-stained lower body, and then I buckled my belt. If anybody saw me through any of this, I didn't see them, and they didn't make their presence known. Hopefully the sun was my only witness. Hopefully.

The Mansion seemed very far away. Still, I had to return to it. Rather than soiling the insides of the Glacier Gloves, I tucked them under my arms as I walked back to 72nd and Madison, taking side streets as much as possible. I didn't mind my fingers being cold; they gave me something else to think about.

Fortunately, Pat was still outside when I returned; I really hadn't wanted to bang on the door in my present state. If he had been inside, I would have stationed myself across the street from The Mansion and waited for

Pat to spot me from a window, and then signal for him to come back down. Instead, he was on his knees, coiling up the water hose.

"Uh, Pat," I said. "You don't have to do that just yet."

"Huh?" Pat said as he looked up from his task.

"I didn't make it," I said.

"What!?" Pat said, rising to his feet.

I took a step back so he wouldn't have to.

"I didn't make it," I repeated, smiling and blushing in disbelief. "I didn't find a bathroom."

"Oh, man!" Pat said, shaking his head as he checked me out. "Dude! Shit, look at you!"

"Yeah, it's pretty bad. Would you mind rinsing me off?"

While Pat prepared the hose, I tried to make out my reflection in Polo/Sport's shiny metal window frames as best I could. Despite their dark fabric, my jeans nonetheless had extra dark streaks down the legs and in back. My sweater and shirt hadn't escaped, either. I couldn't tell if I smelled since it seemed that my nose had gotten used to my new scent, but I'm sure I did. Perhaps the cold was keeping it at bay.

Once Pat had straightened out the hose, reconnected it to the spigot, and turned on the water, he walked over to me. I turned away from him and pulled the back of my pant's outward to create enough of a chasm for the water to run down. I braced myself for the blast.

"Polo!" I said.

We both laughed.

The water felt warm against my skin — although it must have been cold. I was sure I would feel the true temperature soon enough. The stream that emerged at my ankles was a reassuring brown. It was working.

"Pat, I don't care if you can't get it all. Just do the best you can."

"Right," Pat said matter-of-factly. I was glad I couldn't see his face.

I was impressed by how well Pat was handling this. It wasn't his shit after all, but here he was —

"Oh man, this is gross!" he let slip. Of course, I let him slide.

"This is fine, it's fine," I said. "Look, I'm just gonna go home so I can change and get back here."

Pat readily agreed and pulled the hose away.

I figured that even if the water hadn't actually left me totally shit-free, it had at least made my jeans a uniform dark, sleek, and shiny black. Besides,

I was soaked and freezing.

There was no way I could catch a cab, no one would pick me up in the state I was in. Nor did I want to hail one. Central Park and the subway then.

I told Pat goodbye and left The Mansion for the second time. Except now my shoes were squishing. But at least I wasn't hopping.

Walking the block of 72nd between Madison and Fifth, I took my mind off my plight by looking up at the penthouse apartment we clean caddy-corner to the Polo/Ralph Lauren store. The place boasts two stories, a circular stairway, and a very wide picture window in the living room that requires a lot of pole work. A nice place to spend an afternoon. It also has plenty of bathrooms.

As I reached the park, it occurred to me that I should have just come and gone here like a dog instead of going on my W.C. search. I could still see my breath in the morning air. I could also see joggers. In an effort to avoid eye contact, I looked down at my feet. But that only made me more aware of my soaked shoes, soaked socks, soaked pants. Plus, I found myself looking for flecks of leftover shit. I looked up at the sky instead, blue, clear, and cold. The bare trees stood out all the more, as did the two towers of the San Remo and the Majestic apartment houses on Central Park West. I appreciated that the Beresford was a good nine blocks away. I certainly didn't want to be recognized by any of its workers. At least Yakov didn't man the door on Sundays.

About midway across the park, I sensed a vehicle slowly approaching from behind. It being a weekend morning and the park being closed to cars, the sound of this one coming up wasn't hard to hear. Nor was knowing what it likely was: a cop car. They were about the only vehicles that would be driving around at that hour. I wondered if I was about to be taken in.

The charge: not finding a bathroom in time? Being an idiot? No, Officer, you got the wrong guy. Bust the security guard who was asleep! I imagined using my one phone call to ring my parents and tell them why I'd been arrested. I decided I'd call Lars instead. But the cops drove by without even a look.

Emerging from the park, I admired the Dakota and looked up at my customer's window that overlooked 72nd Street. Then I walked down the station's steps and headed for the far end of the platform. I leaned against the white-tiled wall and waited for the subway to roll in. I just hoped that its last car would be empty. It wasn't.

I boarded the C train thinking that I would now lean against the back door — the door with the window that overlooks the tracks and gives riders a view of where they'd just been — so that I could try and keep my smell tucked inside my jeans. But I stopped myself since I didn't want to chance spreading my feces where a subsequent, unknowing passenger would at some point end up.

Though I did my best to once again avoid eye contact, it looked like the others on the train were a mix of up-all-night kids, off-to-work adults, and ride-all-night passengers. At least I had my end of the car to myself. If this was due to me and my smell, I didn't want to know.

In any event, I decided to give my fellow riders an unspoken explanation of my current state by doing my best to appear strung-out, even if I didn't really know how to do that. I settled on glassy-eyed and sullen for my out-of-it look, along with letting my body dangle from the metal strap I clung to. That should do it.

By the 50th Street stop, I gave up on my standing droop since my arms were getting tired. Not caring about anyone now, I claimed an empty bench for myself and curled into a disheveled, smelly, shitty ball. Isn't that what a real addict would do?

Besides, I'd spied a way out, an escape of sorts: the bench had a left-behind New York Press just waiting to be put to use. I flipped it open and covered my face with it.

It wasn't the Village Voice putting "Voices Inside My Head" inside my head, but it was close enough. Actually, seeing the Press always reminded me of how the weekly had once described my band *clear*: that our pop-rock was too honest sounding to ever get us another deal. The writer was right.

My decision to quit the band now seemed so long ago. Though window cleaning kept my hands plenty callused, I knew that not drumming had made my hands a bit softer. I allowed myself some forbidden thoughts. The truth was I missed drumming and I missed the band. I missed that instinctive creativity, that feeling of being in a band, of collaborating on sounds. Maybe it wasn't too late to rejoin Michael and Gary in the studio? But would they take me back? Ahh, it was too late. I had tired of that life before; I would surely tire of it again. It wasn't like we'd been succeeding.

Though I had no idea if anyone was watching me, I wondered if they had seen the Press move when I'd sighed. The train rolled along clacking over the tracks. Looking down at the floor, I could make out people's shoes standing over me, and then quickly moving away. I must have been a pretty pathetic sight.

Since I felt a bit cramped, I uncoiled both my arms and legs slightly. Even though it made me feel like I was in some warped version of *The Sound of Music*, as the train rolled downtown, I did by best to escape my surroundings and my plight by thinking about — if not my favorite things — then at least some pleasant things:

At least I wasn't the heroin addict I was pretending be.

At least I had a home to go to.

At least my shower had hot water.

At least I could go back and finish the Polo job and get paid.

At least I'd landed an internship at 20/20 in time to include it on my Columbia application, which I had to finish and drop off in just over a week.

Appropriately, a window cleaning customer had made the internship possible by referring me to a friend of hers at 20/20 who was a Columbia J-school grad. Between that customer and the recommendation-writing Mrs. S., I'd learned once more that it pays to mention to people what you are up to.

At least I had a month before Columbia's writing test. And taking that was certainly going to be better than if I had to take the GRE.

At least my winter-induced vacation from window cleaning would begin in just a few weeks.

At least being taken to the dump had been pretty easy lately. Since I had decided to apply to Columbia, my dad had pretty much laid off on the interrogations and had been happily asking how my application was coming along.

At least this shitting incident gave me something to write about for my New School class. On second thought....

At least no one would recognize me with this New York Press covering my face.

It took forever to get to 14th Street anyway.

SEVEN

SPRING CLEANING

The loft I found myself standing in, squeegee in hand, was spartan to the extreme. Four oversized arched windows let in blazing streams of sunlight, casting shadows against the numerous grey columns spread throughout the massive white room and across its ancient wooden floor. Apart from the columns, the room was empty save for a metal folding chair in the middle — upon which sat a phone. Maybe my customer was just moving in. But I didn't know. I didn't even know where the customer was, for I had just walked into the room; the door had been open.

As I was preparing to climb up onto the sill to inspect the first window of the job, I was struck at how high off the ground these sills were, close to five feet. And then the phone rang.

"Would you mind answering that?" a woman's voice called out.

I looked back toward her voice but could see no one. Since the customer is always right, since the phone was ringing, but also because it somehow felt all right to pick it up — I turned away from the window and walked quickly over to the chair, which felt farther away than it appeared. It was a huge loft. Maybe its dimensions had thrown me off.

Curiously, the phone was a "bat phone," the grey dial-less model with the red light. I picked up the receiver. Before I could even say "Hello?" a man's slick, over-the-top voice began yelling a recorded message at me.

"Congratulations! You've just been accepted by Columbia's journalism school! Well done!" It was the Moviefone guy.

As I heard these words, my eyebrows shot up, my eyes grew wide, I caught my breath, my heartbeat suddenly pounded — but the announcer didn't let me savor his good news.

"Press One if you plan to attend," he went on, his voice bellowing. "Press Two if you do not."

I woke up instead.

That had been a pretty odd dream. Not that I didn't welcome the news it had brought. Or, really, the hope it had conveyed. Columbia was obviously on my mind, but I wouldn't hear from them until next month; their "yea or nay" letters went out on the first of April.

But still. The Moviefone guy? A whacky-sized loft? The bat phone? The unseen customer? What was that all about? The English major in me just didn't feel like sorting this one out; I could be content with being amused by it. I mean, it wasn't a believable dream, the kind where you wake up convinced it took place — like this one I had with Stewart Copeland a long, long time ago, just after I'd finished high school.

In it, I'm finishing up my night-shift at the American Café, a long-gone restaurant I worked at while playing in *Faith,* during my year off before going to college. Then Copeland walks in. I cannot believe it. After wondering if I should or not, I take a quick break from the kitchen and walk up to his table and introduce myself. Copeland is very friendly, and happy to meet me, and quite pleased that I am such a fan. Moreover, he wants to hear about my band. Since we hit it off, I don't go back to the kitchen so that Stewart (he tells me to call him that) and I can hang out. Eventually he has to leave, but that's cool — I got to hang out with Stewart Copeland! I thank him, go back to clean up the kitchen, go home, go to sleep — and then awake momentarily believing it happened.

Nor was it like my recurring "Ian Dream," where I hang out with him and everything's great — we're apparently in a band of some kind, but it is never clear if it's *Fugazi* or not — and then I wake up. At least I hadn't had one of those in a while.

Having now been awake for a minute or so, I stood up from my bed and took the sole step I needed to reach the wall. Raising the window, I chided myself for still not having cleaned my own panes, and then stuck my arm out into the sunshine to gauge the temperature outside. Since it was early and a Saturday, I didn't think any of my various neighbors would be awake to notice my nakedness. If they did, so what. My art class posing days had gotten me over that self-consciousness long ago.

Actually, I doubted any of the folks from the nearby buildings had ever espied me. From what I could see, they all pretty much kept their curtains drawn all the time to prevent anybody from seeing them, thus making my having curtains unnecessary. This was just as well since my relatively dark apartment needed all the light its three windows could muster. Unfortunately, despite the bright sun, cold and wind wrapped themselves around my outstretched hand. March had indeed come "in like a lion." I just hoped the lamb would show up earlier rather than later. I drew my arm back inside and shut the window once more.

Even as I rubbed some warmth back into my hand and retreated to the bed to cover myself with sheets and leather jackets (why spend money on an unneeded blanket?), I officially declared an end to my winter break — and the start of the spring cleaning season. I smiled at the falseness of my declaration: Spring and pleasant weather remained far off. As for a true winter break, that hadn't really happened either since Pat and I had worked on-and-off in January and February. My time off works this way: because of the cold, there isn't much work to do and what work there is you don't want to do. Still, because it's money, I feel compelled to make what I can when offered the chance. Really, my free time had easily outnumbered my work time for the past two months. I don't consider March to be part of winter. It's just easier that way.

I had two jobs to do that day. If Pat had been in town, he probably would have done them both, but since he had gone home to Cleveland for a family get-together, I had been manning the phones and scheduling the jobs. Between that chore, the increasing number of calls coming, and the passage of what I considered enough time, I called my self-styled hibernation over. Also, my bank balance had dipped pretty low. Nonetheless, I had managed to scrape through another of my window cleaning "sabbaticals." That always pleased me.

I had scrimped, doing my best to spend my time *not* spending money. I'd spent my mornings listening to NPR and my mid-mornings with the paper. I could read for as long as I wanted; any article, every article. Well, not every article. I had routinely tossed the Sports section since I just don't keep up with that. Nor did I read the Real Estate section, figuring that because I didn't have money, why bother; I skipped Travel for the same reason. And, I didn't look through the Help Wanted section since, well, I have a job.

Though I hadn't really relish it, I had also read my nearly waist-high stack of saved A sections of the Times — the papers I set aside since September to prepare for the current events section of Columbia's written test. How I'd enjoyed tossing them out once I'd taken the exam. Had that only been five weeks ago?

I thought the test had gone all right. With my allotted 30 minutes, I'd made a stab at a "news analysis" piece about the worth of the United Nations that had essentially turned into an editorial commending the organization's worth as an international sounding board. With my allotted 20 minutes, I'd worked with a list of reported facts, and written a short feature about a chocolate-lovers convention in New England. With my allotted 15 minutes, I'd worked with another list of reported facts and written a crime story about a con artist in Queens. None of it was my best work — how could it be? — which was why I'd tossed my copy of my test articles into a trash once I'd left the Journalism Building. Out of sight, out of mind.

As for the current events section — the whole point of that newspaper pile — I believed I nailed 24 out of 25 questions in the allotted 25 minutes. The only one I knew I'd screwed up was identifying who James Fallows was. I'd heard of him, I just didn't know what he'd done. Afterwards, a fellow test-taker told me that Fallows once edited The Washington Monthly. Ah, well. I considered the question the equivalent of "insider baseball" and didn't feel too bad.

On really cold days, when I had no interest in going outside, I'd listen to the radio for as long as I wanted, keeping WNYC tuned to not just Morning Edition, but Brian Lehrer's public affairs program, Leonard Lopate's talk show, All Things Considered, or whatever was on. I'd listen to them between sections of the paper, between book chapters.

Or, I'd move the radio dial to, say, Z-100 — a guilty pleasure of sorts, in that I did like hearing what that Top Forty station was playing; I like to know what's popular with "the kids." Or, I'd put on CDs I hadn't listened to in a long time.

Listening to radio programs or music, however, didn't just inform or entertain. Spending my time in this way kept me from spending my time in more expensive ways, like going to the movies, going to shows, or buying CDs. I would go see bands at clubs when there wasn't a cover charge, even though I've long known that sometimes you do get what you pay for. When the Cineplex Odeon at Worldwide Plaza in Midtown offered three dollar movies, I'd go and see one every so often. I went to see The *Usual Suspects* three times.

I wasn't a total hermit, in other words. I'd go out for cold walks or take cold bicycle rides. I'd go up to the Met and pay a dollar to get in; what you pay is voluntary. I'd see friends. If I were meeting up with someone for a meal, I would fill up on yogurt topped with Grape Nuts so that I would only have to spend money on a soup or a salad — not a soup *and* a salad.

I also had my 20/20 internship. The two or three days a week I'd been spending at the show over the past two months had been pretty instructive. If nothing else, I'd learned that people would call back immediately when I left them a message saying I was with the program. My job was to call potential interview subjects and learn what they had to say, and then the segment's producer would decide if they were worth pursuing. This meant talking to, for instance, a woman who sold drug-testing kits to parents so that moms and dads could secretly clip a lock of their child's hair and analyze it. Crazy. I could never picture my parents doing that to me. But then, they never had to.

I did enjoy calling one lady and hearing her talk about how testing your kids surreptitiously was not, in fact, crossing a parental line. I did not enjoy having to call this woman back a final time, however — after speaking with her on at least four or five occasions — to thank her for all her time and insight, but because the story had headed in a different direction, we no longer needed her help. Actually, it hadn't been too bad since I timed my call right and rang when she wasn't home, having only to leave a message.

I'd also liked introducing myself to the executive producer of the show by saying that I had cleaned his windows a couple of times a few years earlier, and how much of a fan I was of his West End Avenue apartment. I think I kind of shocked him. I guessed that most of his colleagues hadn't been over to his place, and yet the lowly intern had. But he was ready with his comeback, replying (correctly) that, as he recalled, his wife thought we'd charged too much. Pat and I had done our best to justify our price, explaining that their replacement tilt-ins with fake mullions were quite time-consuming and delicate. We had to make sure that there was no excess water beneath the piece of plastic that seemingly divides a single pane of glass into six smaller ones. It involved a lot of careful tapping of the mullions to coax out the extra water that collects in the gap between them and the glass. She dropped us anyway.

I'd discovered at 20/20 that I didn't want to do broadcast journalism since it seemed to me that the logistics of shooting, lighting, editing — and all the rest that goes into making a TV news story — would distract me from writing the story. Plus, 20/20 (like most any television show) needed great visuals to drive the plot, which seemed to rule out a lot of good stories. Of course, with print journalism, *any* article needs a good story.

I also appreciated my 20/20 days since they took my mind off not being in a band. This winter break there hadn't been shows to play, or recordings to make. Instead, I had found myself in a nothing zone, one of waiting to hear from school. It felt like a kind of torture, especially on the occasions in the past few months when my window jobs had been close to Columbia's campus. One apartment's ledge on 116th Street, just off Riverside Drive, had even put me in view of the J-school. I'd looked over at the building's seventh floor and wondered how the Admissions office's deliberations over my fate were going.

It is, of course, disconcerting to have one's future — or at least an aspect of one's life — in the hands of others. It happens occasionally, sometimes more obviously or officially than others. Getting into GDS (my high school), getting into Vassar, and now getting into grad school, were the more traditional (and daunting) examples in my past. Jobs I had interviewed for were a bit more rare. There hadn't been a formal interview for posing at the Corcoran's art classes, or with Pat for cleaning windows; a willingness (or desperation as some might think) to do the work was enough. I had interviewed at Bob's Famous where I scooped ice cream in D.C., just as I had at the law firms of Cravath, Swaine & Moore (where I worked as a legal library assistant the summer after my freshman year in college), and at Powell, Goldstein, Fraser & Murphy, where I'd been a messenger for about nine months during that year off from school when I played in *Embrace*.

I had hoped that Michael (and Henry and Wendell) would want me to be in *S.O.A.*; I had hoped that Ian and Joe would have me in *Fugazi*. Michael and Bert and I had sent out demo tapes in hopes that a record label would sign us. And, of course, it wasn't a shame that Fire Records and East-West Records had both liked *Manifesto*. It was simply a shame what they did to us.

Validation. Approval. Credentials. Identity. What others have given me. Rather, what over time I have been a bit too prone to let others give me. And here I was again, in the midst of a new nothingness before Columbia would now — hopefully — validate and approve me, giving me a new credential and identity.

More accurately, I'd been feeling how "in between" I was, with not much defined in my life. If I got into school, great! Really and truly. I would be more than pleased, I'd be ecstatic, I'd be honored, I'd be floating. It would be quite an accomplishment. But if I didn't get in, what then? I would be a college-educated, window-cleaning, ex-musician, grad-school reject — with no idea of what to do next. Ouch.

I glanced at the clock on the wall by the door, and seeing that it was already eight o'clock, reached over to the old leather suitcase in the tiny corner closet at the head of my bed. I pulled out a pair of boxers and started to dress. Once I had put on some jeans, I walked the five steps it took to cross the room and pressed play on the CD player. *Semi-Gloss*'s six-song EP, "Teenie," would serve as my shaving soundtrack.

Until a week ago, waiting to hear from Columbia had been the only thing that had been defining my nothingness. Then, a Vassar friend had called to say that his band needed a new drummer, and a drumset for that matter. Was I interested in playing in *Semi-Gloss*?

Listening to the first track, the suavely rambunctious "Wild For You," I found myself shaking my can of shaving cream like a maracas, as I prepared to remove a week's worth of stubble. I found Jordy's offer tempting, so much so that I had insisted that we meet shortly after we'd talked so I could get some copies of *Semi-Gloss*'s CDs. I had listened to them a lot in the past few days. They were fun songs about being at the beach, about being in love, about walking around New York City. Quite different from Michael's darker, introspective fare with *Manifesto* and *clear*, and not at all as agenda-driven as anything *S.O.A., Faith*, or *Embrace* had done.

Apart from their tunefulness and Jordy being a friend, *Semi-Gloss* was also a band with a buzz. Dirt Records had put out the well-received "Teenie" a few months earlier, which found fans and critics easily taken with their sound. Now the label was about to release *Semi-Gloss*'s upcoming self-titled CD. And where might that lead them? The band managed the hat-trick of meshing surf music's giddy effervescence, lounge music's laid back cool, and *The Velvet Underground*'s...no, not their grittiness or their drone, but Nico's breathy vocal stylings. I just wondered if *Semi-Gloss* was trying too hard. Tonight, I'd have a better idea once I'd practiced with them at Jordy's loft in Chinatown.

And just how would that go? Would I speed up the songs? Would the four of us click musically? How strange would it be playing without Michael? Very strange, if the past held any answers. At school I had played in a few informal groups and it never seemed to work. They didn't seem serious. But perhaps *Semi-Gloss* would be the exception. They were a real band after all. One with a buzz.

As it turned out, *Semi-Gloss*' other two members, Greg the bassist and Verena the singer-keyboardist-chanteuse had also gone to Vassar, though at school I had only hung out with Jordy, who played guitar and wrote most of the songs. It occurred to me: would an all-Vassar band hold a certain charm, or at least some novelty value? No, I doubted anyone would care. I put down my maracas, squeezed some cream into my hand, and lathered up my stubble.

I wondered as I began shaving away my Kris Kringle beard and my own reddish whiskers, would the envelope be thick or thin? I had begun to fixate on whether a thick envelope was going to arrive from Columbia. When the Dean of Admissions had proctored the writing test, he had said not to bother opening a thin missive from the school. Fortunately, he had shared these words of wisdom with us after we'd taken the test and not before.

As for deferring from the J-school, that was simply not a possibility. Though Vassar had let me take two years off during the course of my education — to drum with *Faith* one year before I'd began, and after my sophomore year to be in *Embrace* — Columbia made it clear that if you chose not to go once you'd been admitted, then you had to reapply. My putting off picking up the application last September by walking down Central Park West instead of across 72nd Street had been the closest I could come to deferring anything with them.

Along with calling an end to my winter break and the "Moviefone" dream, my shaving on a Saturday had also set this day apart. Usually I don't shave on a weekend, and usually I let my beard go until my neck begins to itch, meaning I had a few days more to go. But the first of my two window jobs that day required that I be clean shaven: I was about to return to Sylvia's loft. Well, her boyfriend's loft. He had called for another cleaning. As a tribute to my would-be seductress, I wanted to look presentable. I did my best not to cut myself. The whiskers on my neck tend to nick pretty easily.

I rang the boyfriend's buzzer, pleased that I hadn't been late to his place, despite a C train that had taken its time pulling into the 14th Street station and a walk over to Broadway that took longer than I'd thought. Though I was pretty certain Pat hadn't cleaned this Lower Broadway loft during last fall's cleaning season — I knew I hadn't been back since the previous May — the windows wouldn't be as dirty as the first time I'd come. Compared to a couple of years worth of grime, ten months of build-up would seem easy.

I was buzzed in and looked to the top of the stair's landing, realizing that it would be just as well if this job went quickly. For there, standing at the loft's doorway, was the boyfriend. When I had spoken to him while setting up the job, he'd said that he'd see me on Saturday, but it hadn't really registered that he would actually be there. I didn't associate his place with his presence. The black wool turtleneck I had chosen to hide the blood on my neck with suddenly felt quite warm as I walked up the steps. The warped, ancient stairs creaked once more.

At the doorway, we introduced each other.

So this was the boyfriend — in person. He wasn't what I expected. Instead of the beefy, frat boy, jock-jerk I had envisioned last spring, here stood a slim and polite young man. Yes, he was wearing khakis and a Polo shirt on a Saturday morning, but compared to a suit and tie, that was casual, and at least his clothes were worn, even frayed.

And he seemed nice enough. So much for imagined first impressions.

"Would you mind working as quietly as possible," David said as we walked into the living room that looked the same as before. "My girlfriend likes to sleep in."

"That's fine," I said. I wasn't about to say that I knew this about her already. "I'll just do the bedroom windows last." Sylvia's being with him began to make sense.

After David offered me coffee, he left me alone, retreating to the couch in the back of the loft, the one by the TV, to read the morning paper. I worked in silence. As I had thought, the windows weren't that dirty. They remained as delicate as before, especially the front window that now boasted an air conditioner. Instead of cleaning the panes twice, I only had to do them once. The same was also true outside — where I remembered to take my crowbar with me.

I resented the air conditioner. For when an A.C. unit is installed in a window frame such as this, one where the window doesn't tilt in but only goes up and down, the unit's presence causes an overlap between the lower and upper windows. Since the lower window frame must be raised to accommodate the air conditioner, where the upper and lower panes cross over each other results in a patch of glass that I cannot clean entirely: the outside of the lower window; the inside of the upper window. Over time, the glass becomes a seemingly free-floating rectangle of dirt I always find frustrating.

Some people replace the lower window with one custom cut to fit the space so that no overlap exists. But that is pretty expensive. Most often, replacement windows come in the form of tilt-ins. These oversized versions can be very unwieldy and dangerous since they are so large and weigh so much. Plus, since most buildings remove the belt hooks when they install the tilt-ins, this means yet another set of my favorite kind of windows to clean has been eliminated. I consider oversized tilt-ins a killjoy.

Fortunately, most customers — Sylvia's boyfriend among them — don't seem to mind their dirty rectangles, or at least understand that nothing much can be done to clean them; pouring water into the gap only does so much. I always think these imperfections are taunting me.

While my work itself went relatively swiftly, not talking to Sylvia (or her boyfriend for that matter) also contributed to my quick pace. Still, as I worked, I pictured Sylvia in her black skirt and white blouse sitting at the table reading her magazine; Sylvia looking up at me from the table from beneath her dirty-blonde hair; Sylvia clutching the crowbar; Sylvia running her fingernail along my arm. On my water breaks I looked first toward the bathroom door, knowing that the offered-up shower stood behind it. Then I looked towards the bedroom door knowing that Sylvia was in there asleep. I doubted she was wearing anything.

When I'd finished the front windows and began cleaning the tilt-ins that remained in the rest of the apartment, the boyfriend — though I knew his name, I couldn't think of him any other way — took his reading to the living room that I'd just completed. In my mind, Sylvia tagged along with me as before. Then, a few windows later, the time had come: only the bedroom remained.

"Well," I said to the boyfriend as he sat on the couch and I rinsed out my chamois in the kitchen sink. "I've just got that last window to do."

"Right," he said. "I'll be right back."

The boyfriend rose and walked toward the bedroom. He opened the door slowly, quietly, and leaned into the doorway.

"Hey, honey," he said in a low, comforting voice. "Time to get up. The window cleaner's here and he's got just this window to do.... Okay."

He closed the door and walked back towards me.

"She'll be right out." I wondered what kind of robe Sylvia would throw on. A classic white in terry cloth? A kimono?

After a few minutes, the bedroom door began to open.

The moment had arrived, the three of us together. Would it be awkward? Amusing? Though it seemed unlikely, I could see Sylvia hinting at my last visit. Perhaps she'd mention her need for a shower? Perhaps she would note that I wasn't so dirty this time. Nah. If we had actually slept together she might go that route. But since Sylvia's and my goodbye had come courtesy of my turning her down, this was definitely going to be awkward. I braced myself for the ice princess.

The bedroom door opened a little more and out walked a young lady dressed in slacks and a fair isle sweater, her black hair pulled back in a ponytail.

"Sorry for taking so long," she said.

Instead of an English accent, she had an American one. Instead of Sylvia, she was somebody else. A new girlfriend. Amusing had won out after all.

"Not a problem," I said. "I'll be done very soon."

As I walked past the happy couple, I could only smile. What had happened to Sylvia? What had gone wrong? Had she tired of New York? Had she tired of her boyfriend? Had she been found showering with, I don't know, the guy who'd installed the air conditioner? Answers I would never know; questions I could never ask. But that was okay. I liked the mystery, and knew that the explanation wouldn't be as satisfying. Besides, my asking about her would definitely make for an awkward moment.

After cleaning the last window, however, I did ask David if I could use the phone. I needed to return a client's call. The customer from the housing project in Harlem had called a couple of times the day before wanting to arrange another cleaning. I walked towards the back of the apartment, wanting to be out of earshot of the lovebirds as I dialed the number. I hoped that I could leave a message for Mrs. Jones. I took a deep breath as her phone began to ring, and then she picked up as if she'd been sitting by her phone just waiting for me to call — as if she already knew.

"Hello?" Mrs. Jones said. Her voice sounded polite but strong, a cheerful force of nature.

"This is Ivor Hanson from Shields Windows returning your call. You wanted your windows cleaned again?"

"So just where have you been? I was beginning to think you weren't going to call me back."

"No, no. I got in late last night and didn't want to call you too early today, that's all." This was a lie, but a pretty believable one. I had happened to check Pat's machine just after she had called, but hadn't been ready to call her back then. I had broken out the calculator instead.

"I appreciate that," Mrs. Jones said. "But you should know that if you want to hang on to a customer, you should call them back right away — the day they call you. That's just how it works. So then, when can you come?"

"That's just it," I said, shutting my eyes tightly and making my free hand into a fist.

Feeling myself squirm, I was grateful she couldn't see me as we spoke. Mrs. Jones could, however, hear my hurried words. "I can't come. Because Pat Shields has decided to move to Los Angeles, he's shutting down the New York office — so that's pretty much the end of it. I'm really very sorry about all this. We've just been telling customers as they've called in."

Phew. At least I got that out. Now, how would it go over? I cringed at the ensuing silence on the other end of the phone. Finally, though I am sure that only a few seconds had passed, Mrs. Jones replied.

"I'm very sorry to hear that," she said. Mrs. Jones didn't sound upset, just resigned. "You gentlemen did such a good job on my windows last time you were here. Who am I going to get to clean them now?"

Just don't ask me to do them, I thought, just don't ask me.

"You might try Frank's," I said. "I've heard they're okay. I'm sure they are in the phone book."

"I appreciate your trying to help me out. And good luck to you out in California."

If she thought I was going, too, so much the better.

That had gone much better than I had thought. As I hung up the phone and walked back toward the kitchen, I wondered if Mrs. Jones knew I'd been lying to her the whole time.

I don't mind dropping customers, or "firing" them as Pat and I put it if the clients don't take the news well, I just hate not telling them the truth. Still, I wasn't about to tell Mrs. Jones that her job wasn't worth our time. I had sorted it out, done the numbers. Even with her ten dollar tip factored in, her time-consuming windows took so long that I only ended up making ten dollars an hour up there — half of what I usually make, half of what I need to make to get by. Aside from that, her windows were a big drag that I didn't want to deal with. Pat would understand. When we'd worked at subsequent jobs with pain-in-the-ass panes, we'd been grateful that at least they weren't Mrs. Jones' windows. Then again, perhaps I wouldn't tell Pat about my decision.

I put the phone back in its cradle and felt like a heartless jerk. I remembered Mrs. Jones saying how hard it had been to try and convince other window cleaners to come up to her part of town. Now I was one of them. At least I was a somewhat justified heartless jerk since both money-wise and work-wise, doing those windows didn't make sense. As I said my goobyes to Sylvia's ex-boyfriend, I realized we had more in common than his ex-girl-friend and taste in furniture: we were both capitalists at some level.

Outside on the street, just like last time, I didn't look up and admire my work. This had nothing to do with paying some sort of homage to Sylvia. I just didn't want to see the rectangle of dirty glass staring down at me. Then, even though it was a time-waster, I decided to catch a 6 train at the Spring Street station and ride it up to Lexington and 68th Street. Since I did have a chunk of time before my next job — an apartment in Schwab House up at 73rd and West End Avenue — I thought a walk across the park would be another way to officially recognize the arrival of the spring cleaning season. Even if I was still wearing gloves, at least they weren't Glacier Gloves.

As I crossed Lexington Avenue and headed toward Fifth and the park's 72nd Street entrance, I glanced at the spot by the subway stairs where I had tossed my shit-stained boxers. I liked walking around New York and seeing places that had meaning to me and wondering what meaning they might hold for somebody else. Perhaps someone had died at my boxer spot? Or made love? Or proposed marriage? Or broken up? Or written a song? Or been arrested? Or come across my boxers? Or left their own pair?

A few blocks later, I saw that I wasn't the only one welcoming spring at Central Park. The sun had inspired a good number of others to come out, despite the relatively cold weather. People biking, people skating, people with dogs; they sped, they zipped, they trotted by. I enjoyed my relaxed pace, letting my surroundings define my experience and not the other way around. I simply saw, I simply walked, doing my best not to respond. Not to think "what a beautiful day" or "what a magnificent tree that is," but to let it all happen before me.

"Ladies and gentlemen, I'd like to direct your attention to the young man in the leather jacket and green bucket!"

I looked up. A horse-and-buggy driver, who had pulled over to the side of the road so that his passengers could more easily take photos of the park, was looking my way — along with his passengers and a group of tourists who happened to be standing nearby. He was a middle-aged guy with a gut, dressed in the 19th century riding outfits some of those buggy drivers favor, especially if they are hams like this one.

"Not Sting!" the driver declared.

I smiled. Very funny and even flattering, I guess. I'd always thought Sting was pretty handsome. And Sting did own an apartment in a nearby building on Central Park West — 88 CPW, I'd heard — so his being in the park was a possibility, if remote. Though I'd never done his windows, one of my clients had once been his masseuse.

"Not in the least!" I yelled back. I could go along with his joke.

"No, folks," the man continued, "this is one of New York City's window cleaners en route to his next job!"

Dead-on accurate, I thought to myself. That really is what I am. I'm not Sting. I'm not Stewart Copeland. I'm not a rock star. I'm not even in a band. But the cameras clicked anyway. Some of the people even waved. I think what was going on was that these people were impressed that I was a window cleaner. They had a symbol of the city standing right before them, complete with props. Instead of waving back, I turned my back on them.

"Yeah," I yelled. "And I'm running late!"

I wasn't, but I had to get out of there.

I used to be convinced that musical success was going to happen to me. And though I knew it wasn't going to happen with *Faith* — Chris was a bit of a wild child and, besides, I was off to college — then it would happen with some other band I would eventually be in. Then *Embrace, Manifesto,* and *clear* had run their course. Maybe now with *Semi-Gloss*?

If this possibility with *Semi-Gloss* didn't exist, I knew it would be the moment that showed me I had truly let go of music. This wasn't like the subway and the Voice — that was admitting something was over. This wasn't like the subway after the Polo job — that was missing something that I had admitted was over. Just now someone had mentioned *The Police* and for a brief moment my not being in a band didn't matter!

Except that, thankfully, the *Semi-Gloss* chance did exist. And *The Police* and my not being in a band did matter as well. And I was glad that they did. Memories, experience, they make up in large part what we are, or what I am. I could have told Jordy, "No thanks, but thanks for thinking of me," when he'd called about my playing in *Semi-Gloss*. But I hadn't. I knew that I still wanted to be out there: onstage and in the recording studio. And that I always would.

That morning I had played along to *Semi-Gloss* with my shaving can. Even if the possibility of being in that band didn't exist, I would have been playing along to most any song by anybody. But I wouldn't play along with one of my old bands. I would never do that. At least not yet.

Compared to that, shaking a Noxema-brand maracas to *Semi-Gloss* wasn't so bad. And they did have a buzz. And we all got along. So who knows, maybe we would make it big. What was I thinking? I wasn't even in the band, so why even think about it? Besides, *Semi-Gloss* didn't even like distorted guitars.

I was headed west, toward the river and West End Avenue and Schwab House, the antithesis of the Dakota. Rather than being a building of ornate design and a world famous landmark, Schwab was an apartment building that seemed to strive to have no personality at all. It's an anonymous pile of bricks built in 1948 that takes up an entire city block, taking its name from the actual Schwab House, the beautiful French chateau-style mansion that originally stood there and was torn down for its successor.

I'd always found the carried-over name a bit disingenuous. How could this slab of a building of 300-plus apartments think it could simply take the Schwab House name for itself? The two structures were in no way alike.

I also found it odd that a good number of the tenants in Schwab House hung a picture of the original Schwab House on their walls. Sure, they did have an obvious connection to the place, but if I lived there and had that photo around me all the time, I'd just be reminded that I didn't live in that ornate mansion, but in the plain building that destroyed it. Maybe if today's Schwab House were more attractive, I'd feel differently. For instance, the Beresford apartment house replaced a hotel by the same name. And I do love mid-Century starkness — with Lever House, the Seagram Building, and the buildings of Brasilia being some off-the-cuff examples. Schwab House is simply mid-Century plainness.

Pat and I were more or less the exclusive window cleaners in the building, or at least the window cleaning company that Schwab House's management recommended when a tenant called for a referral. Because we got a good bit of business from the building, usually going there a couple of times a week — more often than if we had cleaned the original Schwab House's windows — we gave those who lived in the building a special deal, charging them a buck less per window than our usual price.

I walked into the West End Avenue Entrance, modest glass doorways at the foot of some large slate steps, beneath a long blue canvas canopy. Even though Schwab House goes by the old mansion's address of 11 Riverside Drive, there is no entrance on that side of the building. I liked regarding this as a tribute to the ghost of the original Schwab House. As I approached, I waved to the doorman on duty, a middle-aged, heavy-set guy standing behind his lectern.

It's funny. Schwab was originally intended for middle-class tenants. It set out to be a humble place, a plain place, a low-key place. As the Upper West Side became a more desirable place to live, as real estate prices jumped, the feeling of the building had changed; it was becoming more upscale. The building now had a gym and a playroom. New elevators had also been installed. I had caught glimpses of their wood paneled walls and brass trimming interiors when their doors had opened to let tenants in or out.

Compared to the modest metal walls painted tan that had been there before — compared to the rest of the building, for that matter — these new
boxes seemed too much, too monied. I'm sure they must have cost a lot.
The building had even dropped a lot of dough on slick new Service Elevators with shiny steel walls and black trim. It's not that I considered Schwab
House downtrodden, I just liked its worn-in, unpretentious feel and wanted
it to stay that way. At least the lobby's walls hadn't become ostentatious, not
yet at any rate. The same old prints of Roman ruins still hung there from
decades earlier. I was sure their days were numbered though.

   I walked down the hall to the Schwab House offices, putting my bucket
down outside the door in the waiting area. Before, this space had been filled
by worn fabric-covered couches, but two stuffed leather sofas had taken
their place. My bucket seemed out of place, even here.

   I waved "Hello" to Carol, the receptionist, since she was on the phone
doing her best to calm an irate tenant about a shower leak, and then wrote
in my name, my company's name, the day, time, and the apartment I was
off to in the log book atop the reception area's counter. I filled out a sticker
with my company's name and the client's apartment number (another new
upscale addition). Apparently Schwab House was taking cues from the Dakota, though this sticker I didn't care about holding onto.

   I waited for the Service Elevator to arrive, its doors being just a few
steps from the doorman. I was grateful that I didn't have to go back outside and then use the stairs to the basement floor (and the true Service
Entrance) and wait for the Service Elevator in the basement, thus making
me out of sight of the tenants. I'm sure some residents wanted this, but at
least Schwab House management hadn't gone that far.

   The new Service Elevator arrived. Though I found it slick and hi-tech, it
did get me up to the eighth floor much faster than the old one had.

   I walked down the hallway to my customer's door, wondering how long
the corridor's light-brown walls, dark-brown carpeting and grey doors
would last. Compared to the elevators, they seemed too downscale for the
building now. Having arrived at the apartment door, I knocked and waited.
After a few minutes, an elderly man opened it.

   "Good afternoon, young man," he said, his voice a wispy rasp. "Won't
you come in?"

   As I did so, I noticed that the apartment was dark, spare, and quiet, not
unlike its owner. He was a retiree, who looked to be in his mid seventies,

a reserved gentleman with bright eyes and polite ways, but not a ready smile. His weathered face was thin and narrow, his silver hair was thick and combed back. He had a craggy elegance. He turned, and I followed him into his place. I admired his slow but dignified stoop. Actually, a bit of his dignity had to be attributed to his clothes. His three-button brown wool shirt with a pronounced collar, his dark-green slacks and his tan wallabies made him appear to be heading out for a civilized hike in the woods.

"Help yourself to the sink," he said pointing to kitchen, still with his back to me. "For your bucket and for a drink." And then he shuffled on, returning to his study. I filled my bucket and myself.

I had been prepared for some ingratiating small talk, but he obviously didn't seem inclined to chat. Instead, he just wanted his windows cleaned. That was fine, too. At least he wasn't a hoverer. Though I take being left alone as a sign of respect and trust, in this case I also wondered if it might just mean he didn't want to be bothered with shadowing me. He moved pretty slowly after all. Despite this compliment of solitude, however, I wanted to talk to him. He seemed so knowing.

I took my bucket into the living room. Even with the sun shining outside, the place remained in shadows. At first, I blamed this on the massive oak furniture that took up so much space and seemed to soak up any available light. Looking around, I realized it also stemmed from all the books on display. This wasn't an apartment as much as a bibliophile's musty lair. Shelf upon shelf brimmed with volumes old and new, along with dozens of postcards from major cities, and photographs of flowers, buildings, and people placed amongst the paperbacks and leather-bound collections of novels, histories, and poetry. On the floor sat neat stacks of more books skirting the edges of the walls. It seemed their owner couldn't get rid of them, but couldn't quite make space for them either. Like many New Yorkers, he had settled in as much as the apartment allowed. I moved a few stacks away from the windows and onto a Persian rug that filled the middle of the room.

Fortunately, the first of the apartment's tilt-ins behaved themselves. The ballasts all worked so that when I raised the windows, they stayed in place, and when I tilted them in, they stayed level. Not surprisingly, there weren't any child-guards to deal with. I cleaned the insides, then tilted the windows in and cleaned the outside panes. Unlike other tilts, since Schwab's windows are pretty light and aren't that big, leaning them against my shoulders or the palm of my left or right hand doesn't strain my body too much. I can clean the windows with my free arm without much trouble, just as long as I can reach for my squeegee and chamois without much effort. Even so, regardless of a window's size or weight, long arms come in handy. I finished the living room's two windows, the kitchen's one window, and the bedroom's two windows pretty quickly — despite the thick dirt on the glass and having to move a good deal more books on the floor to keep them far from my bucket, now filled with increasingly dirty water. The glass hadn't been cleaned in quite a while.

Because Pat and I cleaned so many apartments in the building, and because there are so many apartments there, Schwab House epitomizes for me the fact that behind every door I walk past in the hallway — or behind every window I see from the street — lives somebody with their own story. Though not at all psychedelic, I'd always liked comparing Schwab House to the sequence in "Yellow Submarine," when all sorts of strange people and beasts are found behind the doors of an odd, old mansion — along with *The Beatles*.

There was the old guy who had lived in the building for decades and had told me how, when he was a teenager, he'd worked as a bellhop at a hotel on Long Island. One night, a certain aviator stayed at the place before he attempted to fly solo to France. "Yes," the old man said, "I was Lindbergh's bellhop!" Before retiring for the night, Lindbergh told "his" bellhop to wake him up at three in the morning — and so he did. The two of them went outside and checked the weather. After a few minutes of looking up at the sky, Lindbergh decided it was okay to fly and took off later that day. A few weeks passed, and the bellhop's boss called him in and showed him a telegram from Lindbergh thanking the hotel for its hospitality and asking the hotel's manager to give the bellhop a ten-dollar tip.

"That was a lot of money back then," my customer reminded me.

Then he showed me how his story hadn't shown up in a celebrated bio of Lindbergh that had just come out. "Can you believe? Such a story and it's not in here!"

I told him the book would have been much better if it had, and that hopefully a later edition would correct this oversight. I doubted this would happen, just as the long-ago bellhop did — but that's the sort of thing you say to a customer who has just told you a highlight of his life. Then, his wife told me how she had been a hairstylist for Jackie Onassis. When I complimented her on her blinding platinum-blonde hairdo, she smiled. "I don't give into grey," she told me. "Not yet. Not ever."

There was the customer who was just a teenager when her husband had died in the D-Day invasion. She had never remarried; she had never gone to France to see his grave in Normandy. She still had his picture hanging on her living room wall.

There was the customer who had survived the Holocaust. A previous Super had told me that a number of survivors lived in the building over the years. This woman was a young girl at Buchenwald and never really understood why she had been "allowed" to live. Looking at her, I kept thinking that just beneath her shirtsleeve was her identity number tattoo. But you'd never know it, you'd never guess it. She was just an old lady living a simple life on West End Avenue, who was getting her windows cleaned on a spring day and offering me a glass of water after I finished every window.

And so on, floor by floor — all in the same building, all behind their own doors, all of them with windows that needed cleaning.

I joined the old man in the last room, his study. Here, the books had taken over. Unlike in other rooms, I had to remove stacks of books from the windowsills, putting them on top of the books already piled on the floor. After finishing the study's two windows, I looked out over the white pebbles covering Schwab's underground garage entrance on 74th Street, half expecting to see some of his books down there.

I looked back in and saw that the old man had his checkbook out, ready to fill in the amount as he sat at his desk. My chance at conversation had arrived.

"How long have you lived at Schwab House," I said as I chamoised the last window's edges.

"A few years," he replied in his quiet rasp. "I moved here after my wife died. We'd lived on the East Side our whole lives, and after she passed away, I knew I couldn't stay in that neighborhood. I needed a new life. So I moved across town and came here."

"What sort of field were you in?" I asked as I leaned against the windowsill and crossed my arms. This was beginning to feel more like an interrogation than a conversation, but he didn't seem to mind.

"I did all sorts of things over the years," he said, slightly pushing the checkbook away as he settled slowly into his desk chair. "I went to sea for a while, then I went into business and made a fortune. Then I lost it all. And so I started to make my fortune again. But then halfway through, I thought 'To hell with this,' and walked away. Best thing I ever did, walking away."

Though I could see him smiling now, the way he said "walking away," it seemed pretty clear he did not want to elaborate. Who was I to press him? I was, after all, not even a guest in his house, but a workman performing a service. I sometimes forget that, finding myself wanting to minimize the window cleaning, even though that is what I am there to do.

"I must say that you have a pretty impressive amount of books," I said to fill the silence.

"Oh, yeah," he said, returning himself slowly to his desk and putting his hands back on the checkbook. "We never had kids, but we did have our books. Obviously, I just can't bring myself to part with them."

"Do you write?" I asked, motioning to an ancient typewriter on his desk.

"Well, yes and no," he said as he opened a rickety desk drawer to pull out a pen. I wondered if it would be a Cross or a Montblanc. It was a black Bic. "I do write, but I don't consider myself a writer. I'm a poet."

"I read poetry from time to time," I said. "I like Sharon Olds and e.e. cummings and Norine Niedecker. I like how they do so much with so little, how they —"

I cut myself off when I saw my customer frowning.

"That modern stuff is not for me," he said. "I'm a traditionalist. You know, rhyme and meter. I've written that way since my first collection came out in 1936."

I paused, considering this. "May I ask how old you are?"

"I'm ninety," he said. "Been retired a while, but I'm working on my next book. It will come out next year as a small volume. I'm just sorting out what should go in it. How much do I owe you?"

"Forty-nine dollars please," I said as I stopped leaning and stood straight. I didn't like asking for money while slouching. "And you can make the check out to 'Shields Windows.' This building gets a special deal. We charge seven dollars per window and you have seven windows."

"That's nice of you," he said, looking up at me. "Since you expressed such an interest, before you go, let me get you something."

As I put his check in my wallet, he pulled open one of the desk drawers from which he removed a manila folder. He placed this on his desk, then opened it and methodically leafed through the sheaf of papers it contained.

Each was filled with typewritten words. Instead of the neatness that a computer and printer make possible, overstrikes and mark outs obscured the lines of words, making them a typewritten scrawl.

"I write these out by hand first, but then I work on them on my old Underwood here," he said. "I can barely read my handwriting even when I try to be neat."

"Me, too," I said.

After narrowing his choice down to three possibilities, he chose one sheet and looked it over. He nodded approvingly, and signed his initials "I.I" at the bottom of the page, handing the piece of paper to me.

"Call it a memento," he said. "Read it when you get home."

I looked down at the poem he had selected for me, something called "Hunting."

"Why, thank you, sir," I said. "Thank you very much. I really look forward to reading this."

I shook his hand and then tucked his poem inside my copy of the day's Times, which I had in my courier bag. I didn't want his page to get crumpled. Instead of emptying my bucket in his sink, I decided to pour it down the slop sink in Schwab's basement. It was my present to him. I gathered my tools and bid him goodbye.

"Thanks again, sir," I said as I closed the door to his apartment. "See you when they're dirty."

"My pleasure," he said. "Just remember: You can't go wrong with rhyme and meter."

Instead of waiting until I got home, I read my memento on the Service Elevator as it took me down to the building's laundry room.

On the subway ride downtown, I sat and regarded my tools. I'd realized something while at 20/20. Whereas the cubicle I worked in was in the middle of a long, large room, the senior producers had offices with windows. When I couldn't look out and see the city, I felt lost. Fortunately, the producer whose office I worked nearest to usually kept his door open pretty wide, so I could look out and take in the Upper West Side pretty readily. On my fourth or fifth day there, I realized I wasn't really looking down Columbus Avenue, or across at Lincoln Center, I wasn't even looking *out* his window, but *at* his window. The glass was pretty dirty. I missed my squeegee.

As the subway rolled on toward Canal Street and *Semi-Gloss*'s rehearsal space, I braced myself for the possibility of their turning me down — just in case. Did I really want to play in the band? Or did I just want to play? Or was I wanting to put off going to Columbia? Assuming I got in. Assuming I joined the band.

I did know that there was a very good chance that I could be "too rock" for *Semi-Gloss*, just as *Semi-Gloss* could be "too mellow" for me. Did I really want to be in a band that didn't view distortion as a guitar's best friend? And media buzzes come and go. But did I want to forgo this chance? Did I want to be turned down again, a la *Fugazi*? Whatever happened, even if I didn't end up playing with *Semi-Gloss*, they could have my drumset. That bass drum-coffee table had to be avenged.

EIGHT

The phone rang. I opened my eyes and looked at my watch. Barely seven am.

Was it Pat calling to say the morning job had cancelled? But then early morning phone calls didn't usually wake him up; I'd rung him enough at such times to confirm a day's schedule to know.

"Hello? Hello? Hello?" I said before I picked up the receiver, to make sure I didn't sound like I'd just woken up when I actually answered the phone. "Hello?"

"Hi, Ivor. It's John."

John was John Heasly, a friend of mine since I was five years old. His family had lived down the street when we'd lived in Arlington, Virginia, as kids. Following high school, John went to Notre Dame as part of ROTC, but left the program to study industrial design — before ending up majoring in American Literature. A couple of years after that, John had attended Northwestern's journalism school and was now working at USA Today in Washington.

"John! Hey!" I said. "What's going on?"

John and I didn't call each other that often, preferring instead to send the occasional letter or postcard. So, he must have had news of some kind.

"Nothing's going on with me," John said. "Same old, same old. Work's work and D.C. is D.C. Look, I'm off to the paper and wanted to call before I get swamped. Two friends of friends of mine down here just heard they've gotten into Columbia and I was wondering if you'd heard anything yet?"

"No, I haven't!"

I hadn't meant to yell, but his question felt like a toothache, an impacted wisdom tooth coming in.

"It's driving me crazy," I continued. "I don't know what's going on! I mean, it's the fucking tenth of April, and they sent the letters out the first of the month!"

"Really?" John said. "Wow. I.... Huh. I don't know what to say. Maybe you should call them and see what they can tell you."

"Yeah, I don't know. Maybe."

But I'd feel like such an idiot. "Hi, can you tell me if I got in or not?" It's like when the band went to England for the first time, and we tried to get some shows while we were over there. I was calling venues out of the phone book. It was horrible. I had a spiel I'd say — something like, "Hi. We're a band from America, and I was wondering if we could play at your club." Of course it never worked.

"There has to be something going on," John said. "You'll hear from them, I'm sure."

I hung up the phone and lay back down in my bed, covering my head with my pillow.

Maybe the school sent the out-of-town letters first? I smiled at my rationalization. Maybe some postal worker just didn't want to deal with hundreds of thick acceptance letters and hundreds more thin rejection letters, and had simply thrown his huge, stuffed USPS duffel bag into the Hudson before continuing on his rounds? Maybe my fate was the waiting list once more. That's how it had been with Georgetown Day in high school, and with Vassar. Maybe I wasn't going to get in.

What if that was it? I didn't have a Plan C for my Plan B. I mean, I did only apply to Columbia. That was it. I'm in New York; it's in New York. It doesn't require the GRE; I live in fear of the GRE. Come on. I'm the window-cleaning, struggling musician who finally wised up! I'm the oddball applicant from out of left field! That was the plan! It made so much sense.

But I had no clue as to why a letter — thick or thin — had not yet headed a total of 113 blocks to me.

I lay in bed, in all the silence my apartment could muster. Still, I could hear the clock ticking on the wall and the ceiling fan whirring overhead. The room even rumbled a bit, courtesy of the subway.

Getting in — it was hitting me, meant more than I thought. It wasn't just because I really didn't know what else I would do. I really did need to go. Not to write award-winning magazine articles, not to win the Pulitzer Prize, not to fill up a year. I just wanted to go for myself, to see if I could do it, to see what I could learn. I wanted to look at writing in a new way. Not as a term-paper-writing English major, not as someone enamored of words — but to look at the world through journalism. To hear stories, to tell stories. To get stories. To get the truth. To get in.

I rolled the pillow off my face so I could get some fresh air, keeping my eyes closed against the sunlight that had begun to enter the room.

Of course, I also wanted to go to Columbia to please my parents, and to have my own damn Ivy degree. Now I was going to come off as the fool. The son who took a gamble but then didn't get in. The next trip to the dump was not going to be a fun one.

"So, son, you kinda blew it, huh?"

"Yeah, I guess so. I just figured I'd get in."

"Well, as we used to say in the Navy: You never assume anything but the watch."

"You're right." My dad almost always seems to be right.

I certainly had to plead guilty to putting all my eggs into one basket. Make that putting my only egg in one basket.

This was not how I wanted to start my day. I rolled out of bed and got on with it. I had to get to the Upper East Side for a different sort of window cleaning.

I hoped the rope tied around the cameraman's waist wouldn't be needed. Odds were, he wouldn't fall from the 31st floor, or even drop his video camera. He'd also been the first to admit that he'd never filmed anyone while standing on a ledge "half-in, half-out." His camera did seem much larger and unwieldy now than when we'd planned this shot a few minutes earlier in the apartment. At least the ledge was a bit wider than his shoes.

I actually felt worse for the interviewer. Though he was standing safely on the modern high-rise's living room floor, he held the end of the cameraman's rope in his hands. If the cameraman lost his balance, would this guy be able to save him? Or would he, too, drop to the street.

I thought of the viewers of NHK-TV in Japan, who apparently wanted to know about people in New York City with unusual jobs. Compared to these two guys, my role of answering questions while cleaning a window seemed exceedingly easy. And not just because I'd been in this situation a number of times before: standing on a ledge and looking into a camera, or beyond a camera. My squeegee had never felt so light and maneuverable. Moreover, the bright sun, clear sky, and — finally! — warm temperatures were doing their part to make the day enjoyable. Spring had arrived. The trade off, then: wonderful weather that brings a lot of exhausting work. But which also brings in a lot of money. And, today, an interview.

"SO. WAT MADE YU BEKUM A WINDO KLEENUR?"

"I was broke," I said, after taking a moment to make my way through his sentence. "I'd just moved to New York and I needed some work. I needed a way to support myself so I could play drums in my band."

"AHH, OK. SO AR YU FIXED NOW?"

I laughed just to be safe, as I mopped down the upper part of the window pane. "I'm certainly not broke," I said. "I mean, I do have some money now. I make enough to get by."

The me-in-need-of-mending imagery aside, his question did make me wonder if I was indeed "fixed now." On balance, I would have to say I wasn't. For here I was — the poster boy for downward mobility once more, or at least the oddball window cleaner again before the cameras — this time for Japan! Add NHK-TV alongside The New York Times, CNBC, Brazil's TV-Globo, National Geographic Television, NY1, Extra!, Fox TV, and The Learning Channel.

Ask about my bands, I thought to myself, even though I'm not even in one. Yes, I was "too rock" for *Semi-Gloss*. Even so, I had given them my drumset. Jordy had called me at 20/20 to give me the news that, after four practices, the band had decided to keep looking. I hadn't been that surprised. I had sped some songs up and played others too loudly. Still, I was disappointed.

Who likes getting turned down for anything? Where was that Goddamn thick letter from school? And when was this guy going to ask me about heights?

"WAT IS THE HI-EST YU HAVE EVA BIN TU KLEEN A WIN-DO?"

"The highest I've ever been is fifty-six stories," I said, pausing for a moment from squeegeeing. But then my interviewer made a squeegeeing motion with his hand, and I resumed my work. "There's an apartment building we do down on 38th Street called the Corinthian. And I go that high up there. It's pretty wild to be higher than the helicopters that fly by. Doing windows that high — it's not about the money or the view anymore. It's about pushing yourself. But that is about as far as I want to push myself."

Like the other times I've washed windows for the cameras, this pane was going to be incredibly clean by the session's end since I would have cleaned it at least six or seven times as the questions were asked (or re-asked) and the footage was shot (or re-shot). When the Times photographer had taken his photos of me hooked to the International Ladies Garment Workers Union building down on 7th Avenue and 28th Street, it was the first time I'd ever been out on a ledge for longer than it took me to clean the window. Instead of the typical five minutes or so, I was out there for close to forty-five. As the time passed, I became increasingly aware of how high up 25 stories was, how narrow the ledge was that I was standing on — half the length of my shoe — and how grateful I was to the hooks I was belted onto. I also knew that I would be that much more happy once I went back in.

"HAV YU EVA KUM CLOSE TO FALLING?"

I finished mopping the top of the window once more, then looked down at the street far below. The cameraman smiled.

"Let me think about this for a second," I said, kneeling down, picking up my mop and wetting the window's top section once more. I didn't want to move down to the middle section of the pane since I figured my crouching wouldn't look as graceful and could actually have been dangerous for the cameraman to mimic. "I guess I'd have to say that I haven't come so close to falling that I took it as a sign that I should stop window cleaning. But then, I do wonder if you ever do get such a sign."

I liked my answer on that one. These interviews could get pretty old, pretty quickly. While I did appreciate that the fascination with window cleaning didn't seem to end — it's not like I'd ever been interviewed for being an ice cream scooper or art-class model — I wasn't so keen on the questions I had to routinely answer. This guy had been nailing them all.

I could have turned down the interview, but — I admit it — I liked the attention. Wasn't this part of my fifteen minutes of fame that Andy Warhol promised us all so long ago? My being better known for squeegeeing than drumming was my problem to get over, along with knowing that irony is not so great when it happens to you.

"AR YU SKARED WHEN YU WORK?"

"It depends," I said, instinctively pausing upon hearing his words. I gripped the pane a bit harder. "It depends on the window I am doing, or the ledge that I'm on. I'm always a little afraid since that keeps me alert. When a window or a situation is really dangerous, it's like a car accident, in that time slows down. It takes forever to finish the window, it just seems to become wider."

"HOW LONG HAV YU BIN KLEENING WINDOS?"

"I've been a window washer for six years now. But with any luck, I'll be studying at Columbia University's journalism school in the fall. I am hoping to hear from them soon."

I didn't mention my lack of a letter. I didn't want to think about it. I didn't want to tell Japan about it.

"WAT AR SUM OF YUR FAVOREET BILDEENS IN NU YORK?"

"I've got those all over town," I said, beginning to squeegee the pane once more. I told him about the Dakota, about the Polo/Ralph Lauren Building (but didn't go into being locked out of the Rhinelander mansion). I told him about Tom Hanks' surgical booties and Sigourney Weaver's American Express card. I told him about dropping the air conditioner out the Park Avenue apartment, and my customer whose father was a window cleaner. I even mentioned mourning the bass drum-coffee table. I gave him "Ivor's Greatest Hits," as the pane got cleaner and cleaner.

"WAT IS THE BEST APARTMENT YU HAV EVA BIN IN?"

"I would say that the most spectacular place I've ever cleaned windows in is a five-story penthouse in the Beresford, over on Central Park West. See that building over there with the three towers? Well, this place has one of those towers as its top floor. It's just amazing."

I then ran him through the apartment's five floors and told him how we knew we wouldn't be asked back since the tower's windows weren't perfect.

"That kinda made it special, you know?" I said. "A real once-in-a-life-time experience. At one point, I took a break and looked out over the park from one of the terraces just to appreciate being there."

After saying all that, I figured they'd drop my answer since it wasn't that happy a story and also because they probably wished they could have filmed there instead of where we were. I tried to make up for this.

"You know," I said, "this apartment here is kinda neat in that they modeled the bedroom after a Piet Mondrian painting. It's got sections in blue and red and yellow and black. It's pretty wild."

I looked at the cameraman as I squeegeed away and hoped the interviewer didn't have another question.

"THANK YU VERI MUTCH," the interviewer said. "WE WILL NOW FEELM YUR FREND."

The cameraman handed his camera to the interviewer and then gingerly lowered himself down from the ledge. Once he was back on the floor, he tugged at his rope, took back his camera, and then walked with the interviewer across the room. It was Pat's turn. I got on with cleaning the window.

I wondered how NHK was going to use my interview. When CNBC aired a profile of me, it followed the piece with some analysis by a career counselor pushing his self-help book. He couldn't believe I wasn't working at a record label in case success with my band didn't pan out. "That window washer's a dreamer," the guy said, "he's got his head in the clouds. Literally!" Though I didn't agree with him — why would I want to work at a label? — being criticized on national television was a mixed blessing at best. At least it was only cable. Still, my mother had thought the author had made some worthwhile points. Lesson learned? Not to watch such shows with my parents. And, perhaps, to begin charging my mom and dad full price when I cleaned their windows, not the usual half-off.

When Brazil's TV-Globo had done a story on me — like CNBC, they had been inspired by the "About New York" column in the Times — I had trotted out some of my ancient Portuguese from when my family lived in Rio for two years, when Lars and I were ten. After answering exactly one question — What was the highest I'd ever been? — the interviewer asked me to please answer the questions in English.

I didn't have such awkward moments regarding the Times "About New York" column, which told the story of Ivor, the struggling musician who cleans windows by day to drum by night. The article ran in the local and national editions of the paper, as well as in The International Herald Tribune. It was great: I was everywhere.

That day, I enjoyed pointing myself out in the paper to my customers, friends called to say they had seen the piece, and people who got my number from the phone book rang to ask me to do their windows. One person called and wondered how she, too, could be written up in the paper.

The day after the piece ran, complete strangers stopped me on the street. That was fine, that was flattering. One man raised his arm, pointed me out, and said, "Hey, you're the window cleaner!" He then announced to everyone on the crowded Soho sidewalk: "Hey, people, this guy was in The New York Times! He's the window cleaner!" Some passers-by stopped, then quickly scurried on their way as the man continued shouting, "He's the window cleaner, he's the window cleaner!" I left as well when it became apparent that my fan was a bit deranged. Okay, so one awkward moment.

I rushed off to the next job — a gallery in the building that's now home to Rem Koolhaus's Prada store — whose doorman also recognized me. While out on the ledge, I heard a woman call out my name. I looked down to Broadway six stories below, but no one was looking up at me. Perplexed, I returned to my window cleaning, then heard my name called again. "Ivor! Up here! Across the street!"

I looked over my shoulder, and there in a building across the way, a woman and her staff were all at their office window. She clutched a copy of the Times and yelled, "We read about you in the paper! Good luck!" No more was said, but no more was needed. I smiled, waved, and went back to work. Very cool.

Apart from the same-old-story interviews, was the question of photo shoot locations. It was, of course, supposed to be perfect — meaning something high up and dangerous and preferably involving belt windows: the classic New York City window cleaner look, with the Empire State Building or the Chrysler Building in the background that would instantly convey quintessential Manhattan. My boss didn't have that many clients whose windows fit that bill. Though I used the office in the I.L.G.W.U.

building twice (once for the Times, once more for TV-Globo), shortly after the second shoot there, new tilt-in windows were installed, meaning no more belt hook derring-do.

Setting up a location means that I call a customer whose apartment or office has the appropriate windows, height, and view, and offer to do their windows for free, in exchange for a film crew taking over their place for a little while, usually a couple of hours.

Today's shoot was in an apartment in the East 80s. This was a long-time customer, but the first time we'd ever shot there. Pat had set it up, but I don't think Ted was too keen on us being in his place at first. He was going to be at the office while we filmed, and I think he feared for the well-being of his Mies van der Rhoe day-bed in the living room and his other Art Deco furnishings — if not his Piet Mondrian bedroom. Pat had played up the glamour of the shoot. Just imagine: your living room will be seen all over Japan! Even so, I think the NHK guys were a bit disappointed.

They couldn't complain about the altitude or the view of Midtown. Still, half-in, half-out windows just aren't as dramatic or as iconic as belt windows. To his credit, the cameraman was certainly making them seem as dangerous as possible — or at least putting himself in danger. I doubted the rope would've really save him, but I hadn't said anything. Why make him or the interviewer even more nervous?

Even though I have celebrity customers and celebrity buildings, it doesn't follow that I am a celebrity window cleaner. That is just as well. I mean, really, what would that mean? The window cleaner known for... window cleaning? "Ivor Hanson, the window cleaner of New York City!" That's not the case at all. For that to be true, I would have to dedicate my life to the profession, and be someone who could clean any window in town — including scaffolding jobs.

Most importantly, the window cleaner of New York would want to clean windows. Pat, my boss, has a fantasy that if he ever wins the lottery, he won't quit his job — at least not right away. For his last year of work, he'll have his limo take him to his window cleaning appointments. Perhaps that would be part of being the celebrity window cleaner of New York City. I'm just a window cleaner sporadically in the public eye.

I can see why TV shows, magazines, and newspapers have done stories on me. I'm not your "typical" window cleaner. To the show's producers, I guess, I'm articulate and look all right on camera. And I'm an Admiral's son,

Vassar grad, ex-struggling musician now heading (hopefully) towards grad school, heading towards being a writer.

In regards to any media interest, I want window cleaning to be a part of the story, not *the* story. Then again, I don't really like the ex-musician part, since it makes me feel that the most important part of my life was long ago, back then.

New York Lotto once cast me for a print advertising campaign that featured "working" people who had just "won the big one." There was a "plain Jane" secretary, an Asian fishmonger, a Jamaican taxi driver, and, me, the window cleaner. My photo shoot took place on the roof of the Lincoln Building on 42nd Street, since the photographer wanted the Chrysler Building looming over my shoulder. The only problem was that by standing on the cornerstone of the roof's retaining wall, I had no window to clean or window frame to hook onto.

But I was cool, I was professional, I was vain, I could handle it. I settled onto the three-foot by three-foot cornerstone, quietly awaiting my instructions, and quietly ignoring that to my right and behind me, I was inches from the edge and a drop of nearly sixty stories. The photographer's assistant approached me with a light meter at the end of his stretched out arm. He came closer and closer so he could get an accurate reading. It didn't matter that I was standing a good couple of feet above him on the retaining wall. It didn't matter that he was a good couple of feet from me. I snapped.

"Get the fuck away from me!"

The words just escaped from me, erupted from me, startling everyone on the crew, especially the kid, and myself. He'd apparently entered my space. Funnily enough, the photographer didn't want to take a picture of me washing a window. Instead, he wanted me to hold my squeegee-topped pole in one hand and my chamois cloth in the other and look like I had just won a million dollars — ignoring that I was actually only being paid $400. To achieve the look he wanted, I needed to flash a big smile, with my eyes closed and my head tilted slightly upward — ignoring that my closed eyes and tilted head could induce vertigo.

Instead of picturing myself falling, I concentrated on my photo soon appearing on telephone booths and the backs of buses. I thought about the leather pea coat I would buy with the money. I ignored the wind. The two hours I spent atop the Lincoln Building were among the longest in my life.

Though I got my jacket (and wasn't pushed over the side by the wind), my photo never ran. Apparently, some higher-ups at New York Lotto didn't like the look of the ads and nixed the second wave of the campaign, which I was to spearhead. At least I have my jacket.

National Geographic Television leant me a camera to film myself working for a few weeks for a feature on dangerous jobs. The deal was that I would hand over the film, and based on the amount of footage they used in the finished piece, I would be paid anywhere between $500 and $2,000 dollars. I filmed a lot, five tapes I think. It was mostly at a building in Dumbo that then housed New York State's Department of Labor, where, incidentally, I once came across the cleaning belt of a window cleaner who had died in a fall. It did make me stop and think — but only about the guy's bad luck. One Main has classic views of Lower Manhattan since it stands between the Brooklyn Bridge and the Manhattan Bridge. Just as important, the building's ninth-floor ledge extends out at least two feet. I might as well have been standing on a sidewalk up there, as Pat filmed me from inside. At a different location, I caught Pat on film accidentally dropping a very precious ceramic lamp when he moved it to clean a window. Appropriately, the next shot showed Pat apologizing to the camera. Even so, that customer never asked us back. Shortly after I handed over all my footage, however, a new executive producer took over the show and dropped the segment on dangerous jobs. I got $100 for returning the camera.

After I finished cleaning the window I'd been on, I moved to the next window in the living room, the one by the Mies day-bed. While I cleaned that one, I got the word to stay in place so that the camera crew could go down to the street and get footage of Pat and me from the sidewalk, thirty-two stories below. I fought the temptation to wave.

After thanking the NHK guys and saying goodbye to them once Pat and I had got back down to the street, the two of us split up to do separate jobs. He headed over to First Avenue to do some tilt-ins, and I walked down Second Avenue to 86th Street, where I'd catch the crosstown bus so I could get over to the C train, which I'd take downtown to Tribeca.

Fortunately, the crosstown bus to the West Side pulled up just as I arrived, a rare instance when our schedules coincided. I settled into a seat in the back, on one of the benches that has its back to the window, and faces sideways, the kind that fold up for wheelchair-bound riders. Such seats give me more room for my bucket, which I placed at my feet. I closed my eyes for a moment's rest and pictured the NHK interviewer holding the rope that was wrapped around the cameraman's waist. If only the segment showed a shot of that!

I opened my eyes after a block's travel, as the bus's stop-and-go made it hard to keep my eyes closed. Too many jarring interruptions for me to really relax. Sitting across from me was a young kid, probably around five or so, eyeing my bucket. He had blonde hair and blue eyes, wore khakis and a Polo shirt. His mother, a true Upper East Side type wearing smug sunglasses and pearls, took no notice of her son. I could see from his smile and his furrowed brow that he found my tools interesting.

"You want to know what they do?" I asked.

"Sure," the kid said, his voice a little rougher and deeper than I expected. Looking up at me, he didn't seem on the spot, like I had caught him looking at my things, just appreciative that I'd noticed his interest.

"Okay then," I said, leaning forward over my bucket to get at its contents. "This is my mop," I said, picking up the bigger of the two that I carry with me. Over the years, I learned from customers' kids that they like looking at my bigger tools, but prefer handling the smaller ones. "I use it to wet down the windows that I clean. It holds onto the water so I can get a lot of glass wet with it."

The kid smiled and nodded his head. I moved on, but not before noticing that the adult riders in the back of the bus were also taking in my impromptu lesson. I, however, stayed focused on the kid.

"And this is my squeegee," I said, picking up my 22-inch blade. I hoped the copper gleamed, but I had my doubts. "This is what I clean the windows with," I said as I made a left-to-right motion. "This is what I take the water off the glass with."

Another smile. Another nod.

"Actually," I said, putting down the "22" and picking up my other three squeegees, "as you can see, I have these other squeegees, each one a different size. That's because window panes also come in different sizes."

Another smile. Another nod.

I put the squeegees back down, then fished out my chamois.

"And then," I said, "there's my chamois cloth. It lets me get rid of streaks and also lets me get rid of little drops of water that sometimes stay after I've cleaned the glass." I pointed to black streaks and blotches on the beige cloth I had in my hand. "As you can see, it gets pretty dirty."

The kid's smile and nodding were quite vigorous.

"You like that one, don't you?"

The kid blushed and then smiled once more.

"Did you know," I said, "that Curious George cleaned windows at one point?"

"Really?" the kid said. "Cool."

"Yeah," I said, "he had a squeegee and mop and a bucket, too."

"Okay," I continued, "last but not least. This is my pole." Instead of letting it lean against my shoulder as I had been, I now grasped the midpoint of my four-foot-long brass pole with the black rubber handle. "By putting my mop or squeegee on it, and by extending this pole to make it longer, I can clean windows that I can't reach with my hands."

And then the kid spoke. "Sounds fun," he said. "Call my mom. Make a playdate."

Those of us in the back of the bus laughed because we couldn't stop ourselves.

The kid laughed, too, glad he had made us laugh, even if he didn't quite know why.

I smiled as I looked at his mom. Even though she didn't remove her sunglasses, I could feel her disdain. Her silence, her lack of laughter, her lack of a smile, let me know that there would be no "playdate" with her son. In other words, she wasn't about to ask for my number so I could come over and clean her windows.

Perhaps she had a long-time window cleaner. Perhaps she didn't want her son to be so interested in mops and squeegees and chamois. Maybe she feared that I would somehow taint him. He was the one who had relished my dirty chamois. Besides, if he really wanted to be a window cleaner, I would do my best to talk him out of it. I'd done it before with the kids of other customers, their ages ranging from five, to fifteen, to recent college grads.

Her silence brought the bus's laughter to an end. I looked back down at my bucket. The other passengers looked away. Her son looked up at his mom, but then he, too, looked away. I think he knew I wouldn't be coming over either. A few moments later, the bus made its stop at Fifth Avenue, and the two of them got off.

I looked away from the bus's back door and looked out the window at

Central Park. Maybe the mom was just in a bad mood, or at least preoccupied. I liked to think that on another day, she would have laughed right along with the rest of us at her son's remark. I had my doubts, but it remained a possibility.

The headphones of the bus rider who'd sat down where the kid and his mom had just been were pounding out a hard-to-ignore dance beat. Almost against my will, I found myself tapping my foot. With *Semi-Gloss* turning me down, it had been hitting me yet again that for a while now, when I'd gotten home and put down my bucket, I didn't really have much else going on. I had things to do. I read, I saw movies, I listened to music. But I didn't have a band to play in. I didn't have an application essay to work on. I didn't have anything else that was me.

I got off the bus at Central Park West and then descended to the subway platform and caught the downtown C train to Chambers Street.

Another loft. Not that I was surprised. This was Tribeca and the customer did live on Chambers Street. The odds were pretty good that a large open living space was what I would find. I wasn't expecting a townhouse, in other words. But I wasn't so sure what the windows would be. Though the building was old, I'd forgotten to check the window frames from the street.

As I stood on the first of six windowsills that lined the front of the apartment, I silently rejoiced that these oversized windows still had the original panes and frames, still had the original hooks for me to latch onto. Excellent. While I had appreciated the previous job's sleek, new, and relatively safe switchers, I was now pleased that I didn't have to deal with being half-in, half-out. Nor did I have to deal with a camera crew. I could tend to my favorite kind of windows — old, tall "belts," with wide ledges to boot! — without answering distracting questions. What with this being a new customer, I could be the one asking the questions once more.

So far, I hadn't learned that much about the client. Part of this was due to the apartment's size. It was so big. This meant that as I cleaned the windows and she did the dishes, instead of being just across the room, she may as well have been across town. There was also the client herself. Her pensive demeanor made talking to her in a voice loud enough to be heard feel somehow inappropriate; it felt like yelling. I would be interrupting her thoughts. I took my cue from the quiet loft itself — there was no stereo, no radio on — and worked away without saying a word.

I was also hesitant to speak up because English was not her first language. She spoke English very well, but her accent was there, and she didn't try to hide its up-and-down, sort of stop-and-go Northern European lilt. Somehow this made her seem delicate.

I looked away from my window once I'd finished squeegeeing it. She stood at the sink in silence. She kept to herself. It was as if I wasn't there. I didn't take this as rudeness, as she had been perfectly polite, if not gracious, when she'd let me in. She seemed the kind of person who — were some sort of window mishap to occur — would respond by asking, "What happened?" and not, "What did you do?"

She had timeless features, undeniably Nordic; blue eyes that bordered on being grey, sharp cheekbones, and blondish hair that may have been getting a little help staying that way. Perhaps she had looked this way all her life. Older looking when she was young. Young for her age when she was older.

Unlike a lot of lofts in New York City, or, at least a good deal of the lofts that Pat and I cleaned, an artist actually lived in this one. Two easels stood near each other along the wall running perpendicular to the six windows that looked over Chambers Street. One had a canvas covered with dark brown, green, and orange splotches, while the second easel's canvas remained untouched by paint. A stack of canvases leaned against the wall, next to at least a dozen cans of paint. Were they "his" and "her" easels? I had noticed a large pair of work boots by the door, so I figured she had a husband or a boyfriend. Along with the easels, small, intricate metal sculptures on stands had been placed around the room, and large abstract paintings hung on the walls of exposed brick.

While I was out on the ledge doing the first window's exteriors, I looked in and saw that once she'd finished with the plates and silverware, she went about the loft cleaning up. She made the stack of Art In America magazines on the coffee table neat once more. She dusted off the light-brown leather couch and its matching chairs that didn't just look lived-in, but nearly beaten-in, adding to the place's artistic shabbiness. As she made her way amongst the maze of creativity, she'd pause at the blank canvas, consider it, and then move on. I wondered what it would become.

Once I came back into the apartment, but before I began to work on the second window, I decided to speak as she swept the kitchen floor.

"Have you lived in the States a long time?" I said.

I cringed when I saw that my words had startled her. At least she hadn't dropped the broom.

"A little while," she said, going back to her chore. "Actually, I have been here longer than I think, some years now already. But New York is like that. It speeds up time."

I stood on the second sill and began wetting down the window with my mop.

"Where were you before you were here?"

"I grew up in Finland," she said as she resumed her sweeping. "I lived in a small tiny town north of the Arctic Circle. My family raised reindeer. That's what we did. Growing up, I'd always painted for the fun of it. Eventually, I realized I was pretty good at it and started taking it seriously. I started studying it in school. Along the way, I got married to a nice young man from my town, someone I had known since I was a child. We were such good friends. We had two kids. We all had so much fun. But then I had to go."

I thought for a moment. I pictured her facing her husband one day when he had come home for the night from the reindeer farm. I imagined that they kept their herd in their backyard, and that they could be heard bleating (or whatever sound it is that they make) in the background. He'd just finished shearing them. Or perhaps he'd just delivered a newborn.

Anyway, she'd been working on a painting for some weeks and knew that once she finished it, she'd have to talk to him, she'd have to tell him. I imagined her telling him that she had to leave. That this little town north of the Arctic Circle wasn't for her any more. That she needed to move to the city and pursue her art. That she needed to be happy. That she needed to leave. That she felt horrible about leaving her children behind, but that motherhood wasn't for her after all. But they would be okay. She knew that they would be better if she wasn't their mom. She and her husband had married far too young, had had a good time, but now, well, now things were different. She had outgrown her life and needed to move on.

"So," I began, wondering how I would ask my question. I decided to go with the words she had given me. "Why did you have to leave?"

She said quietly but firmly, "They died in a car accident."

I was about to squeegee the window, but now I stopped and turned to face her. She had finished sweeping and was leaning against a kitchen counter, looking not at me but through me, out beyond the window.

"I'm so sorry," I said.

"Thank you," she said, focusing her eyes on me. "Thank you very much. It was quite hard and so, so sad. Eventually I left and went to study art in this country at Yale, and it was there that I met my second husband, and that is how I am now in New York."

"Wow," I said, not entirely convinced that saying "Wow" was the right thing to say. "I am very happy for you."

I returned to facing the window, squeegeeing it clean. As I began to chamois away the streaks, I heard her voice from across the room as she swept once more.

"You know, here I am, so lucky in my life. Most people don't find one true love ever, and I did. Then, after I lost that love, I was lucky enough to find a second person to love that way. Who would think that could happen? And he is an artist, too. He made the statues you see here. I am so lucky."

"Yes," I said as I raised the window and headed out onto the ledge. "Yes, you really are. That's great."

"But New York," she said, "New York can be so hard, you know? When it snows here, I wish it would be serious. I want real snow. And it can be so loud. They pick up trash here sometimes at five in the morning, or in the middle of the night. I don't understand. It is not quiet here, like my home. It is not cold here, like my home. But what am I talking about?"

I slowly pulled down the window so that I could do its outside panes.

"You certainly know more about full-blown winters than I do," I said.

When I came back in from the ledge, silence had returned to the apartment. Since she did not resume our conversation, I did not either. Instead, we each resumed our respective wordless chores. When I washed the remaining four windows, the only sounds came from my squeegee. I wondered if perhaps her past was weighing on her mind. It certainly was weighing on mine — what tragedy and change had done to her.

Once I had stepped in from the last ledge in front, I realized that I did need to break the silence.

"Ma'am," I asked, "do you want the windows in the back cleaned?"

"Yes, I would," she said as she stood in front of the blank easel. "They're quite dirty, too."

I walked across to the loft's far side, to a window that was undeniably in need of a washing and would be easy to do. Though it looked out on a back courtyard, cleaning it would let in a bit more light.

To the right of this window was a small room which had its own window, but one almost hard to spot since the ancient rusted shutters outside it had been pulled closed. I could make out a small couch against the wall, alongside a stack of storage boxes.

"Would you like this one done as well?" I asked.

"No, thank you. I never have that one cleaned," she said from the easel. "That is the one room I keep dark, as dark as I can. It is where, when I need to go back, I go to. There is no light and it is quiet and that is what I need sometimes."

I closed the door to the room.

"Whatever you want," I said solemnly.

I cleaned the one window. While out on the ledge, I looked at the darkened room's shutter and hoped for her sake that it would remain on the building for a long while.

When I finished the window, I rinsed out my mops and chamois in the kitchen sink and gathered my tools together. She wrote me out a check for the windows, and I bid her goodbye.

I wondered what my next visit would be like. Would she tell me more about her past life, or her current one for that matter? Or, because I now knew a bit about her, would it be a silent window cleaning? I certainly didn't know, and I was fine with that. I had something to look forward to, another little mystery to savor. Did this mean that investigative journalism was not for me?

The next job had been sad. It turned out the customer — another new one — lived in the same Greenwich Village apartment building as the nurse with cancer. Unlike the nurse, she had a front apartment so that the sun shone right into her living room. When I'd asked if she knew how her downstairs neighbor was doing, I'd learned that the nurse had died two weeks earlier. On my way home, I wondered if the nurse had "pure light" when she'd passed away. I doubted it. Had Ella Fitzgerald been playing when she passed away? I hoped so.

The phone rang and I opened my eyes. I sat up in bed and stumbled across the floor on my knees, to the phone on my desk. I glanced up at the clock on the wall. 9:30? I'd been asleep for three hours?

"Hello? Hello? Hello?" I said as I reached for the phone.

Was it John calling to say a third friend of a friend had just gotten in? Maybe it was Lars calling from work. We hadn't talked in a couple of days.

"Hello?"

"Ivor! Ivor! It's Ursula!"

Ursula was my sister who had moved to Maine after living in my place the previous year. Her calls weren't as rare as John's, but she had a penchant for not always calling me back when I called her. And here she was calling me.

"Hey Urgie," I said. "What's going on? You sound exci—"

"Ivor, I got your Columbia letter!"

"What?"

"I got your Columbia letter! I got it! The mail forwarded it to me up here."

"Is it thick or thin?" I asked, demanded. "Thick or thin?"

NINE

Though I was running late, I lucked out — when I finally arrived, the maid at the Upper East Side apartment was engrossed with her afternoon soup. This maid was pretty cool. She did get mad if you weren't on time, but since Pat was the more likely one to be tardy, I usually only had to hear her raised voice about him and not me. If she ever was annoyed with me, I'd do my best to steer the conversation toward Trinidad, where she was from, and where she and her family were building a house.

As I filled my bucket from the pantry's old, deep basin, her voice called out from the TV room, just off the dining room.

"Would you please clean Matt's room first? He'll be home from school soon."

"Yeah, sure," I said. Since I could hear the commercial break ending, I knew better than to continue our conversation. Instead, I waited in silence for the water to reach the bucket's halfway point and then made my way to the son's room.

Though I knew it didn't make a huge difference in the end, I always liked doing this apartment from front to back. Part of this was simple greed. Since the living room, the study, and the master bedroom all had two windows each, it made sense financially for me to claim these windows for myself if Pat were to meet up with me here. As you know, the more windows I clean, the more money I make. As it was, the son's room had two windows itself plus a bathroom window, as did the daughter's room, who had gone off to college (to Vassar of all places; small world). The dining room, the TV room, and the kitchen each had three windows. It didn't really matter, especially since today Pat had his own jobs to deal with, and I wouldn't have to share these windows.

Starting with the living room windows made the apartment go faster. It seemed that the apartment flowed in that direction, from front to back. Starting in the son's room placed me downstream.

As ever, the kid's room seemed bathed in blue. The wall-to-wall shag carpeting was a dark, dark navy blue, while his sheets and pillows were in a slightly lighter shade, as were his walls. I'd wondered if it had been this color his whole life. Not that I could recall his sister's room having been pink, but this was certainly an instance of it's-a-boy blue. And though I thought the carpeting soaked up most any light that shone through the room's windows, I had certainly appreciated its deep, stain-hiding color when I'd accidentally spilled some dirty water all over it a couple of years earlier.

Unlike my previous visits, however, in addition to blueness, something else now helped define the room. Just across from the bed stood a large, dark-grey electronic drumset. Unlike a real drumset — a drumset made of wood that needs to be deep and large and round to make noise — this kit's "drums," its bass drum, snare drum, tom-toms, floor-tom, and, yes, even its electronic cymbals, didn't need to be. Instead, they all looked more like a collection of hexagonal drum heads (even the cymbals) mounted together and then all plugged into a mixing console, along with a speaker. Instead of a drumset, it seemed more like an insect. At least the drumsticks resting on the snare were wood.

As I cleaned the room's interior panes, I stared at the drums in the window's reflections. I hadn't been this close to a set since *Semi-Gloss*. I felt both attracted to and estranged from the kit. What was it doing here? Perhaps it was just as well to get this room over with. I now only had the outside to do.

Being out on the fire escape, cleaning the window's exterior panes meant I was outside looking in and had an even better view of the drums — and of Matt walking into his room. We waved at each other as I squeegeed and he put his book bag down on the floor and then picked up the phone on his bedside stand. At least it wasn't a floor-tom.

While the windows along the back of the building didn't offer much of a view — they looked out on a school building just across the way — these windows did offer the kids inside the school looking out, a view of window cleaners on a ledge. Even though the classrooms sounded quiet, I looked around as discretely as I could to see if anyone was watching me, but the place looked empty. If there was a summer session, it hadn't kicked in yet. Or perhaps the kids were out on a field trip somewhere.

When school was in session, however, I would invariably notice the latest batch of kindergarteners spying on me from their classroom window; their surveillance techniques usually involved a lot of giggles, "Shhhhs," and even hand waving. Usually they'd duck when I first waved to them and then they'd laugh to themselves for having escaped my view. They'd eventually peek out the window again, and I would wave once more. They would wave back and shyly call out "Hi." As I popped out from window to window along the apartment's back wall, the kids would begin to ask questions like, "Are you scared?" or yell out "Wow!" and "Cool!" as I mopped and squeegeed away. This lasted until the teacher noticed what was going on and presumably feared that her students would try this at home or in the classroom itself — despite the child-guards. No such contact today. I worked in silence and solitude.

Once I'd finished leaning over the fire escape to reach Matt's small bathroom window, I raised one of the bedroom windows and let myself back in just as he was hanging up the phone.

"How's it going?" I said as I stood over my bucket and wrung out my chamois. "I haven't seen you in a while."

"I'm doing all right," Matt said as he sat on his bed. He was on the verge of becoming tall, his adolescent frame seemingly prepared to shoot upwards towards adulthood. But his face — with its brown eyes and freckles, framed by his short brown hair — wasn't quite ready to join in. He still seemed pretty young.

"What grade are you in now?" I asked. "Well, wait, that's not right, it's the summer. What grade did you just finish?"

"I'm gonna be in tenth this fall," he said quietly. "It should be okay."

"So what are you up to this summer?" I asked as I picked up my bucket and began to walk back to the living room and get back on track, in order, and at the top of the stream.

"I'm going off to camp pretty soon, which will be great," he said. "But wait! Didn't you used to be in bands?"

I stopped at the edge of his room.

"Yeah, I was," I said, turning around to face him. "But that was a long time ago."

"But you play the drums, right?" Matt asked. "I'm pretty sure you told me that once." I smiled and nodded my head. Good memory, kid.

"Yes, that's true," I said. "And by the look of it, I'd say you're playing the drums now yourself."

Matt blushed, seeming to see the drumset in his room for the first time.

"I've got this set," he said. "But, really, I like the guitar a lot more."

I then saw the guitar case at the foot of his bed for the first time.

"Hey," he said. "You wanna jam?"

I put down my bucket.

"Yeah, sure," I said. "Why not."

A part of me did want to play, if only to make up for my *Semi-Gloss* audition. A part of me was curious about the kit before me. I'd never played on an all-out electronic set before.

As Matt took his guitar out, I settled onto the drummer's stool, or drummer's throne as it is also known. My right foot instinctively tapped at the bass drum pedal, just as my left foot tried out the hi-hat pedal. So far, so good, even if my feet weren't making the sounds they were used to. Instead of, respectively, the drum's satisfying thud and the cymbal's warm but sharp "Sshhst," I heard a hard, harsh clacking sound. My feet might as well have been hitting a kitchen counter.

I picked up the drumsticks. They felt cold and smooth and slightly foreign. My fingers wrapped themselves around the Regal Tip 2B's — the traditional size for a beginner — comfortably enough, and I could feel them remembering.

Since I was using what is called a "match grip," my index fingers and my thumbs were pressed against their respective sticks, while my remaining fingers merely grazed them. My hands were trying to find just the right balance between tight and loose, the perfect grip in which my hands and the sticks disappear into the rhythm so that I am only aware of the song I am playing, not what I am holding, not what I'm hitting. I tapped at the faux snare drum before me and heard the kitchen counters once again.

"It'll sound better if you turn it on," Matt said.

"Oh right," I said. "Of course."

Turn on the set. How funny. I'd turned on Michael's drum machine for years, but never a drumset. I pushed a button on the mixing board and a red light came on along with the noises that my feet were producing: processed, sterile sounds. But how else were they going to be? At least I was actually playing, actually sitting at a kit.

"So what do you wanna do?" I asked once I saw that Matt had plugged in his guitar and turned on his amp.

"I don't know," Matt said, leaning against his bed. "Just play around."

"That's cool," I said. "Do you have a song you really like playing, like by one of your favorite bands or something you wrote yourself?"

"Yeah, sure," Matt said. "Whatever."

"Let's play that." I said. "If you want. Whatever you want."

"Okay," Matt said. "But I gotta tune first."

While Matt looked down at the guitar tuner he'd plugged into his guitar, I looked over at him and smiled. This had the potential to be pretty cool, a chance to show both of us a magical aspect of music. How, even though I was over twice his age, this difference wouldn't matter once we began to play, once we began to rock. It wouldn't be me and him, it wouldn't even be us, it would just be the music we were playing.

Matt's guitar now sounded tuned and my hands felt warmed up.

"You ready?" I asked.

"Yeah, sure," he said.

"Why don't you just start playing," I said, "and then I'll come in."

I could tell we were now both hesitant about our jamming. I could feel the worse-case scenario floating over us, or at least over me: a "would-be" and a "has-been" making foolish rock noise in a kid's room on the Upper East Side. But I didn't want to say anything like, "Don't worry, it'll be fine," since that would kill our "jam" for sure.

"All right," Matt said. "Here goes."

He stepped away from his bed and started to lightly strum his guitar. Tentative mid tempo sounds came out — basic, polite chords. I waited through a couple of beats to see where he was going with it, listening to whether he was going to speed up or slow down, feeling out what kind of beat his song wanted. But Matt stayed steady and so I joined in, playing a typical rock 'n' roll beat: Boom-bap! Boom-boom-bap! Boom-bap! Boom-boom-bap!

I was pleased as I played that Matt hadn't looked startled when I'd started to play. Hopefully that meant that he'd played with someone before. I did see, despite his looking down at the guitar to make sure that the fingers on his left hand were going to the right places on the fret board, his smile. Hopefully that meant that he was enjoying himself. I closed my eyes.

The song sounded a bit like a slowed down version of "Johnny B. Goode," traditional rock 'n' roll fare that you'd expect a beginner like Matt to play. The song bore on, essentially rounding itself through three slightly different parts, notes that weren't that far from each other on the fret board.

I kept the Boom-bap! Boom-boom-bap! coming, but when I sensed that the time had come for the next chord change, I'd hit a cymbal as we went into it, or even did a drum fill. I kept my eyes closed the whole time, since I felt that keeping them open would somehow put more pressure on Matt.

I also knew that I didn't want to see myself playing. It wasn't just a matter of witnessing my playing with, well, this kid — but playing at all. In the midst of the music, I suddenly felt like I had gone against my word, broken a promise somehow. I had decided to stop playing, I had given away my drums, but here I was playing anyway. And liking it okay.

Still, I kept my eyes closed so that this scene could remain unseen and, therefore, unreal, or at least a bit less real. Just sound, not vision. Opening my eyes would have put more pressure on myself.

Though I didn't want to, I started to picture myself on some of the stages I'd played over the years. D.C. Space and the old 9:30 Club down in D.C., various dives in London like the Power-haus and the Mean Fiddler, and places like C.B.G.B.'s and the Mercury Lounge in New York. Spotlights cutting through cigarette smoke, stale beer mingling with applause, the backs of Michael and Bert as they played and sang before me.

I opened my left eye a skosh to see what Matt was doing and noticed that he was looking at me a bit baffled and miffed, apparently wondering why my eyes were closed, and wanting to end the song. I nodded my head and at the end of a few more Boom-boom-baps! hit the crash cymbal, and the song was over.

"That was a bit longer than I usually play it," Matt said.

"Sorry about that," I said. "Just sorta got carried away back there. But that was good."

"It was all right," Matt said. "I liked your rolls."

"Thanks," I said. "So are you in a band?"

"Just a sec," Matt said, "I gotta tune."

I smiled. "Ivor, the chatty drummer" had returned. Hadn't heard someone say that to me in a while. Actually, Jordy had with *Semi-Gloss*.

"No, not yet." Matt said after a minute or so of fiddling with his tuner. "But some friends at school and I are thinking about getting something together."

"That's cool. You should try it. You wanna play something else?"

"Yeah, sure," Matt said. "I've got this other song we can do."

Matt started to play again, and this time his strumming was more forceful, even aggressive. Not that he was hitting power chords, or getting feedback or distortion, but just that his guitar sounded fuller. From the way he was pinwheeling his arms, it was apparent he liked Pete Townsend. But since it was the same speed as the last one, I played the Boom-boom-baps! once more. And because it seemed appropriate, and because he had complimented me on my fills, I did a bit of a Keith Moon impersonation and played like I don't really like to, treating the drums like a lead instrument, treating the song like an excuse for an ongoing solo. I also kept my eyes open, and saw Matt playing with his eyes closed and flashing a toothy smile.

We hadn't been playing the song for too long when it began to feel like we had. Part of this I blamed on the song, since this one meandered, as well — with three chords quite different from the first song, but all related to each other nonetheless, and all kinda mundane. My wrists were also getting sore. Well, that was quick. I waited for Matt's signal to end the song and, for his benefit, brought the thing to a close with an over-the-top, clichéd assault on the tom-toms and cymbals.

"Wow, that was cool!" Matt said. "I mean, really cool."

"Thanks," I said. "Thanks a lot."

I had to be careful now.

"So," I said as casual as possible, "are you taking any guitar lessons?

"Oh, yeah," he said, now quiet and looking back down at his guitar. "They're okay. But they're not like this."

"I know what you mean," I said. "Drumming by yourself isn't as fun as this either. But it's cool that you're taking them since they'll just make your playing in a band that much more fun."

"Yeah, I guess," Matt said, his head still downwards. I felt like I was grilling him.

"I don't wanna sound like your mom or dad," I said. "But taking lessons and practicing is really gonna help you." I stopped myself from saying "get better." Instead I said, "But you know that."

"Yeah, I know."

"Your lessons will be fun, too, eventually. Really."

"I sure hope so," he said, looking back up at me. "Do you want to play another?"

"Sure."

This time Matt leaned over and turned up his amp and began his best *Clash* imitation, striking his guitar so that jagged and harsh chords came out. It was falling short, but it was better than the other songs. He was only a kid starting out.

I kicked in with some punky half-beats, and Matt responded to the Boom-bap! Boom-bap! Boom-bap! Boom-bap! by attacking his guitar and twirling around. I smiled. When Matt and I went into the chorus, I hit the table-top-like "cymbal" for his benefit and, as if on cue, he leapt into the air. We played on. I wasn't going to tell him about record contracts, I wasn't going to say a word about record label machinations, A&R clowns, or the need for a good lawyer. As for his band, I wasn't going to talk about those fabled "personal and musical" differences that do in so many groups. I wasn't going to say a word about the Voice listings, I was going to keep quiet about lugging equipment to shows.

Of course, as a guitarist, he didn't have it as bad as drummers do, but it still had to be a drag. Before hailing a cab, I would put my drums to the side so that the cabbie wouldn't know what he was getting into: filling his trunk and his front and back seats with the cases for my bass drum, snare, toms, cymbals, and stands. I hoped my large tip would make amends. Usually though, I just tried to get out of this entire hassle by contacting a drummer from one of the other bands that were also playing at the club that night. By offering him $20 to use his bass drum and toms, I could show up with my snare drum, bass drum pedal, and cymbals. They usually agreed — my money probably rivaled the guy's share of his band's take by the end of the night. Or at least it was a few beers.

I also wasn't going to mention seeing *Fugazi* a couple of weeks earlier. They'd come to town, and I'd surprised myself by deciding to go to the show. I figured the time had come to face down my feelings about that band, and then see what happened. I guess I was hoping for, I don't know, a cleansing? A moment of letting go, of being done with it once and for all. Watching the band perform had been all right. They were really good, as usual: as impressively tight and aggressive as they were heartfelt and honest. I found myself once more wanting their tunes to be more melodic and catchy. But that quibble certainly didn't stand in the way of my still wishing that I was up there playing with them. Even so, I was glad they didn't play "Waiting Room."

Afterwards, I'd gone backstage, and it might as well have been a D.C. reunion back there. People from Washington's punk scene who had moved to New York and had come to the show were milling around, as were a number of folks who had come up from D.C. with the band. At one point, I talked briefly to Ian and that had gone all right, too. But then, I'd basically just said "Hi." Mostly I just looked around the back room and saw the people hanging out in chairs and couches, saw the drinks and food laid out, saw the well-wishers talking to the guys in the band. Saw the life that I thought I was going to have. When I left, I knew that if anything, I hadn't faced down my feelings. They'd continued to face down me.

I looked up from my drums — Matt's drums — since it felt like the song's end had arrived, and when Matt and I made eye contact, I knew that this was so. Four beats later, silence filled the room. He looked flushed.

"Man, that was great," Matt said. "Wow."

"Yeah, that was good," I said. It was almost true.

Matt leaned against the wall and looked over at me.

"Why'd you stop being in a band?"

I rested the drumsticks on my thighs and wondered what to say.

"I guess I'd just done it long enough."

"But you were making records and playing shows right?"

"Well, yeah, sure, that's right," I said. "Well, actually, I had made records and had been playing shows, but...."

"But what?"

Ever been screwed over by a record label? I wanted to ask. Ever had a band fall apart that you didn't want to? Ever felt like you weren't getting anywhere? But I kept those words at bay.

"It was just time to try something else," I said instead. "Just time to do something else."

"That's too bad," Matt said.

"Yeah, I guess you're right," I said. "What else do you want to play?"

Matt thought for a moment, as he looked back down at his guitar.

"Can we play that first song again?" he said. "I think I wanna change it some. I've got an idea for the chorus."

"Yeah, sure," I said. "That sounds good."

My pattern of Boom-boom-bap! Boom-boom-bap! returned, and this time Matt was a bit better. He didn't hold back like the first time, though I attributed that to his now being warmed up. More importantly, the new part did work better. It descended a notch in a kinda catchy way, giving the song a new feel, making it feel like, well, a song.

I was glad that he wanted to play some more since I knew that if I had kept talking, I could have come close to spilling out the stuff I didn't want to. Who knew if this kid was going to continue with his guitar lessons, or start that band with his classmates, or just mess around with the guitar, or even get better if he did stick with his lessons. I knew from his asking me to jam, I knew from seeing his smile when he played, and his twirl and leap, that he had some kind of dream about music. Neither of us had said the word "rock star," but then I don't think either of us had to. Regardless, I wasn't going to say anything to threaten or dampen his dream if I could help it. Even if it meant four songs of relatively painless torture for me. Actually, I was having an okay time as long as I concentrated on the novelty of the two of us playing together, the oddness of this electronic drumset, and keeping a beat.

Keeping a beat, playing well, even if it was for this just-starting-out kid. I wasn't trying to be a martyr. The point wasn't being a nice guy or an obliging window cleaner. Fixating on keeping the beat just made things easier at that moment. Wandering off from the Boom-boom-bap! Boom-boom-bap! Boom-boom-bap! Boom-boom-bap! simply wasn't worth it.

Man, was I glad to be back out on the ledge, and not just as an escape from the drums. Really, I was glad to be out on this ledge. I considered this customer's place the epitome of why I clean windows. Here I was, strapped to the window frame of an elegant and large apartment in a pre-war building, one just off Fifth Avenue, no less. I looked through the living room window and admired the classic understatement in its moulding, and how the walls welcomed both Western paintings and Asian prints. The room's generous size (like most all of the apartment's rooms), could easily have swallowed up my 13th Street studio a couple of times over. As it was, it easily held a couch and some chairs, as well as a grand piano and a nearly incongruous set of bongos. The apartment felt quite well-to-do throughout, but also comfortable; a showcase, for sure, but also one that felt lived in; upscale, but not pretentious; obviously refined, while also pleasant and unintimidating. Like the people who lived there, but who were usually not home when we did the windows — another bonus.

Moreover, this apartment had held on to its original windows, belt-hook windows made of sturdy wood and old glass; a few of the panes boasted those in-the-grain ripples I really do treasure. Further, despite their age, these windows opened and closed easily. They behaved themselves. Nor were the windows cut up into smaller panes, but were simple, slightly oversized one-over-ones. The ledges were in fine shape, clean and uncracked, the hooks were strong and secure. Plus, the windows never really were that dirty in the first place since these customers usually called Pat for a cleaning every couple of months.

Finally there was the view, truly one of my all-time favorites.

Once I had pulled myself up and out onto the ledge of the north-facing window of the mother's corner-room study and secured myself to the frame's hooks, I leaned back and looked out over East 90th Street, savoring a view only possible while leaning away from the building.

Look Ma! No hands!

I set the work at hand aside. My squeegee dangled in its holster; my chamois cloth remained in its loop at my waist. My mop sat seemingly abandoned on the ledge, ignored by my shoes just inches away.

Directly next door, the gothic Church of the Holy Rest offered up a delicate and intricate rose petal window of stained glass. Caddy-corner across the street, I looked down on the stately Cooper-Hewitt Building, the former mansion that now housed the National Design Museum. Its immaculate gardens provided a gentle (if not genteel) patch of greenery. Directly across the street, meaning directly behind me, a row of elegant turn-of-the-century townhouses filled the block. This could have been the view a hundred years ago.

Still looking to my right, I took in Central Park's trees and the men and women running alongside the glistening reservoir. Across from the shimmering body of water stood the brooding towers of the Eldorado. That's where the daughter who'd gone to Vassar now lived, though we didn't clean her windows.

Everywhere I looked was a special sight on its own, but with all of them before me now, all of them seemingly just for me now, these little snapshots became prized mementoes. This view wouldn't be possible if I weren't wielding my squeegee.

The old mantra of "mop, squeegee, chamois" remained, but here at this job, at least I also knew that the windows weren't going to hassle me. I felt in control, felt I could relax, felt I could really enjoy what the city had to offer.

Even though I knew the belt hooks were secure, I checked them for a telltale hairpin. I just like the ritual — how it involves danger, clues, and a kind of secret. Many people aren't aware of the hooks on window frames, let alone those with paper clips. But I am.

I looked around. Up at the sky, its blueness dotted with occasional white puffs. Down at the brick, glass, and cement that comprised the building's lower floors, seeing how each stacked upon the other to form the structure I was not just hooked to, but in some way felt a part of. I looked, too, at the far-off, far-down sidewalk. Yes, that's where I'd splat, that's where I'd die. But that chance seemed so remote, so unthinkable that I didn't regard the pavement as a foe, or my fate, or my resting place. Instead, I saw it as what the oblivious passers-by — the people who walked under me without looking up, without knowing I was there — trod upon and were weighed down to.

Then I gazed across town. Central Park's mighty trees, the wind-swept reservoir, then the brooding towers of the Eldorado framed by the crisp sky and the shiny, bright sun. It's easy to see why Icarus died.

After finishing on the Upper East Side, however, I had not soared over the scenery that I'd admired earlier. Instead, I'd had to settle for experiencing that view on foot, crossing Central Park with a walk along the reservoir and then catching a downtown C train at 96th Street, a few blocks north of the Eldorado. I met up with Pat at a new customer's worn-in townhouse in the Village, where we were now on the top floor cleaning some pretty dirty and old windows, wooden six-over-six "switchers," which were not easily switching because, well, they were old and wooden.

Rather than behaving as designed, the top windows did not come down easily, just as the bottom windows did not go up easily (thus letting us clean the panes from above and below without having to step out on the ledge). No, we were having to force the window frames to move along their tracks, knowing that they would be at least as hard to shove back into place. If not harder. A drag. Particularly because these windows were making a lot of screeching sounds that not only drew attention to what we were doing, but made it appear that we were damaging the windows. Which we weren't. At least not seriously.

Pat had gotten to the place first — and by place, I mean the entire townhouse. I don't care where a townhouse is in Manhattan or even what shape it is in. That people have whole townhouses to themselves in this city will always blow me away. By now Pat had done the heavy lifting of "client relations:" introducing himself to the new customer, some guy named Newfield, sweet-talking him about his residence and livelihood, and talking up Shields Window Cleaning as a good, fast, and careful outfit. I wondered if this time out with his spiel Pat had referred to his small company as a "boutique" window cleaning company, one highly skilled and highly attentive that only worked with the best customers. Though it was a pretty accurate description of what we did, the line always made me laugh. It sounded like our squeegees should be gold-plated.

I'd pretty much only said "Hi" and "How are you?" to Newfield when he'd answered the door, before making my way up the stairs, leaving him behind on the ground floor. But he'd struck me as a gruff, no-nonsense kind of guy. I must admit that I'd never heard of him before, but looking around his place, I readily discerned that he was a well-known journalist who over the years had written for the Village Voice, had been close to R.F.K., had written about Don King's career as a boxing promoter and impresario, and that he now worked as a columnist for The New York Post. Newfield came across as an old-school newsman, one who bit down on a story and didn't let go until he had nailed it. Though I hadn't seen any ashtrays about, if the guy smoked cigars, I wouldn't have been surprised; I bet he would call them stogies. I guessed that he had bought his home back when townhouses in Greenwich Village were actually affordable, decades earlier.

I'd left Pat in the top floor's front room, where he was dealing with another set of troubled "switchers," and had made my way to the floor's back room, to Newfield's study. Here, the windows weren't the problem. At least not yet. Instead of switchers, I had cut-up casements to contend with. But before laying a hand or mop or squeegee on them, I had to get *to* them. In my way stood a large, oversized desk that didn't look that moveable even with Pat's help. I didn't really want to move the desk, since standing on it would help me reach the windowpanes that much easier. No, the problem wasn't the desk but what was strewn upon it, piles of paper that covered nearly all the table's surface.

Before me lay an array of the way the written word is preserved. Typed, hand-written, printed. Fresh, gleaming papers that might have been printed out and stacked there just moments before, mixed with yellowed papers that had obviously been sitting there a while, perhaps years. Manila folders and large beige envelopes took their places as well, along with dozens and dozens of small, letter-sized envelopes, all stuffed with more papers. Newspaper clippings, magazine clippings, some with Post-it notes attached, others bearing paper-clipped additions were placed here and there, too. Reports, letters, notes, journals, books, magazines, notebooks, ledgers, all sorts of documents, including those small pieces of paper stating who had called when and had left a message. Photographs — some small snapshots, some 8x10s, had their place in these piles as well.

If there was order here, I could not fathom it. Over the years, I had moved enough piles off customers' desks so as to reach windows (and not to drip onto the piles themselves) to know that one existed here. I knew, in other words, that this mess of piles would have to be preserved across the room, on the floor, one stack at a time. I did a quick count. Five piles across, three piles down, meant fifteen piles. Great.

I started excavating the site with the desk's top left corner and worked my way across the first row, wondering how many stacks it would be before a pile on the desk — finding itself suddenly without the support of its neighboring pile — would simply topple over. It took exactly two. Just as I was about to move the third pile (a stack of files, graph paper, and newspaper articles), it fell to the right, cascading over the other awaiting piles, mixing itself with them. Damn! Well, so much for exactitude. Though I tried my best to recreate the stack, the odds were pretty good that at least one item of the spilled pile had not made it back and had ended up in another pile. Order had been lost. Confusion had set in. But so be it: I had some windows to clean. I moved onto the next pile. And the next. And the next. And so on, until I was done.

Once I'd finished getting the desk cleared, I admired the grid of dust left behind on its surface. I was tempted to play a round of tic-tac-toe with myself, or even call Pat into the room and challenge him to a match. I filled enough of the boxes with X's and O's to suggest a game in progress and secretly declared it a piece of art, one that would last until I put the papers and all the rest back in place.

Believing I now deserved a break, I walked across the hall and stood in the doorway of the front room where Pat was working. Because he wasn't in a perilous position, I knew I could speak without endangering him — startling him into a fall or a dropped squeegee. Pat was standing on the floor, his back to me, touching up a window with his chamois.

"And they said it couldn't be done," I intoned, doing my best take on a melodramatic voice-over.

"Couldn't be done," he said without looking away from his work. "Oh wait, let me guess. Couldn't be done, couldn't be done. Wait, wait. I got it. You managed to get that desk cleared in there?"

"Bing!" I said. "Correct!"

I must say that I was a bit disappointed that Pat had gotten it right; I had wanted to stump him. But I was nonetheless pleased that he knew exactly what I was referring to. Call it window cleaners speaking in shorthand.

"Yeah," I said. "I couldn't believe that table. But wait. Come and take a look. I gotta say I'm pretty impressed with how I —"

A yell erupted from the study.

"What is going on here?! Who did this?!"

Pat and I flashed each other the look of horror and shock we have when a customer unexpectedly gets mad at us: eyes wide, mouth clenched, back suddenly straightened. I fought the need to run to the client with the desire to simply leave. But I also thought: Is he mad about the tic-tac-toe?

Pat and I scrambled into the study, coming upon Newfield standing over my carefully laid out stacks on the floor.

"Did you do this?" he demanded, looking right at me.

"Yes, sir, I did," I said. In such situations, it's always best to use the word "sir." I could feel myself fighting to stay in the room, trying not to detach myself from the scene like I did with that dropped air conditioner. I would stay here. I would.

"I didn't want your stuff to get wet," I said. "Plus I had to get to the windows."

"Listen here," Newfield said. "You never touch a reporter's notes! Never! You don't touch them, you don't move them, you don't read them. You don't do anything to them. You understand that?"

"Yes, sir," I said. "I'm sorry."

"You can't just come in here and move my notes around," Newfield said. "You just —"

"My guy screwed up, Mr. Newfield," Pat said, doing his best to politely cut him off. "I should have gotten the okay from you first. It was my mistake."

"No, really, it was my mistake," I said. "It won't happen again."

"You're damn right it won't happen again!" Newfield yelled and then turned and walked out of the room.

Pat and I looked at each other for a moment.

"Whoops," I whispered. "Sorry about that."

"Hey," Pat said, "we're here to clean the windows."

Pat then returned to his windows and I to mine.

Okay, so I shouldn't have moved his notes without asking. But he could have made it clear that his notes shouldn't have been moved. Or touched. Or read. I'm not a mind-reader. And only so much of a note-reader. I walked over to my bucket, knelt down to pull out my small mop, and then got to work on the cut-up panes. Still, I had learned a little journalistic lesson.

A couple of weeks earlier, I had gone up to Columbia for the journalism school's welcoming reception for incoming students. The event was held in the majestic Low Library, which brimmed with students, teachers, alums, and really good food. After an hour or so, I declared the event a success — for I felt lucky and smart and special and wanted. And full. The vegetable wraps were really tasty.

Taking a break from the commotion of meeting fellow prospective students — one was a farmer from Vermont, another was a theatre director here in New York, someone else was at a small daily in Connecticut — I made my way over to the Director of Admissions, a tall, lanky guy with glasses and a moustache. He'd proctored the now long-ago written test back in January, and had declared that if a thin envelope arrived from the school in April, to not bother opening it.

"Mr. MacDonald!" I'd said, shaking his hand. "I just want to thank you for letting me in. This really is one of the best things that's ever happened to me. I mean, I still can't quite believe it. Thank you!"

"It's my pleasure, but it wasn't just my decision. We've got a whole team that goes over the applications. So, it certainly sounds like you're coming here in the fall."

"Oh, yeah," I said. "That is the plan. Definitely."

"And what is your name?" Mr. MacDonald asked.

"I'm Ivor Hanson," I said. "I —"

"Oh really?" Mr. MacDonald said. "Just a sec." He turned away. "Joan! Joan! I'd like to introduce you to someone. The window cleaner is here."

I knew that I would be calling my customer, Mrs. S., the next day. It's good to have friends in high places. In my case, the seventh floor of an East Side apartment building was high enough.

Newfield's place went by pretty quickly and smoothly after the fiasco in his office. His windows behaved themselves for the most part, but more importantly, our customer left us alone. As we finished up in the kitchen, having rinsed out mops and chamoises and sponges in our buckets and prepared to depart, I thought I'd try and show him that I was more than an idiot window cleaner who stupidly messed with his stuff.

"Sir, I have to ask," I said. "Apart from not moving a reporter's notes, have you got any other tips for someone who is off to Columbia's journalism school in the fall?"

"Columbia?" Newfield said. "Is that so? Huh. Well, you see, I've always thought that journalism was something you did, and not something where you sat in a classroom and were taught."

I smiled. Now, in addition to being an idiot window cleaner, I was apparently a sucker.

"From what I understand," I said, "the school really stresses getting its students out into the streets so that they make New York City their classroom, and then use the classroom as a newsroom. Or something like that."

"Really?" Newfield said. "How nice. You know, every couple of years Columbia asks me to come up there and teach a class. But I've always said no. You wanna know why?"

"Sure."

"Because I don't believe in consumer fraud!"

I paused for a moment, wondering how to respond.

"Well," I said, "I guess I won't be seeing you in September."

TEN
[right]**DOUBLEWIDE**

I looked up from the tiny table I'd just sat down at and checked the ancient clock on the wall against the beat-up watch on my wrist. If *Doublewide* was going to be on time, they would be here in fifteen minutes. Time enough to down my lentil soup and hand my bowl and spoon back to the guy behind the counter so that I'd have space enough to go over the questions I'd written out in my notebook earlier in the day.

The guys in *Doublewide* had chosen the location, and it was perfect: the grimy but cool B&H Dairy diner on Second Avenue, just south of St. Marks Place. Rundown, dimly lit, decades old, and so narrow that the six tables lining the wall felt in the way. At the moment, I had the place to myself.

I knew I couldn't fit all of that in my profile of *Doublewide*, so I'd probably settle for "an East Village greasy spoon." The music editor at Time Out New York had stressed that I had only a max of 300 words "to play with" — and a minimum of 275.

I had to capture the essence of this band in just a few paragraphs. Getting, as one of my J-school professors had put it, "the flinty facts." I figured I had to describe the group's sound (while avoiding the _____ meets _____ cliché); cite a telling lyric; say how long they've been together; tell what they're trying to do with their music; get a pithy quote or two from the guys.

I looked down at the notes I had scrawled a couple of months earlier, when I'd happened upon a *Doublewide* show. I smiled to myself: I really did have to work on my handwriting.

My time at Columbia hadn't improved that! But I had learned a lot from my teachers. I now had my degree. And my $18,500 debt. And on my desk at 13th Street, lots of notes stacked in various piles. I readily admit that my piles weren't as plentiful or as exacting as Jack Newfield's. They could spill onto each other and it wouldn't be the end of the world. Even so, I'd come to appreciate what he'd been talking about — well, yelling about — the previous summer. Piles exist for knowing where those flinty facts are. *Doublewide* had its own little pile.

I reached down to the floor and fished my mini-cassette tape recorder from my courier bag. Another sign of having been at school. I wasn't going to misquote anyone today! More to the point, I wasn't going to miss out on a quote because I couldn't read my notes afterwards. To insure this, I popped into the machine the two new batteries I'd just picked up at the magazine shop next door.

"Testing, testing, one, two, three," I softly spoke into the microphone as I pressed the record button and the tape rolled. "Testing, testing."

I paused.

"Check, check," I said. "Check one, check two. Could I have a little more slap-back on the vocals, please?"

It was what Michael, my former bandmate invariably said into the mic during sound checks.

Then an over-the-top deejay interviewer suddenly took over me, making my voice super-slick, like Tom Waits's character in *Down by Law.*

"Hi there, folks. Welcome to the show and thanks for tuning in. Okay, today we're talking with *Doublewide*. They're a rock band here in New York City who took their name from a kind of mobile home. The extra-fancy, extra-wide kind. Very cool, very catchy, guys. All right. So tell us: Is this your way of latching onto the white trash vibe that the kids are so into these days? And when did the band get togeth—"

I looked up from the recorder as two men in their twenties walked through B&H's door and approached me. They were Jake and Keith, the main guys from *Doublewide*. Man, I hope they hadn't heard me. I switched the machine off. I didn't want to waste any more of the batteries.

Jake was just shy of being stocky, with a big grin and an open face, black shoulder-length hair, and black horn-rim glasses. Keith's slightly bedraggled blonde locks, tee shirt, and worn-in shorts gave him a surfer look, as did his broad shoulders and the silver locket around his neck. Neither of them sported attitude, however, just enthusiasm.

I stood and put out my hand and braced myself for some pain: my re-emerging window cleaning calluses remained tender, as they weren't quite finished being blisters.

"Jake," I said, noticing his low-key jeans and tee shirt, "I almost didn't recognize you without your orange jumpsuit."

"Oh, yeah," he said, giving me a firm grasp. "Stage clothes. They're fun."

"Seriously though," I said as the three of us sat down at what now seemed a miniscule table, "I'm so glad you guys could make it. Thanks again for talking to me."

I'd managed to avoid the word interview.

"Are you kidding?" Jake said. "We wanna thank you for asking to interview us in the first place."

"My pleasure," I said. I'd forgotten how grateful bands can be when given the chance to be in print. How grateful I'd been. After the first *Faith* show, for instance, when I was in high school, some kid had written in his Xeroxed fanzine how good we had been, and how he was sure we would blow away most any band we shared a bill with. If only that had been the case for all of our shows. Still, it had certainly made me happy — and wanting more press.

"Do you mind?" I asked, picking up the tape recorder and waving it slightly. "I just want to get it right."

"No, that's cool," Jake said. "Ask away. This'll be fun."

The interview wasn't going badly, as I'd feared it might. Indeed, it was going pretty well. I was getting answers to my questions, and furthermore, Jake and Keith were agreeing with my take on their group: that *Doublewide* was an unapologetic pop band that had no problem performing ultra-catchy, melody-driven, hook-laden songs. And that they were big fans of '70s pop-rock, like *Big Star*, and even, dare I say it — but then their songs did have keyboards all over them — Elton John (but early Elton) — they had no problem with that either.

Since I was trying to make my questions feel more like a conversation than an interrogation, I was taking longer to nail down the who, what, where, and all the rest, than I actually needed to. And because this meant a good bit of back-and-forth on our parts, it also meant a good bit (okay, a lot) of talking on my part. But that was okay. I like talking to people (probably more than I like listening to them, and definitely more than I like writing down what they have to say).

Moreover, I did have specific things to say, things I wanted to be known. Like that I was more than just a music writer. I felt the need to impress on Jake and Keith that I had...well, "street cred," to use a term I don't like. That I had not only played in bands myself, but that they had been influential groups.

In other words, I wanted to hear Jake say, "You were in bands with Henry Rollins and Ian Mackaye? Wow!" And when he did say words along those lines, I was quite pleased. Who wouldn't be? I also knew that by telling them about *S.O.A.* and *Embrace* (and *Faith* and *Manifesto* and *clear*) I was risking them asking (or at least thinking): So what are you doing talking to us? If I were in their shoes, that thought would cross my mind.

"So," I began, flipping my notebook to the next clean, pristine page that was about to be made close to illegible. "You guys have been together nine months and you've got some great songs, like 'Spaceman' for instance. That chorus — 'Won't you bring back my sunshine?' — is just so catchy. I remember writing down the word 'effortless' the first time I saw you play."

"Thanks," Keith said, genuinely pleased. "It's all about the melodies. We don't waste any time. It's: Let's hit 'em with the hook!"

"Like an aluminium bat!" Jake added with a swinging motion and a laugh, nearly causing the table to tip.

"Right," I said, writing this down more slowly since I knew I had just got myself something quotable, while also asking my next question. "What I'm wondering is: you've got these songs; you're playing out; people are coming to your shows; you're in the studio working on a demo — any labels interested in you guys?"

"Well," Jake said, pausing slightly. He seemed reticent to speak. "Yeah. A couple. A couple of majors, a couple of indies. They've been checking us out. A few of 'em have even seen us more than once. But no offers yet."

"Just a lot of talk at this point," Keith said. "We'll see what happens."

"But," Jake quickly said, "let me be on tape as saying that we are quite happy to be talking to them. We're flattered."

"I bet," I said. "Of course. Who wouldn't be?"

"Would you mind leaving this stuff out?" Jake said. "It might not look so coo—"

"Oh, don't worry," I said, pointing at the tape recorder. "Not a problem. I won't put it in. I'm just curious. Just make sure you get yourselves a good lawyer. That's my advice. Actually, if you want, I could see if my band's old lawyer would be interested in talking to you."

"We've got someone helping us out," Jake said. "Most definitely. Thanks, though. Thanks a lot."

"Okay," I said. "That's cool."

What was going on here? I'd just offered to help them get a lawyer? I'd just let them have a say in what would be in the piece? Where was my journalistic objectivity? A month out of school, and I was already walking away from my degree? What was I doing? Interviewing these guys, or hanging out with them? Befriending them?

Honestly, I wasn't really practicing journalism. This tiny little profile I was writing was really just one step away from being a press release, and my being a public relations flak. The difference was that this puff piece was appearing in a magazine and not a press kit. I was doing a happy smiley piece, not an exposé. I couldn't really say anything bad about the band. I mean, the point of this "Preview" piece was to get people to go see their show. Time Out wasn't interested in me writing up a lame band. And neither was I.

This was a taste-maker piece. I guess I could write something like, "in their best songs, *Doublewide*...." But I'd have to see what those 300 words could accommodate. I doubted I'd do it anyway. It would just go over as arrogant.

Plus, I genuinely did like Jake and Keith and the music *Doublewide* played. I wanted to help them get some press, I wanted to help them succeed. If that meant writing what I essentially considered P.R., or offering up my band's former lawyer, then so be it. If I'd known any managers, I would have suggested them, too.

Despite my desire to help the guys in *Doublewide*, I envied them. Labels interested in them? Indies and majors? It didn't matter that Fire Records became interested in *Manifesto* about nine months after we started playing out. It didn't matter if nothing ended up coming of *Doublewide*'s label interest. What mattered was that I wanted to be a part of their success. Actually, that's not quite right. I just wanted a bit of their being in a band to rub off on me.

I took a long swig of water — as I needed to stall a moment or two: The "wannabe" rock star inside me wanted to have his say.

Get out of here, I thought, leave me alone. But the guy in the motorcycle jacket wouldn't go away, wouldn't disappear underfoot. He just rolled his eyes and mouthed the words "pathetic."

Fuck. Now I was stumped. Until then, I'd thought that my "rock star jealousy" had been exclusively reserved for *Fugazi*. And why not? They were a critically acclaimed, commercially successful punk band that epitomized independence and honesty. They were cool and adamant and serious and humble, too. No wonder I'd hoped, and had tried, and had wanted to be their drummer.

Compared to *Fugazi*, *Doublewide* was...was just a puny little pop band heavily influenced by Elton John, for Christ's sake. Sure, their tunes were sing-along friendly, but so what. "Won't you bring back my sunshine?" Give me a fucking break.

No, give *Doublewide* a break. At least Jake and Keith were in a band. Which was more than I was. And besides, Jake and Keith weren't trying to be *Fugazi*.

I'd been quite taken by that first show I'd seen and the others since then. They were tight and fun and entertaining. If they hadn't been, I wouldn't have pitched them to Time Out. I wouldn't have arranged this interview, I wouldn't....

Still, as I placed my glass down on my notes, I couldn't quite shake the feeling that, though I was writing — creating! — I considered the people that I was writing about as the ones who were actually doing something. What's the line? Journalists witness history; others make it. *Doublewide* was making music. I'd watched them play. And now I was merely telling people about them.

I thought of John, the former A&R guy from East-West Records, and asked myself, is writing my second chance or my second choice? I knew the answer even as I was asking the question. And the answer was easy: it was both. I had to accept this, even appreciate it. After all, at least I had a choice. Still, accepting and appreciating this choice and this chance of mine — this "new life" of mine — was proving to be a lot harder than I'd thought. A lot harder.

"Well," I said, looking up at Jake and Keith. "I think I've got plenty to work with. I'm just sorry this ran a little long for you guys. Do you mind if I turn this off?"

"No, that's fine," Jake said, stretching his arms. "I think I'm all talked out."

Maybe it was because we all had water to drink or that we just wanted to put off dealing with the sticky summer afternoon, but none of us moved to stand up. Looked like we were hanging out after all.

"I'm curious," I said. "What do you guys do to get by? That is, if you don't mind my asking."

"Not at all," Keith said. "I play in pit bands when they need subs."

"You mean for Broadway shows?" I asked. "Wow."

"Hell yeah!" Jake said. "Pretty cool, huh? Like the song says: 'On Broadway!'"

"Yeah," Keith said, smiling, seeming slightly embarrassed by Jake's plug for him. "Just like. Actually, the gigs are pretty great. I'd just like to get more of them."

"And what about you, Jake?" I asked.

"Oh, man," Keith said, taking his turn to tell of Jake's job. "I could never do what Jake does. I really don't understand how he does it. See, Jake's a —"

"It's not that bad," Jake said, tapping Keith's shoulder. Being the showman, he wanted to draw out the suspense. "It just took some getting used to, that's all. You definitely can't be afraid of heights, though, that's for sure. Besides, it's fun. And it's a real New York City job, if you know what I mean."

"So what do you do?" I asked. I had a feeling I already knew.

"I'm a window cleaner."

"Can you believe it?" Keith said. "He's high up there and everything."

"Really?" I said. "That's so funny."

"Huh?" Jake said, noticeably raising his eyebrows. I recognized that slight defensiveness.

"Oh," I said, "it's just that I clean windows, too."

"No," Jake said. "You're kidding. Right?"

"No, really," I said. "I do."

If I had seen a bit of myself in that kid I'd jammed with on the Upper East Side last summer, than what was I seeing now? Some sort of doppelganger?

Jake and I talked shop for a bit. It turned out that he, too, had been working for a friend of his for the past couple of years and that he, too, liked cleaning ancient belt windows best of all. As far as close-calls, Jake had had a few, but nothing as bad as dropping an air conditioner out a window. Then, once we had finished comparing notes, we said goodbye.

As I sat back down while watching them leave, I was beginning to believe that I would be squeegeeing for a while. If the $50 that Time Out was paying me was any guide, it was going to be hard to make freelance writing pay the bills. Not that I didn't know that already; not that I hadn't been warned, you could say. But, you know, it's one thing to be told something, and another to actually experience it. Even so, I was doing my best to ignore the nagging similarities between being a struggling writer and a struggling musician.

For that matter, I was also trying to ignore what my father had said to me when we'd talked on the phone a few weeks earlier: "Son, wasn't the point of going to Columbia so that you could land a real job? You don't want to get sucked back into window cleaning."

After recovering from my shock at "going to the dump" over the phone, I'd told him that I was working on getting a real job, but that I first needed to get some clips together. I figured that would buy me some time until our next such talk.

A real job? The thought of me going to a real job made me cringe. Even if it were for a magazine or a newspaper, working nine-to-five was still nine-to-five. Actually, from what I'd gathered from classmates who were journalists before going to Columbia, magazines and newspapers weren't nine-to-five, but more so.

Okay. So I apparently didn't want to be tethered to a real job, a career job, a job that defined me for sure — not even one that involved writing. Didn't that leave me shackled to my squeegee?

Even though I hadn't played in a while now — let's see, it had been basically a year since I sat behind that electronic drumset on the Upper East Side — not playing still haunted me, still made me think I was...a failure. *Doublewide*'s playing (and apparent success) was just rubbing this in my face. Of course, it wasn't their fault. Jake and Keith were just being in a band.

Hadn't I moved on from playing? But if that were so, why did not drumming still smack of giving up and giving in? At this point — having quit the band, having given my drums away, having gone to grad school, and, now, having pitched my first piece — I just didn't think it would. Would I always feel a bit like a quitter? Yeah, probably. I wasn't playing, was I?

Along with discussing my getting a real job, my dad had called to ask me to play in his band. I would back him for what apparently was turning into an annual benefit concert for the historical society my mom headed out on Long Island. The previous year, my dad had sung his saloon songs accompanied by his friend, Caroline, on piano. Now he wanted an all-out band and had found a bass player whose girlfriend would sing a few duets with my dad — and, hopefully, a drummer — me.

I felt both honored and on the spot. Sure, I was pleased he had asked me to perform with him. The two of us onstage, father and son. That would be special. I wasn't about to say no. Even though I knew it wasn't an order — it wasn't like with the earrings — I also felt like I couldn't say no. Turn down my dad on something like this? How would that have gone over?

Something else, however, had given me pause: What if I screwed up the songs? The music would certainly be a far cry (or yell) from my punk bands that "the Admiral" had occasionally seen perform in the past. We wouldn't be playing songs like, say, *Faith*'s "Don't Tell Me." Its lyrics were to the point: "I don't want to hear your problems/Don't tell me!/I don't want to hear your shit/Don't tell me!" Even with the verse and chorus repeated and a guitar solo, the tune lasted all of forty-five seconds. But what a forty-five seconds! "Don't Tell Me" had an excellent buzz-saw guitar riff, a breakneck pace, and a shout-along chorus. I loved playing that song.

I had studied some jazz, but that was back in seventh grade. I would have to dig out my Chapin's "Book of Jazz Exercises" and see if I could keep that triplet beat going on the cymbal. Actually, I was pretty sure that I'd keep the beat. Even if I didn't, due to the hall's echoey acoustics, I would be performing with wire "brushes" instead of wooden sticks. It's a quieter way to strike the drums and would make any of my mistakes that much harder to hear.

Compared to Caroline, who was a natural at the keyboards, and Jim, the bassist, who made his living gigging around New York City, who was I? A former punk and rock drummer who hadn't played in a while. Moreover, I would undoubtedly be wearing a suit and tie for the show. That would probably feel just as odd as backing my dad on "You're the Top."

At least picking my squeegee back up hadn't been so bad. I must say that after a year away, I'd been enjoying feeling the brass handle back in my hand — my calluses notwithstanding — just as I'd liked seeing favorite customers. Earlier that day, I'd cleaned the windows of Ann-Marie, a gourmet chef whose varied career has included serving as the personal chef for Jacqueline Onassis, starting a cooking school, having a cooking show on television, and writing cookbooks. Now Ann-Marie prepares and hosts private dinners for corporate clients in her Murray Hill townhouse.

When I am there, I seek out on her office wall a framed holiday letter of thanks from Jackie O: "Merry Christmas Ann-Marie and thank you for all you do for me." This hard-to-forget charming little rhyme is typed out, but then below it is a hand-written note praising Ann-Marie for her contribution to the household, the children's well-being especially.

Ann-Marie is also known for her Chocolate Normandie, a rich chocolate dessert. I had had some Normandie earlier that day, once I'd finished the job. It had worked out that Ann-Marie had made lunch for me and her intern and her cleaning woman (and herself) that afternoon, a spicy pasta and vegetable dish.

As for Ann-Marie's windows, I appreciated the replacement panes that opened inwards like doors and her quite accessible skylights. But these didn't make up for the 6 ten-feet-high, arched mirrors mounted on the dining room walls. They were at least twenty feet off the ground, with very narrow spaces for me to tiptoe along. "Tricky," to say the least — more so for my having been away from them for at least a year. As I mopped, squeegeed, and chamoised the glass, my reflected image in front and behind me made it quite clear where I was. Back on the ledge.

At least I was making money, steady money.

I couldn't say that about freelancing. There were so many freelance writers out there. Looking at bylines in, say, The New York Times, Rolling Stone, New York, Spin, and The New York Times Magazine, had replaced my looking at band listings in the Voice. Except that I could feel myself more readily intimidated by this totem pole of publications and writer's names, than the clubs from before. Maybe this was because I was just starting out? Maybe it was because I'd already gotten squished by the music biz? I guess that's why returning to Windowland felt so good. It was something I knew, something that — as odd as it sounds — didn't scare me.

I picked up the tape recorder to put it back in my bag. Because I was curious, I rewound the tape so I could hear a bit of it.

"— claim to fame, you could say, was that its singer was Henry Roll—"

Me talking about *S.O.A.*

I rewound the tape some more.

"— when I hear 'Spaceman,' it seems to me that you guys are —"

Me again.

I rewound some more.

"— first time I saw *Doublewide* play I remember thinkin—"

Me again.

Were Jake and Keith even on this tape?

Some years earlier, someone somewhere (in England, I think) had come up with a quiz that, based on the respondent's answers to a couple of humorous questions, told them which "early" D.C. punk band they most closely resembled. When I'd taken it, I'd learned, appropriately, that I was one of my old bands:

"You are *THE FAITH*! You are so underrated, it's sad. You are shy but hold a lot of anger and power inside of you. You may seem kind of snotty but it's mainly misunderstanding. Also, you are highly self-involved in the projects you undertake, you are a go-to person. Don't worry, everyone will come to their senses and start paying attention to your awesome talent in no time."

I guess it's my being "highly self-involved in the projects I undertake" that was keeping Jake and Keith from being heard. At least I could skip over a lot of the tape when I was searching for band quotes. I gathered up my stuff and put it all in my bag. Then I took out a section of the day's paper.

Since I'd already read through and discarded the A and Arts sections earlier in the day, I looked down at what I'd pulled out: Business Day. I look through this mostly to see what the record companies are up to, insofar as what the Times finds newsworthy. But there was nothing to be found. And then my eyes caught sight of a headline: "Self-Cleaning Windows to Be Sold in U.S. This Year."

I pictured some sort of newfangled and high-priced contraption that would emerge discretely from a window frame, and then clean the window like a giant windshield wiper. Instead of a Rube Goldberg device, both a British company called Pilkington and the American company, PPG, (and even an unnamed Japanese company) were making windows that had a permanent coat of titanium oxide applied to the glass. Huh? Titanium oxide, I learned, helps rainwater run off glass in what the article called a "continuous sheet," which means that dirt doesn't have a chance to gather on the glass.

Fortunately, a spokesperson for a trade group called the Soap and Detergent Association, as well as the Chairman of the Remodelers' Council of the National Association of Home Builders voiced their skepticism. They didn't believe a huge market existed for such windows, since the titanium oxide coating added 20% to the price of a basic window — which already cost between $200 and $600.

Okay, so they weren't exactly or even actually self-cleaning windows. I mean, these titanium oxide windows did not involve mops and squeegees and chamoises. And they were expensive to buy. So I didn't feel that replaced, that threatened. At least not yet.

Still, self-cleaning windows were what the top guy at Pilkington called "one of the holy grails of window manufacturing" — and now they were here. My life on the ledge seemed to be coming to an end regardless. If that were so, at least I knew one thing: just as whenever I hear a song, I drum along to it in my head; whenever I see a window, I will sort out how to clean it.

As I stuffed the Times into my bag so as to finally be on my way, I wondered: why hadn't the reporter interviewed a window cleaner?

THE END

THE AUTHOR WISHES TO THANK: Christina Carlson — wife, mother, buyer of cat food, and international civil servant who took me (and *Ledge*) from New York, to Geneva, Kosova, Bougainville, and back again. I am forever indebted, grateful, and lucky.

My family — who have put up with this book for quite a while now. Thanks, bobbi.

Teachers of mine. GDS's Kevin Barr, Mike Kirchberg, Barbara Churchill, Gary McCown, and Leigh Sherrill; Vassar's Lorrie Goldensohn, Karen Robertson, Dan Peck, and Pat Wallace; The New School's Candy Schulman; Columbia J-school's Sam Freedman, Michael Shapiro, Judith Crist, and Sig Gissler; Little Compton's Luke Wallin; they all make writing worth pursuing.

The many, many customers who have let me into their homes and their lives over the years. They've allowed me to experience New York City in a unique way — hopefully without leaving a streak.

The New York Times, for Connie Rosenblum's "City Section," Michael T. Kaufman's "About New York" column, and Fred R. Conrad's photograph.

Lars Hanson, Seth Greene, Bridget Kinsella, Tom Cushman, Gabrielle Brooks, and especially Eric Obenauf for helping to sharpen *Ledge*.

Eric, Eliza, Vin, Brian and everyone at Two Dollar Radio for their commitment to *Ledge*.

Johnny Temple, of Akashic Books, for sending Two Dollar Radio my way.

Pat Shields, for teaching me how to wield a squeegee.

The countless windows of New York City that all need cleaning at some point — preferably twice a year.

A portion of the proceeds from each copy of Life on the Ledge sold will be donated to:

FILMMAKERS IN MEMORY OF SHAYNE WORCESTER

Filmmakers in Memory of Shayne Worcester was established to honor an artist, writer, poet, and dear friend to many people.

On May 26, 1999, Shayne was shot and killed while visiting friends in San Francisco. In his honor, this foundation was established to make annual donations to YES TO YOUTH!, a non-profit organization which provides after school programs in media and sports for youth in Maine. YES TO YOUTH! was selected as our beneficiary to both honor Shayne's passion for the arts and to support the organization's resolve in fostering safe and educational environments for young people. The fund will be managed by the Maine Community Foundation.